D0114681

THE CREATION
CONTROVERSY

THE
CREATION
CONTROVERSY
Science or Scripture in the Schools

Dorothy Nelkin

W·W·NORTON & COMPANY
New York   London

Published simultaneously in Canada by George J. McLeod Limited, Toronto.
PRINTED IN THE UNITED STATES OF AMERICA.
An earlier version of this book was published in 1977 by MIT Press.
The text of this book is composed in 10/12 Times Roman, with display type set
in Baskerville. Manufacturing by The Hadden Craftsmen, Inc.

FIRST EDITION

Library of Congress Cataloging in Publication Data
Nelkin, Dorothy.
    The creation controversy.
    Includes index.
    1. Bible and science. 2. Creation. 3. Evolution.
4. Religion and science—History of controversy—United
States. I. Title.
BS651.N39   1982   261.5'5'0973   82–7840

ISBN 0-393-01635-8   AACR2

W. W. Norton & Company, Inc. 500 Fifth Avenue, New York, N.Y. 10110
W. W. Norton & Company Ltd. 37 Great Russell Street, London WC1B 3NU

1 2 3 4 5 6 7 8 9

To Erica

Contents

Abbreviations   11
Preface   13
1   Introduction   17

I The Context   23

2   A Science or a World View? Historical Notes
     on the Teaching of Evolution   25
     Evolution and the Nineteenth-Century Soul   26
     Antievolution in the 1920s   30
     The Legacy of the Scopes Trial   33

3   Science after Sputnik   39
     The Federal Government's Role   40
     The Biological Sciences Curriculum Study   44
     Man: A Course of Study   47

II The Science-Textbook Watchers   55

4   Textbook Watchers and Space-Age
     Fundamentalism   57
     Forbidden Subjects   57
     The Conservative Ministries   59
     The New Censors   63

5   The Scientific Creationists   71
     The Bible as Science   73
     Creationist Organizations   77
     The Activists   84

6   Political Tactics   93
     In School Boards and Commissions   93
     In the Streets   95

In State Legislatures   97
In the Courts   100

III Disputes   105

7   Creation versus Evolution: The California
     Controversy   107
     Creationist Demands   109
     The California Solution   112

8   The Proper Study of Mankind . . . : Evolution
     and the MACOS Dispute   121
     "We're all animals, kids are taught here"   122
     The Politics of Local Protest   124
     MACOS: A National Debate   127
     The Tip of the Iceberg: MACOS, Accountability,
     and the NSF   132

9   Legislating Science in Arkansas   137
     The Legislation   138
     The Trial   139

IV Science and the Resistance Ideology   149

10   Censorship by Surrender   151
     Manipulated Media   151
     Publishers and Profits   153
     Conflict Avoidance in the Schools   154
     The Scientists' Response   156

11   Social Sources of Textbook Disputes   165
     Disillusion with Science and Technology   167
     Challenges to Authority   170
     The Ideology of Equal Time   173

12   Science and Personal Beliefs   185
     Images of Science   185
     Problems in the Communication of Science   189

Appendices   199

1   Decision, *The Rev. Bill McLean* v. *Arkansas*
     Board of Education   199
2   Public Knowledge of Science: Report of a Survey

by the National Assessment of Educational
Progress   229
3   Proposed Creationist Revisions of the California
Science Framework for 1976   234
Index   237

Abbreviations

AIBS   American Institute of Biological Science
ASA   American Scientific Affiliation
CBE   Council for Basic Education
BSCS   Biological Sciences Curriculum Study
CDA   Curriculum Development Associates
CRS   Creation Research Society
CSRC   Creation Science Research Center
EDC   Education Development Center
ESI   Educational Services Incorporated
ICR   Institute for Creation Research
MACOS   Man: A Course of Study
NABT   National Association of Biology Teachers
NAEP   National Assessment of Educational Progress
NSF   National Science Foundation
PSSC   Physical Science Study Committee

Preface

This study began simply out of curiosity about the creationists as a group of people who represented themselves as scientists while challenging the most sacred assumptions and norms of the scientific establishment. As the disputes developed over the teaching of evolution theory and its presentation in textbooks, and over Man: A Course of Study (MACOS), a course in the social sciences based on evolutionary assumptions, the creationists' demands, which had seemed so out of step in the 1970s, emerged as an expression of basic and rather widespread criticism of science and its pervasive influence on social values. Thus, the study turned to analyze the creationists dispute as an expression of this new concern.

Science is attacked these days from both the left and the right. The disputes described here represent a reaction from a highly conservative population; but interest in local control and increased participation and objection to the dominance of scientific values and the role of expertise will be familiar to people located anywhere along the spectrum of political ideologies. The textbook disputes provide a means of exploring the relationships between science and its public and of examining how the growing criticism of science can bear on public policy.

The research for this study was facilitated by the cooperation of many groups. These included scientists, creationists, teachers, educational administrators, parents of school children affected by the disputes, and book publishers. People from the following organizations provided material from their files and cooperated during extended interviews: The National Association of Biology Teachers, the Biological Sciences Curriculum Study, Education Development Corporation, Curriculum Development Associates, the National Science Foundation, the National Association of Educational Progress, the National Education Association, the Council for Basic Education, the Institute for Creation Research, Education Research Analysts, the American Scientific Affiliation, and the Creation Science Research Center. In addition, biologists, schoolteachers, fundamentalist ministers, politicians, congressional aides, and individuals involved in controversies throughout the country cooperated in interviews, providing useful documentation on their perspectives. As in any controversial situation, a number of those who were interviewed may disagree with my analysis, but I very much appreciate their cooperation and have attempted to use their material fairly.

I also appreciate the criticism received from scholarly colleagues who have spent considerable time reviewing drafts of this manuscript and some of the articles and seminars developed from it; these include William Blanpied, Harvey Brooks, Gerald Holton, Everett Mendelsohn, Larry Moore, Mark Nelkin, Gerard Piel, and Will Provine. Articles from the manuscript have appeared in Gerald Holton and William Blanpied, *Science and Its Public* (G. Reidel, 1976), and in *Scientific American,* April 1976. Editorial criticism in preparing these articles and the many letters that followed their publication were extremely helpful.

Support for this study was provided in part by a National Science Foundation research grant on science policy. Some of the writing was done during a semester at the Political Science Department and the Center for International Studies at MIT. I would like to acknowledge their hospitality and invaluable assistance. Finally, I appreciate the support of my colleagues at the Cornell University Program on Science, Technology, and Society.

THE CREATION
CONTROVERSY

1

Introduction

In 1981, the states of Arkansas and Louisiana passed legislation requiring that the creationist account of the origin of life be taught as a viable scientific alternative to the theory of evolution. The Balanced Treatment for Creation-Science and Evolution Science Act was the culmination of more than ten years of struggle by the "scientific creationists," fundamentalist groups who believe that scientific evidence supports the Genesis account of creation, and that considerations of fairness and academic freedom require it be given "equal time." Although a federal judge ruled, in a powerful and unambiguous decision, that the Arkansas statute was unconstitutional, a similar act is under consideration in some twenty other states.

The creationists entered the policy arena in 1969, when they convinced the California board of education to issue new guidelines for its public-school biology courses, recommending equal time for the Genesis account of creation. They have since demanded equal time in school boards, textbook commissions, state legislatures, and the courts.

Creationists reached the United States Congress in 1975, when an epidemic of community controversies over a social-science course based on evolutionary assumptions forced congressional reevaluation of the massive federal effort to modernize precollege science instruction. They have lobbied for a broader congressional debate on the federal funding of museums, national parks, and educational institutions that exclude creation theory when dealing with the origin of life.

They have also reached the president of the United States. Seeking fundamentalist votes during his electoral campaign, Ronald Reagan told reporters that evolution theory has been seriously challenged: "It is not believed in the scientific community to be as infallible as it once was believed. But if it is going to be taught in the schools, then I think that the Biblical theory of creation should also be taught."

By 1980, scientific creationists looked back with enthusiasm on a "decade of creation." A number of school boards and curriculum committees were avoiding biology and social-science textbooks that collided with religious beliefs; many public-school teachers were exposing their students to the "scientific" evidence for the Biblical study of creation; state legislatures across the country were considering laws requiring balanced treatment of creation theory in biology classes and textbooks; and textbook publishers were significantly reducing the treatment of evolution theory in their new editions.

The creationists also looked back with satisfaction on a decade of considerable public attention. Major news outlets had published feature stories on scientific creationism which, if not always flattering, provided welcome publicity. So too did their legislative and judicial battles. When Arkansas and Louisiana passed their Balanced Treatment acts, the controversy became a new and widely publicized test of the constitutional separation of church and state. Judicial defeat in Arkansas (the Louisiana case is not yet in court at the time of this writing) has not deterred the creationists. They present themselves as a beleaguered group rejected by a scientific establishment protecting its turf. They have drafted new legislation called the Unbiased Presentation of Creation-Science and Evolution-Science Bill. And they have intensified their efforts to bring creationism into the nation's public schools.

The emergence of scientific creationism as a significant political force is a dramatic expression of the renewed concern with moral and religious values in American society and the related ambivalence toward science. Science is often perceived as a dominant world view that threatens traditional values and suppresses essential elements of human experience. Indeed, at a time when the accomplishments of science have fostered faith in the value of rational explanations of nature, there are concentrated efforts to reinvest the educational system with traditional faith. At a time when the evolutionary concepts of biology are among the more firmly established generalizations of modern science, public demands for the teaching of alternative explanations of human origins have exercised remarkable influence. At a time when the complexity of the modern technological enterprise requires specialized expertise, there are increasing demands for lay participation in science education by groups insisting that education must reflect community and religious values. These are some of the paradoxes manifest in the persistent dispute over the teaching of evolution and the content of textbooks.

The science textbook watchers have targeted courses that were developed in the 1960s to bring the concepts and methods of modern scientific research to the nation's public schools. The National Science Foundation has funded fifty-three science curriculum projects, bringing university scholars together with professional educators to create textbooks and other course materials. For years this effort was welcomed as a major and important reform, "a victory of human reason over obscurantism," a "renaissance movement," in education. But in the late 1960s, in a society increasingly concerned with the social implications of science, university scholars and professional educators became an "arrogant elite," imposing their values on the American school child. Critics accused the NSF, once a source of intellectual enlightenment, of promoting "value-laden" materials, and pressured the foundation to review courses produced under its sponsorship and to increase lay participation in course evaluation. By 1982, the science textbook watchers had destroyed the science education activities of the NSF, putting an end to twenty years of science education reform.

Why, one must ask, in this science-dominated age, is there such concern with science education? Why has the old resistance to evolution theory gathered new momentum? What issues have converged to force public recognition of complaints long ignored as merely the rumblings of marginal groups of religious fundamentalists and right-wing conservatives? How have small groups of "believers" been able to intrude their ideologies into educational establishments and in some cases to control the educational apparatus that determines science curriculum?

Public-school education is among the most volatile areas of public policy, and efforts at reform can count on opposition. Conflict thrives on the persistent concern of parents about what influences their offspring and on considerable public ambivalence about the role of education. Should schools emphasize individual intellectual development or should they be responsible for the transmission of culture? Should they convey basic knowledge or provide useful skills? Are they to generate new values or preserve existing ones? Should they promote social change or protect the status quo?

The history of American educational reform has reflected an abiding faith that schools are a means to remedy social problems and to bring about social reform. Education is often viewed as an ideological instrument, a means of changing social perceptions, such as racial or sexual prejudices. The perceived importance of education as an instrument of reform is also the basis of a powerful conservative reaction among those who seek to protect traditional ideologies. Curriculum reform often becomes the focus of bitter disputes over the values to be conveyed to the young.

Yet, with the notable exception of the Scopes trial (often thought to be the last vestige of the great struggle between religion and science), there have been relatively few public attacks on science teaching. Following World War II, science, perceived as neutral and associated with material progress, was dissociated from value questions of interest to textbook watchers. The pervasive influence of science in advanced technological societies suggested that traditional religious beliefs no longer had significant bearing on science education policy.

In the late 1960s, however, attitudes appeared to change. Growing concern with the misuse of science and the harmful effects of technology led also to criticism of scientific rationality. The interest in nonrational and supernatural explanations of nature was reflected in the proliferation of cults and sects based on Eastern mysticism. Less visible, but perhaps more important in the long run, was a significant growth in fundamentalist churches, especially in the very centers of high-technology industry, such as urban Texas and southern California. In these areas, many conservative citizens expressed disillusion with the "decadence of scientism" and the bureaucratic authority that seemed to remove their sense of local power. The dominance of scientific values and the consequent decline in Christian teaching, they claimed, were responsible for contemporary social ills. These people form the financial, social, and political base for the science textbook disputes. Their answer to the uncertainties of a technological society is not to reject technology but to return to fundamentalist religion and traditional beliefs. It is in this context that evolution theory has become the focus of prolonged and bitter attack.

Scientists tend to associate the questioning of scientific rationality with alienation, crackpot ignorance, or pathology. They label those who persist in their criticism of scientific explanations as "irrational," "marginal," "out of touch" with modern society. The battles over science textbooks, however, cannot be easily dismissed as social pathology, for the challengers are people far removed from the deprived and marginal subcultures long associated with pentecostal sects; they are sober and solid, often technically trained, middle-class citizens, employed in white-collar jobs. Their ideas are squarely in line with Horatio Alger myths of individualism and self-determination, for they are seeking order, certainty, and some measure of independent control over their lives. Many of the textbook watchers identify themselves as scientists, arguing that alternative Biblical explanations can be scientifically validated. If the conservative groups who participate in these movements feel a sense of deprivation, it is their sense of decreased power, and their loss of local control to technical bureaucratic institutions. If they are marginal, their marginality is more philosophical than social, for they are engaged in an ideological battle to preserve their values against "the forces of irreligion, agnosticism, and secularism."

Yet the textbook disputes are less a manifestation of antiscience attitudes than a reflection of a much broader concern in contemporary American society with the social, political, and cultural implications of science. Criticism of science textbooks expresses the growing tensions in the relationship between science and society as public confidence in the unmitigated benefit of science wanes. Similar to many disputes over such diverse scientific and technical developments as fluoridation, nuclear power, or biomedical and genetic research, the creation-evolution controversy exposes concerns about the increasing role of technical expertise, the dominance of professional bureaucracies, and the neglect of local interests, and it illustrates how such concerns are translated into political and administrative decisions.

This study explores the complex spectrum of motives and perceptions underlying contemporary criticism of science as expressed in the arena of public education. Part I briefly portrays the historical context of present-day disputes, discussing those aspects of the early reaction to Darwinian evolution and its introduction in the schools that have recurred in contemporary conflicts. To provide more background on the textbook conflicts, Part I also describes the science curriculum reform movement. Part II discusses contemporary textbook watchers, analyzing their social and political base, and their political tactics. Part III describes three major disputes. Finally, Part IV analyzes their impact, the social and political concerns underlying the collision of values over science education, and the relationship between science and personal beliefs.

I

THE CONTEXT

[Science] wrote an end to the ancient animist covenant between man and nature, leaving nothing in place of that previous bond but an anxious quest in a frozen universe of solitude. With nothing to recommend it but a certain puritan arrogance, how could such an idea win acceptance? It did not; it still has not. It has however commanded recognition; but that is because, solely because, of its prodigious power of performance.

—Jacques Monod, *Chance and Necessity*

2

A Science or a World View? Historical Notes on the Teaching of Evolution

The metaphysical assumptions and moral implications inherent in aspects of evolution theory have been a source of conflict for over a hundred years. Pre-Darwinian biologists based their science on theological assumptions. Science was rooted in religion; its purpose was to prove the existence of God, using as evidence the design and purpose in nature. Darwin introduced an explanation of biological change that excluded the necessity of supernatural intervention and incorporated elements of chance and indeterminacy. Thus, Darwin's *Origin of Species* was viewed as a revolutionary document in 1859, although its primary contribution was to organize and synthesize a set of ideas that had pervaded the scientific literature for more than fifty years.[1] A brief review of the reactions to evolution theory in the nineteenth century, and later to its introduction in the American school system, suggests the persistence of certain concerns about its underlying assumptions and social implications.

Evolution and the Nineteenth-Century Soul

By 1800, theological explanations of human origins such as those of Archbishop James Ussher, the seventeenth-century prelate who established the year of origin as 4004 B.C., were already being seriously questioned as studies in biology and geology generated a variety of evolutionary hypotheses. For example, as early as 1796, James Hutton had attributed geological features to physical causes, introducing the principle that uniform geological agents operated during all periods of history to provoke continuous change.[2] By the 1830s, Charles Lyell had elaborated this uniformitarian hypothesis and laid the groundwork for modern geology by describing the development of the earth over many ages.[3] Other evolutionary theories appeared; the concept of catastrophism, associated mainly with Georges Cuvier, suggested that change occurred by sudden cataclysms that destroyed life and gave rise to new waves of increasingly complex living forms. Later, Lamarck related the tendency toward increased complexity to the influence of environment, which, he claimed, caused adaptive changes that were transmitted to subsequent generations. Others, such as Karl Nägeli, postulated that inner-directed forces guided evolution.[4] Meanwhile, a body of rich geological data accumulated.

Darwin saw evolution as the interplay of three principles: the occurrence of random variation; the mechanism of heredity, which transmits similar organic forms; and the struggle for existence, which determines which variations survive to be inherited. He described natural selection as a plausible causal mechanism for evolution in an environment that directly determines the survival of better-fitted variants (those able to reproduce themselves). Later, neo-Darwinians, benefiting from better understanding of genetics and the statistical analysis of gene pools, would develop evolution theory more in terms of the statistical transformation of populations than of changes in individuals, but in the nineteenth century

Darwin's work provided coherence and organization to a mass of observations and permitted scientists to develop logical postulates concerning the origin of life billions of years ago.

Despite its rich empirical base and the prior history of evolutionary thought, *The Origin of Species* was profoundly disturbing, for concepts of unlimited change and purposelessness, the "twin philosophical implications of Darwinism" distressed the nineteenth-century soul. While evolutionary concepts had been implicit in previous scientific advances, "Darwin brought them into the open when he applied them to the hitherto sacrosanct topic of the origin and destiny of man."[5]

The most active nineteenth-century resistance to the new science came from scientists themselves. The traditional scientific view was locked into a theoretical system based on the assumption that science must justify "the divine presence" and that scientific theories must rest on "a primordial creative power." The historian Charles Gillispie talks of the nineteenth-century debate as "one of religion in science rather than religion versus science."[6] Asa Gray, for example, saw the need of theories to prove an overarching design or ultimate purpose. Louis Agassiz described the obligation of the scientist: "Our task is . . . complete as soon as we have proven His existence."[7] Agassiz accepted the concept of evolutionary change, but assumed that the members of every species shared a common essence and that the essential character of any species was immutable. Natural selection violated this assumption of "fixity of species," as it violated earlier theories of uniformitarianism and catastrophism. Moreover, the idea that blind physical forces could generate change invalidated the assumption of progress toward an ideal state of perfection.

Perceiving science as an inductive process in which the collecting of facts was the only possible basis for constructing a theory, Darwin's critics also attacked him for violating scientific methodology. They argued that evolution was "mere hypothesis; unsubstantiated speculation." There were no concrete facts to demonstrate the existence of random variation, nor were there known transitional links between species. Adam Sedgwick, professor of geology at Cambridge, detested the theory "because it has deserted the inductive track, the only track that leads to physical truth; because it utterly repudiates final causes and thereby indicates a demoralized understanding on the part of its advocates."[8] And Sir Richard Owen, a paleontologist from the British Museum, expressed his disappointment about the inadequacy of observations: "We are called upon to accept a hypothesis on the plea of want of knowledge."[9] Darwin replied to such criticism by defining his sense of scientific method. "I am actually weary of telling that I do not pretend to adduce direct evidence of one species changing into another, but that I believe that this view is in the main correct because so many phenomena can thus be grouped together and explained."[10]

Beyond its impact on traditional science, Darwinism was devastating to conventional theology. Religious traditionalists accused Darwin of "limiting God's glory in creation," of "attempting to dethrone God," of "implying that Christians for nearly 2,000 years have been duped by a 'monstrous lie.' "[11] Evolution theory violated traditional theological assumptions, and, above all, the assumed distinction between man and the animal world. Yet Darwin himself did not reject the concept of a creator, writing that "There is grandeur in this view of life, with its several powers, having been originally breathed by the Creator into a few forms or into one; and that . . . from so simple a beginning endless forms most beautiful and most wonderful have been and are being evolved."[12]

By the turn of the century, both scientists and theologians were increasingly inclined to accept Darwinism as revealing God's purpose, and some elaborate theories attempted to reconcile geology and Genesis. P. H. Gosse, the religious naturalist, developed the omphalos theory that denied there had been a gradual modification of the earth. "When the catastrophic act of creation took place, the world presented instantly the structural appearance of a planet in which life had long existed."[13] Efforts at reconciliation included suggestions that the six days of creation were indeed eras, or that God created fossils simply to test man's faith.[14] Years later, Catholic theologians would reconcile science and religion as "two different approaches to reality, distinct in their methods of thought."[15] Both were concerned with the search for an orderly, harmonious universe, but neither excluded the other. By a sort of truce, it was assumed that religion provided a vision of a world beyond nature, while science was grounded in reality. Efforts to demonstrate the compatibility of religious conviction with modern science, to coordinate "the reality of divine revelation in the Cosmos and in Scripture," to prove that "Christ and not evolutionary process is the only adequate index to cosmic activity and purpose"[16] continue to this day.

By the end of the nineteenth century, the scientific and religious implications of Darwinism were fully matched if not exceeded by its philosophical and social influence. Late nineteenth-century entrepreneurs such as John D. Rockefeller and Andrew Carnegie found natural selection a comfortable sanction for laissez-faire economics. "The growth of large business is merely the survival of the fittest." Industrial competition was not an evil tendency, but "merely the working out of a law of nature and a law of God."[17] Indeed, postbellum America could be described as a caricature of the struggle for existence and survival of the fittest.

Evolution had an extraordinary appeal as a vision of reality. Herbert Spencer, the "cosmic evolutionist," soon applied the concept to society.

> The advance from the simple to the complex, through a process of successive differentiations, is seen alike in the earlier changes of the Universe to which we can reason our way back . . . it is seen in the unfolding of every single organism of its surface, and in the multiplication of kinds of organisms; it is seen in the evolution of Humanity, whether contemplated in the civilized individual, or in the aggregate of races; it is seen in the evolution of Society in respects alike of its political, its religious, and its economic organization.[18]

Later, Julian Huxley described the "evolutionary vision" as a naturalistic religion,[19] and C. H. Waddington, the noted British biologist, saw evolution as "a secure basis for ethics."[20]

In the United States, Victorian culture absorbed the theory of evolution.[21] In 1895, the National Education Association recommended a zoology course that was evolutionary in organization, and biology textbooks prior to 1920 began to introduce evolution theory to secondary schools and college students, often presenting it with extraordinary and perhaps self-conscious assurance. "We do not know of any competent naturalist who has any hesitation

in accepting the general doctrine."[22] "There is no rival hypothesis
to evolution, except the out-worn and completely refuted one of
special creation, now retained only by the ignorant, dogmatic, and
the prejudiced."[23]

Antievolution in the 1920s

The reconciliation between evolution and religion was not to last
in the United States; the conflict became a public issue in the 1920s
—provoked by fundamentalists in the South. Fundamentalism was
an American movement that developed around the turn of the
century as a defensive response to the threatening social changes
brought about by the industrial revolution, and to the cultural
diversity brought about by increasing immigration. Literal interpretation of the Bible became the bulwark against modern ideas.
While the movement was rooted in the ethos of the Methodist
revivalism of the early 1800s, it began to crystallize around the
issue of Darwinism after the publication in 1909 of a series of
pamphlets entitled *Fundamentals.* These pamphlets attacked
"modernism" and, in particular, evolution theory; the idea that
evolution involved discrete accidental changes determined by the
circumstances of the moment shattered fundamentalist faith in
planned and purposeful change. They attacked the theory with zeal
and enterprise, and worried about its implications for Christian
behavior.

By the 1920s, the issue of evolution divided Protestant churches;
fundamentalists denied the validity of evolution, and modernists
sought to reconcile their faith with science. Control over educational institutions was the arena for their battles. The major fundamentalist reaction against evolution took place in "backwoods"
areas, among people inclined to be irritated by the liberal and
disdainful attitudes of the industrial North. Intellectuals of the
time viewed it as a populist, anti-intellectual movement—"a revelation of the backwardness and intolerance of large elements of our
population."[24] Indeed, among Northerners who had reconciled
religion and evolution, the old assumption about the incompatibil-

ity of science and religion seemed almost absurd by the time the Scopes trial brought the issue to national prominence. In fact, the trial was not intended to raise this issue at all. Rather, it was provoked by the American Civil Liberties Union in order to show that Tennessee's antievolution legislation violated the First Amendment. The constitutional question, however, was buried as William Jennings Bryan and Clarence Darrow clashed over questions of religion and morality, and conveyed the resentment between northern liberals and southern conservatives.

Arthur Garfield Hays, who worked with Darrow for the defense, could hardly believe that "religious views of the middle ages" could recur "in spite of railroads, steamboats, the World War, the telephone, the radio, the airplane, all the great mechanistic discoveries."[25] Yet fundamentalists had considerable political influence in the twenties. Between 1921 and 1929, they introduced antievolution bills into thirty-seven state legislatures. These bills were passed in Mississippi (1926), Arkansas (1928), and Texas (1929). Fundamentalists also convinced publishers to qualify statements about evolution in those textbooks that included discussion of the theory by threatening to exclude such textbooks from adoption in the schools.

Evolution was not their only target. The revolt against science also included attempts to prescribe by law that π should be changed from 3.1416 to 3.000, partly because it was simple to use, partly because the Bible described Solomon's vase as three times as far around as across.[26]

One contemporary writer described the prevailing emotional hostility to science as a "cancer of ignorance," a repudiation of the authority and integrity of scientists.[27] But hostility was due largely to the association of evolutionary theory with disturbing social problems of the day. Evolutionary ideology, claimed Bryan, went beyond simple scientific questions and bore on moral values. The force of this argument was great in the 1920s, a comparatively lawless period; popular discussion suggested that the country was "going to ruin." Harry Emerson Fosdick, a liberal Baptist, speaking for "a large number of Christian people" disagreed with many of Bryan's ideas, but fully concurred that "Everyone closely associated with the students of our colleges and universities knows.

Many of them are sadly confused, mentally in chaos, and, so far as any guiding principles of religious faith are concerned, are often without chart, compass or anchor."[28] Social problems were variously attributed to the weakening of loyalty to the church, to postwar letdown, and to prosperity. But blame for "immorality" was also laid on a materialism fed by science and especially by the teaching of evolution.

The Scopes trial reflected parental demands to control the education and the values of their own children. "What right," Bryan asks, "have the evolutionists—a relatively small percentage of the population—to teach at public expense a so-called scientific interpretation of the Bible, when orthodox Christians are not permitted to teach an orthodox interpretation of the Bible?"[29] Scientists, however, had quite a different view about populist control of science curricula. "What is to be taught as science would be determined not by a consensus of the best scientific opinion, but by the votes of shopgirls and farmhands, ignorant alike of science and of the foundation principles of our civil society."[30] While the people of Dayton, Tennessee, defined the issue in terms of their social and moral concerns, the proponents of teaching evolution focused on the rational and logical basis of the theory. Clarence Darrow, for example, tried to force Bryan to a literal defense of the Bible as a scientific and logical document in order to "show up fundamentalism . . . to prevent bigots and ignoramuses from controlling the educational system."[31]

Although Scopes lost his case, the trial ended for a while the public efforts of fundamentalists to ban the teaching of evolution. The textbook crusades that were so influential in the 1920s faded from public view during the Depression, as economic problems and support for prohibition occupied the time of fundamentalist leaders. Antievolution sentiment persisted, but mostly among millennial sects such as Seventh-Day Adventists and Jehovah's Witnesses. Their tracts continued to denounce evolution theory as both incorrect and responsible for "the progressive worsening of crime, delinquency, immorality and even war . . . morals are broken down and for multitudes, faith in God has been shattered . . . evolution has paved the way for an increase in agnosticism and atheism as well as opening the door for communism."[32] During the 1940s and

1950s, fundamentalists were preoccupied with maintaining their own subculture, setting up Bible camps, colleges, seminaries, newspapers, and radio stations. To the extent that they attacked the public schools, they focused more on prayers and sex education than on evolution.[33]

The Legacy of the Scopes Trial

The relative quiescence of fundamentalists concerning the teaching of evolution in part reflected the neglect of the subject in biology textbooks after the Scopes trial. A scholarly survey of the content of biology texts up to 1960 found the influence of antievolutionist sentiment to be persistent, if undramatic, and showed that the teaching of evolution actually declined after 1925.[34] Textbooks published throughout the late 1920s ignored evolutionary biology, and new editions of older volumes deleted the word evolution and the name Darwin from their indexes. Some even added religious material. By the late 1930s some publishers were tentatively introducing evolution, but most, discouraged about market prospects and anxious to avoid controversy, avoided the topic, focusing largely on morphology and taxonomy.[35] In 1942, a nationwide survey of secondary school teachers indicated that fewer than 50 percent of high-school biology teachers were teaching anything about organic evolution in their science courses. Some avoided the subject either because of potential community opposition or their own personal beliefs. At the time, a biologist claimed that "biology is still pursued by long shadows from the middle ages, shadows screening from our people what our science has learned of human origins . . . a science sabotaged because its central and binding principle displaces a hallowed myth."[36] Fifteen years later, biology courses still neglected paleontology and evolution. A major biology textbook devoted only one page to evolution theory, which it called "racial development," and avoided discussion of origins.[37] As late as 1959, Herman J. Muller could write that public-school biology teaching was dominated by "antiquated religious traditions."[38] One hundred years after the theory of evolution by natural selection was firmly established, it was still not an integral part of the public-school curriculum.

Meanwhile, laws forbidding the teaching of evolution in public schools remained on the books in several southern states. In January 1961, a bill to repeal Tennessee's monkey laws, still in force thirty years after the Scopes trial, met prompt and passionate rejection by people who argued that evolution theory "drives God out of the universe" and "leads to communism." "Any persons or any groups who assist in any way to undermine faith in the teaching of the Bible are working in harmony with Communism."[39] In 1967, Gary Scott, a high-school teacher in Jacksboro, Tennessee, was dismissed from his job for violating the state statute. He appealed with legal assistance from the National Science Teachers Association. By this time reapportionment had given greater representation to urban areas in Tennessee, and the law was finally repealed. The sponsor of the repeal measure, D. O. Smith from Memphis, brought to the state legislature a caged monkey with the sign reading "Hello, Daddy," but his humor and the subsequent repeal of the legislation did not mean that the values of Tennessee citizens really changed. This was to become evident when the legislature met again on the issue in 1973.

In Little Rock, Arkansas, Governor Faubus defended antievolution legislation throughout the sixties: it was "the will of the people." But Susanne Epperson, a high-school teacher, challenged the legislation and won a favorable judgment in a local court. "The truth or the fallacy of arguments on each side of the evolution debate does not either contribute to or diminish the constitutional right of teachers and scientists to advance theories and to discuss them."[40] The state supreme court, however, upheld the constitutionality of the law forbidding the teaching of evolution, and it was not until 1968 that the U.S. Supreme Court ruled the Arkansas antievolutionary law unconstitutional. Following this precedent, the last of these laws (in Mississippi) was soon off the books.

Even as the courts challenged the old legislation forbidding the teaching of evolution, textbook watchers were gathering momentum for a renewed attack on the evolutionary assumptions of the new biology and social-science courses being introduced in their public schools.

Notes

1. Bentley Glass et al., eds., *Forerunners of Darwin 1945–1859* (Baltimore: Johns Hopkins Press, 1959).

2. James Hutton, *Theory of the Earth* (London: 1796).

3. Charles Lyell, *Principles of Geology* (London: John Murray, 1835).

4. For selections from Darwin's forerunners and a history of the response to Darwinism, see Philip Appleman, ed., *Darwin* (New York: W. W. Norton, 1970).

5. Langdon Gilkey, "Evolution and the Doctrine of Creation," in *Science and Religion,* ed. Ian Barbour (New York: Harper & Row, 1968), p. 164.

6. Charles Gillispie, *Genesis and Geology* (Cambridge, Mass.: Harvard University Press, 1951). For discussion of this point, see also Ernst Mayr, "The Nature of the Darwinian Revolution," *Science,* 2 June 1972, pp. 981–989.

7. Louis Agassiz, *Essays on Classification* (Boston: Little, Brown, 1957), p. 132.

8. Adam Sedgwick, "Objections to Mr. Darwin's Theory of the Origin of Species," *The Spectator,* 24 March 1860, p. 286.

9. Review of *The Origin of Species* in *Edinburgh Review* III (1860), reprinted in Appleman, *Darwin,* pp. 295–298.

10. Francis Darwin and A. C. Seward, eds., *More Letters of Charles Darwin* (London: S. Murray, 1968), vol. I, p. 184.

11. Andrew Dickson White, *A History of the Warfare of Science with Theology in Christendom* (New York: 1896).

12. Charles Darwin, *The Origin of Species,* II (New York: P. F. Collier, 1902), p. 316.

13. Edmund Gosse, *Father and Son* (London: Heine, 1907), p. 100.

14. For discussion of the reconciliation between science and religion, see Ian Barbour, *Science and Religion* (New York: Harper & Row, 1968), pt. II; Henry Drummond, "The Contribution of Science to Christianity," in *Henry Drummond, an Anthology,* ed. J. W. Kennedy (New York: Harper & Row, 1973); John Dillenberger, *Protestant Thought and Natural Science* (New York: Doubleday, 1960).

15. See, for example, discussion in Paul Chauchard, *Science and Religion* (New York: Hawthorn Books, 1962), p. 148.

16. Carl F. H. Henry, "Theology and Evolution," in *Evolution and Christian Thought Today,* ed. Russell Mixter (Grand Rapids, Mich.: Eerdmans, 1959), p. 202.

17. Cited in Richard Hofstadter, *Social Darwinism in American Thought* (Philadelphia: University of Pennsylvania Press, 1955), ch. 2.

18. Herbert Spencer, "Progress: Its Law and Causes," in *Essays: Scientific, Political and Speculative* (New York: Appleton, 1915), p. 35.

19. Julian Huxley, *Evolution in Action* (New York: Harper & Row, 1953), and *Religion without Revelation* (New York: Harper, 1927).

20. C. H. Waddington, *The Scientific Attitude* (London: Penguin Books, 1941), and *The Ethical Animal* (London: G. Allen and Unwin, 1960).

21. There was, however, a continued current of opposition to science expressed, for example, in the antivivisection movement. See Richard D. French, *Anti-Vivisection and Medical Science* (Princeton: Princeton University Press, 1975).

22. J. Arthur Thomson, *Concerning Evolution* (New Haven: Yale University Press, 1925), p. 53.

23. H. H. Newman, *Outlines of General Zoology* (New York: Macmillan, 1924), p. 407.

24. S. J. Holmes, "Proposed Laws against the Teaching of Evolution," *Bulletin of the American Association of University Professors* 13 (December 1927): 549–554.

25. Arthur Garfield Hays, "The Scopes Trial," in *Evolution and Religion,* ed. Gail Kennedy (New York: D. C. Heath, 1957), p. 36.

26. Howard K. Beale, *Are American Teachers Free?* (New York: Scribner, 1936), pp. 226–227.

27. Chester H. Rowell, "The Cancer of Ignorance," *The Survey,* 1 November 1925.

28. Harry Emerson Fosdick, "A Reply to Mr. Bryan in the Name of Religion," in Kennedy, *Evolution and Religion,* p. 33.

29. Bryan's ideas on evolution theory were influenced by George McCready Price.

30. Holmes, "Proposed Laws against the Teaching of Evolution," p. 554.

31. Frederick Lewis Allen, *Only Yesterday* (New York: Blue Ribbon Books, 1931), p. 205.

32. Jehovah's Witness, *Did Man Get Here by Evolution or Creation?* (Brooklyn, N.Y.: Watchtower Bible and Tract Society, 1967), pp. 168–170.

33. The Christian Crusade, run by Preacher Billy James Hargis, published a booklet called "Is the Little Red Schoolhouse the Proper Place to Teach Raw Sex?" This caused the demise of many sex-education programs in the United States. Other fundamentalist demagogues such as Gerald L. K. Smith associated fundamentalism with nationalism.

34. Judith Grabiner and Peter Miller, "Effects of the Scopes Trial," *Science,* 6 September 1974, pp. 832 ff.

35. Cornelius Troost, "Evolution in Biological Education Prior to 1960," *Science Education* 51 (1967): 300–301.

36. Oscar Riddle, "Preliminary Impressions and Facts from a Questionnaire on Secondary School Biology," *American Biology Teacher* 3 (February 1941): 151–159. This survey, done by the Union of American Biological Societies, was sent to 15,000 teachers, of whom 3,186 responded.

37. Truman J. Moon et al., *Modern Biology* (New York: Henry Holt, 1956), p. 665.

38. Herman J. Muller, "One Hundred Years without Darwinism Are Enough," *The Humanist* 19 (1959): 139.

39. W. Dykeman and J. Stokeley, "Scopes and Evolution—the Jury Is Still Out," *New York Times Magazine,* 12 March 1971, pp. 72–76.

40. Quoted in an editorial, *Science Teacher* 33 (September 1966): 17.

3

Science after Sputnik

As Sputnik was launched in 1957, so was the science curriculum reform movement, intended to build up scientific and technical manpower by bringing modern scientific knowledge to the nation's public schools. Science curriculum reform was an effort to enlist the public education system in the resolution of the problems of the cold war. It was based on the assumption that the public-school curriculum should introduce students to the key concepts and methods of the academic scientific disciplines.

Nearly every social and political cause looks to the school system as a means of effecting social reform. The demand for skilled labor in a growing industrial economy had prompted the movement for manual training in the schools. Concerns with urban migration and the bleak future of agriculture generated the Nature Study Movement. The progressive education movement after World War I reflected Wilsonian visions of a new and better world; schools became "an engine for social benefit," a means to apply the promise of American ideals to industrial civilization.[1]

The new science courses grew out of disillusion with the progressive movement, although they shared many of its ideals. "Our technological supremacy has been called into question," declared Admiral Hyman Rickover. "Parents are no longer satisfied with life adjustment schools. Parental objectives no longer coincide with those professed by professional educationists."[2] American schools, it was discovered, lagged behind their European counterparts, and textbooks hardly reflected the rapid development of modern scientific knowledge. The fragmented and competitive textbook industry, trying to reach a national market, seemed unwilling to run the risk of presenting new science materials for which there was little existing demand. Concerned scientists turned to federal agencies for what was, after all, a problem with national implications.

The Federal Government's Role

The public-school system in the United States is anarchic: about 20,000 school districts operate as autonomous domains serving a diverse population from rural, suburban, and inner-city backgrounds. Anarchy permits flexibility in educational experimentation, as long as it is not costly. However, the diversity of values and differences in priorities in this complex school system limits costly or controversial innovation.

It is customary to deal with diversity by avoiding conflict. For schoolteachers this has meant a considerable reluctance to introduce subjects such as evolution theory in classrooms where religious objections are likely to appear. For the highly competitive textbook industry, conflict avoidance means continual compromise. The industry must produce books that are provocative, but not so different as to be controversial; textbooks must stand out in some way in order to compete effectively, yet be sufficiently standard to attract the largest possible market. Most publishers, operating on a low profit margin, shun experiments and avoid controversy. Major textbook reforms are, therefore, seldom initiated by the industry, and in subject areas of high relevance to national goals, federal agencies felt it appropriate to intervene. This was the situation when competition with Soviet technology brought awareness of the need for technical manpower.[3]

In 1957, Jerrold Zacharias and a group of physicists from Cambridge, Massachusetts, formed the Physical Science Study Committee (PSSC). This group proposed to develop films to teach physics to high-school students, and they received a grant of $303,000 from the National Science Foundation to develop the project. PSSC was the first course in the NSF's science curriculum development program, which soon grew into an important activity within the foundation, and a major enterprise in the history of education.[4] The physics program was followed by mathematics, chemistry, biology, and finally by social sciences; by 1975, NSF had funded fifty-three projects at a total cost of $101,207,000.

Following the success of the PSSC, research scientists worked with educational experts to prepare course materials that reflected the knowledge and methods of modern science.[5] The new curriculum thus tried to remedy the authoritarian textbook presentation of science. Students had long been fed "objective facts" and "proven laws of nature" through textbooks based on the assumption that science was simply an inductive process. Scientists themselves had rejected this approach; the role of theory was less to explain than to predict. Students, claimed the curriculum reformers, must therefore be taught to use theory as an instrument of prediction and to participate in the process of scientific discovery. The new curriculum focused on the methods of science and introduced students to the research process. Pedagogical techniques followed from the idea that the student must be an active "scientific investigator" rather than a passive recipient of materials provided by teachers. Moreover, the materials were to be "teacher-proof," conveying accepted concepts of science regardless of local opinions or local circumstances. The science courses thus not only updated materials but tried to change the methods of education, focusing less on the learning of facts than on the methods of inquiry and the exercise of individual judgment.

At first the NSF approached the problem of improving science education by supporting projects to develop new textbooks, films, and audiovisual materials as proposed by various educational centers and university departments throughout the country. It very quickly became apparent that the development of courses or books was not sufficient to assure their utilization. Due to the costly nature of multimedia materials and equipment, an initial federal subsidy was needed to implement their use. Teachers had to be trained to understand the new curriculum and to use the new pedagogical techniques.

NSF approached programs for implementation with some reluctance. While concerned with disseminating the material it had sponsored, foundation officers were also aware of the political sensitivity of local school districts to any implementation program that might appear to be "federal intervention." They were constantly under congressional pressure to avoid such "interference."[6]

"You do not interfere unless they ask you to interfere." (Senator Magnuson, 1958)
"I don't want these things rammed down the throat of educators." (Senator Allott, 1964)
"You are not suggesting the philosophy . . . that is being taught? This is a local option of the school district." (Congressman Talcott, 1967)

Federal funds were finally appropriated for three types of implementation activities: leadership projects to train specialists who would influence curriculum decisions and guide local implementation efforts; teacher training projects;[7] and projects to help local schools, in cooperation with colleges and universities, put NSF materials and techniques into practice.

Until the late 1960s the thrust of the new NSF-supported curriculum was to encourage scientific careers. An important early exception was the Biological Sciences Curriculum Study (BSCS), which was directed to a much wider student body and essentially taught "biology for the citizen." Later in the sixties, responding to a general social concern with "science for citizenship," the foundation began to shift its emphasis in other courses as well. The declining need for scientists and engineers had coincided with an apparent disillusion with science and technology and their association with social and environmental problems. Better public understanding of science might, it was hoped, create more favorable attitudes. Again, the public schools were the vehicles for reform, and curriculum was now to be directed not only to future scientists but to citizens in a society in which science was a crucial economic, social, and political influence. This change in perspective, however, also required new pedagogical techniques to make science more palatable to nonspecialized students. Science teaching would have to be oriented around practical problems rather than traditional disciplines, and this implied increased attention to the social and behavioral sciences.

NSF had always approached the support of social-science research and education with caution. The physical scientists who had formed the foundation during the late 1940s and had shaped its development had been strongly opposed to the inclusion of social science among the foundation's activities. They argued that the quality of work in the field, and its political connotations of socialism and public manipulation would undermine public confidence in other scientific activities.[8]

The foundation eventually funded social-science research under the vague rubric "And Other Sciences," but it remained extremely careful to support only "ultra-safe lines of inquiry."[9] Only in 1968, when Congress endorsed the Division of Social Sciences through an amendment to the NSF Act, were the social sciences afforded status equal to other categories of science. Congress was especially cautious with respect to curriculum development. By this time, however, the NSF officers were complacent about the social sciences: in the budget hearings for fiscal year 1966, Dr. Riecken asserted, "The kind of social science materials being produced under our grants are not, I think, likely to be as much trouble as the biologists have had over evolution."[10]

Complacency was understandable. Until the late 1960s science education was relatively immune to attack—with the important exception of persistent efforts to keep evolution out of textbooks. And during the years following World War II, when textbook watchers were most active, even this issue received relatively little attention compared, for example, to questions of patriotism or sex education. The development of the science curriculum, a highly professionalized activity, was hardly a problem to be thought of in political terms. The earliest NSF courses in the physical sciences, developed for a limited group of potential scientists, raised few controversial issues. If there were profound objections, faith in science and its association with material progress overwhelmed them.

Scholars had enthusiastically acclaimed many of the new course materials, and once federal initiatives stimulated a market for these materials, private publishers followed, incorporating many of their features in their own publications. By 1970, about one fourth of all high-school students in the United States were taking science courses based on NSF materials.[11] The program thus brought about widespread pedagogical change, with implications for teachers, students, parents, publishers, testing agencies, local school boards, and other participants in the educational system. Yet the foundation continued to treat curriculum development contracts much as it treated research grants, relying on the professional peer review system to control the quality and accuracy of the work performed under its sponsorship. As in the case of funded research, this meant minimum interference with the course development process.[12] The foundation thus supported curriculum development, but refused to endorse or claim responsibility for the educational value of the materials produced. Its role was to make materials available but not to mandate their use. This was a deliberate policy intended to avoid accusations of federal intervention in local educational policy.

Inevitably, however, dissemination of federally funded materials increased the tension between the federal government and local school districts jealously guarding their autonomy; and between professional educators concerned with disseminating knowledge and parents preoccupied with perpetuating family values. As the science curriculum, reflecting contemporary research, dealt with controversial aspects of evolution theory and its importance for understanding human development and behavior, these tensions increased. By improving the public-school curriculum, the NSF, despite its denial of responsibility, found itself involved not in an isolated neutral research endeavor but in a major social intervention filled with political implications.

The Biological Sciences Curriculum Study

Soon after the NSF funded the physics program, the American Institute of Biological Sciences (AIBS) began to discuss the problem of public education in biology, which appeared to be at least twenty years behind current research in the discipline. Biologists were particularly concerned about the neglect of evolution theory. Population genetics, entomology, and experimental field work in paleontology and geology had brought both refinements to and increasing support for evolution theory. It was confirmed and reconfirmed as a useful scientific hypothesis. Yet, during the Darwin centennial celebration of 1959, a group of selected teachers at an NSF summer institute agreed that teaching evolution was still hampered by deficient texts, inadequate knowledge among schoolteachers, and their continued fear of local religious opposition.

Biologists were appalled to realize that the sophisticated research in the discipline was so poorly taught. Biology is, after all, a key course in general-science education. Over 90 percent of American high schools offer a biology course, and an estimated 80 percent of all high-school students enroll in the subject; for most, it is their only exposure to science. After the centennial, a group of distinguished scientists from the AIBS formed the Biological Sciences Curriculum Study (BSCS) at the University of Colorado to develop a modern approach to the teaching of biology. NSF provided the center with $7 million.

Unlike physics and chemistry, biology had to be presented at a level where it would be studied by a majority of students.

> A sound biological understanding is the inalienable right of every child who, when adult, will need to cope with individual problems of health and nutrition; with family problems of sex, and reproduction and parenthood; and with citizens' problems of wise management of natural resources and biological hazards of nuclear agents.[13]

BSCS decided to abandon the earlier taxonomic approach requiring extensive memorization, and instead to focus on methods and laboratory research. "Inquiry-oriented" instruction replaced the "pickled frog approach" involving memorization of facts. "The emphasis . . . is placed on the nature of science, on the men who have worked as scientists, and on scientific inquiry. The point is to teach science not as a body of classified knowledge, but as an approach to problem solving."[14]

Finally, the BSCS determined that their work would not avoid controversial subjects such as organic evolution and that they would base the new curriculum on current themes of biology: the change of living things through time, the diversity of types and unity of pattern in living things, the genetic continuity of life, the complementarity of organisms and environment, and the biological roots of behavior.[15]

BSCS set up curriculum study groups involving professional biologists and educators. These had no commercial dependence on the nonacademic marketplace, for BSCS felt strongly that biology books had in the past suffered from the influence of political interest groups and apprehensive public officials.

In 1963, after nearly five years of preparation and testing, BSCS marketed three introductory textbooks for high-school classes. Each volume had a slightly different emphasis, reflecting trends in biological research; one stressed cellular biology, another ecology, another molecular analysis.[16] However, the material overlapped by about 70 percent, and each book was based on evolutionary assumptions as "the warp and woof of modern biology."[17]

In 1961, as a part of its testing program, BSCS had tried out one of the books in Dade County, Florida, and had run into a skirmish when school authorities asked that diagrams of the reproductive system be removed. BSCS refused and the school officials themselves blackened out offending material. BSCS scholars were not particularly surprised at this reaction, but they did not anticipate a religious opposition. It was generally assumed that, while an occasional extremist might emerge, sympathy for scientific accuracy would prevail.

When the books were finally marketed, there were a number of isolated incidents of hostility. School supervisors in several southern states refused to purchase the books. The state board of education of New Mexico insisted that the inside front covers of all BSCS books be stamped with a note emphasizing that evolution was a theory, not a fact, and that this was the official position of the state board. Then a major dispute took place in Texas, a state with a long tradition of conservatism in the selection of textbooks. When BSCS books were submitted for adoption to the state textbook screening committee, the Reverend Reuel Lemmons, of the Church of Christ, a fundamentalist sect claiming 600,000 members in Texas, appealed to the board of education and to Governor John Connally. He called the books "pure evolution from cover to cover, completely materialistic and completely atheistic," and asked his constituents to petition against their adoption.

The campaign against BSCS in Texas continued during the summer and fall of 1964. One critic suggested in a letter to Connally that "the assassination of our late president and the attempt on your life were the vicious attacks of a Godless individual. It is the purpose of this letter to call your attention to a situation in our state which is designed to promote such Godlessness in our public schools through the atheistic teaching of evolution theory."[18] That the assassination took place from the state textbook depository was not ignored by textbook opponents.

The protest reached its peak in October when the state textbook selection committee held a public hearing. Lemmons and his supporters, including two college professors, sought to have the textbooks banned as a violation of the First Amendment. The committee finally approved all three BSCS books, but only after several changes in the books that softened their evolutionary emphasis. These, for example, specified that evolution theory was a theory, not a fact, and that it had been "modified," not "strengthened" by recent research.

Subsequently, nearly 50 percent of American high schools used BSCS materials, which later included films, pamphlets, and other instructional programs. During most of the 1960s, the major problem facing BSCS was less a matter of social protest than the inertia of high-school teachers, who often failed to understand the materials and the methods of science sufficiently to convey the character and use of evolution theory in biology.

Man: A Course of Study

Social-studies courses for upper elementary school children often consist of descriptive presentations of American history directed toward creating "responsible citizens" with allegiance to the values of democracy. Few students are exposed to the study of human behavior until their college years. That this situation was perceived as a problem in the 1960s reflected the contemporary confidence (also evident in the Great Society programs) that social-science knowledge could be useful in coping with major social problems.

In the early 1960s, the American Council of Learned Societies began to grapple with reform of the social-studies curriculum. To meet potential objections, the council first had to reconcile the "new" social sciences with the well-entrenched concepts and goals of the traditional social-studies curriculum. It concluded that social science did not conflict with traditional goals, but rather would enhance them by developing the student's analytic perspectives and respect for "objective knowledge" about human behavior. The controversial issues that were bound to arise could be dealt with in a spirit of open scientific inquiry free from prejudice and ignorance.

Reflecting this belief, in 1963 a group of scholars organized by Jerome Bruner met in Cambridge, Massachusetts, with the Educational Services Incorporated (later called the Education Development Center [EDC]) to discuss the possibility of developing a new humanities and social-science curriculum. The result of this meeting was an exploratory proposal to the NSF. The foundation funded the proposal and eventually granted EDC $4.8 million to develop Man: A Course of Study (MACOS), a year-long program for the fifth and sixth grades using films, tapes, games, and dramatic devices to introduce children to several fundamental questions about human behavior: What is human about human beings? How did we get that way? How can we be made more so?

The program is based on scientific research on animal behavior and on ethnographic studies of human behavior. It focuses in particular on the Netsilik Eskimos, a traditional hunting society from the Pelly Bay region of Canada. It uses these studies to explore fundamental questions about the nature of human beings, their daily life style, patterns of social interaction, child-rearing practices, and cosmology.[19] The main emphasis in MACOS, however, is ethological, focusing on animal behavior. This orientation was more a political than an intellectual decision, a response to the political reality of the educational establishment in which social studies remained dominated by historians. By linking the course to the biological sciences, EDC hoped to avoid interference. This also meant that the course had to be developed at the elementary-school level in order to avoid overlapping the new biology curriculum.

Pedagogically, the course is heavily influenced by Bruner's concept of education as a self-motivated process. Bruner argues that the factors leading to satisfaction in learning are curiosity, confidence, identification with the subject, and reciprocity, or the need to respond to others.[20] Children, claims Bruner, need reassurance that they may entertain and express highly subjective ideas; they learn more by creating answers than by finding them in books. The task of education, then, is to provide a stimulating environment that will give children the opportunity to use their own problem-solving skills. Thus MACOS is open-ended and problem-seeking, based on student inquiry and the free exploration of values rather than on teacher authority. Children are asked to compare and contrast what they observe in films and books with their own experience, and to examine their own values as yet another source of data.

MACOS does not avoid controversial issues. The course includes discussions of religion, reproduction, aggression, and murder, for it is built on the assumption that it is necessary to deal with such problems in a thoughtful and reflective manner. "Oversimplification and dogmatism are twin enemies of creative thought."[21] In controversial areas, teachers are advised to encourage their students to cultivate independent attitudes and warned that the questions raised by the course often have no clear-cut answers.

These "liberal pedagogical assumptions" were themselves destined to alienate those textbook critics who were committed to traditional authoritarian relationships in the school system. But the substance of the course and its underlying assumptions were even more controversial. MACOS presents details of animal behavior as provocative metaphors that help to illuminate features of human behavior. The course thus includes a study of the life cycle of salmon, the family life of herring gulls, and the social behavior of baboons, always inviting contrast and comparison with human life.

For example, in the course of discussing animal behavior, the children are encouraged to ask difficult questions about human society. If salmon can survive without parental protection, why cannot man? What differences do parents make? What do you think are the characteristics of successful parents? What is the value of a group to the survival of its individual members? And what is the value of cooperation as opposed to competition? The course thus assumes a discernible continuity between animals and man that remains difficult for many people to accept.

The analysis of Netsilik culture is intended to convey the concept that humanness is an attained and man-made condition "composed of an environment shaped to suit his needs, a society with common rules and expectations and a spiritual community of mutually held values and beliefs."[22] The study of a distinctive traditional culture that must adapt to a rigorous environment suggests how behavior is shaped by the functional requirements of particular situations. The Netsilik culture offers profound contrasts with American society; it is a society without social hierarchy held together by social bonds and surviving through forms of adaptive behavior uniquely suited to survival in a difficult environment. But an understanding of this culture requires presentation of behavior that seems bizarre and morally repugnant to Western culture (practices of senilicide and infanticide), behavior dictated by the need to minimize the economic burden of maintaining the weak. This, of course, raises touchy moral questions: "How does our society treat the elderly?" "Do you think your parents ever have to choose between pleasing a friend and doing something they believe is important or right?" "How do cosmologies develop out of culture and experience, and in turn influence this experience?" Teachers are asked to raise these questions without making judgments, and students are asked to explore relationships among their families and friends.

The point emphasized again and again in both animal and Eskimo studies is that neither behavior nor beliefs have absolute value apart from their social or environmental context. "Our hope," claims Bruner, "is to lead the children to understand how man goes about understanding his world, making sense of it; that one kind of explanation is no more human than another."[23] And in *Talks to Teachers,* MACOS emphasizes that values and moral principles must also adapt to contemporary circumstances: "The rules by which man will have to govern himself must take into account the inventiveness of man himself, the variability of situations in which he finds himself, and the historic process in which change occurs."[24]

MACOS was clearly treading on sensitive ground, dealing with questions that are the foundation of the most dogmatic beliefs. The course is not only built on evolutionary assumptions, but it denies the existence of absolute values, thus explicitly teaching just those controversial ideas that fundamentalists have long suspected were implicit in the teaching of evolution.

Publishers were well attuned to the sensitivity of the marketplace, and the troublesome features of MACOS became apparent when EDC began to seek a commercial publisher. The course had already been successfully tested and evaluated in 300 selected classrooms throughout the country, where it was acclaimed as a major educational contribution.[25] But commercial publishers backed away; "religious groups would not endorse the teaching of this type of material."[26] Thus, in 1969 EDC sought funding from the NSF for manufacturing and distribution costs.

MACOS was finally published in 1970 and, by the end of 1974, had been purchased by about 1,700 schools in forty-seven states. Sales were yielding $700,000 per year. They were to plummet dramatically in 1975 with an epidemic of community disputes. But more important, this controversial course based on evolutionary assumptions provoked an attack on the NSF that was to end the period of science-curriculum reform.

Notes

1. For an excellent history of the relationship between educational and social reforms, see Lawrence A. Cremin, *The Transformation of the School* (New York: Alfred A. Knopf, 1962).

2. Hyman G. Rickover, *Education and Freedom* (New York: Dutton, 1959), pp. 189–190.

3. Congressional support for educational reform in science was evident in NSF appropriations hearings and in the National Defense Education Act of 1958, which subsidized improved teaching in mathematics, science, and foreign languages. See discussion of legislative oversight of early NSF

curriculum development in National Science Foundation, Science Curriculum Review Team, *Pre-College Science Curriculum Activities* (Washington, D.C.: U.S.G.P.O., May 1975), vol. 2.

4. This program was first called Course Content Improvement Program, then the Curriculum and Instruction Development Program, and later the Materials and Instruction Development Section.

5. The philosophy behind this approach is described by J. J. Schwabb, "Structure of the Disciplines," in *The Structure of Knowledge and the Curriculum,* ed. G. W. Ford and L. Pugno (New York: Rand McNally, 1964), pp. 6–30.

6. NSF, *Pre-College Science Curriculum Activities,* pp. 36–38.

7. By 1973, NSF had supported 7,000 summer institutes, mostly for high-school teachers.

8. See Policy Research Division of Library of Congress, *Technical Information for Congress,* Report to the Subcommittee on Science, Research and Development, of the Committee on Science and Astronautics, U.S. House of Representatives, 25 April 1969, ch. 5.

9. *Ibid.,* p. 103.

10. NSF, *Pre-College Science Curriculum Activities,* p. 38.

11. For statistics on dissemination see Joseph Platt, "NSF and Science Education," *Journal of General Education* 27 (Fall 1975): 188 ff.

12. NSF, *Pre-College Science Curriculum Activities,* pp. 63–65.

13. Bentley Glass, "Renascent Biology," in *New Curriculum,* ed. Robert W. Heath (New York: Harper & Row, 1964).

14. Arnold Grobman et al., *BSCS Biology—Implementation in the Schools,* Boulder, Colorado: American Institute of Biological Sciences, Bulletin #3, 1964, p. 1.

15. Addison Lee, "The BSCS Position on the Teaching of Biology," *BSCS Newsletter* 49 (November 1972), 5–6.

16. The three textbooks, known as the blue, green, and yellow volumes, were published respectively by Houghton Mifflin, Rand McNally, and Harcourt, Brace.

17. BSCS, *Biology Teachers' Handbook* (New York: Wiley, 1963).

18. Hillel Black, *The American Schoolbook* (New York: Morrow, 1967).

19. MACOS material includes sixteen films and about thirty booklets, plus games, posters, and records. A complete list is available in a brochure published by Curriculum Development Associates, Washington, D.C., 1972.

20. Jerome Bruner, *Toward a Theory of Instruction* (Cambridge, Mass.: Harvard University Press, 1966).

21. Education Development Center (EDC), ed., *Talks to Teachers* (Cambridge, Mass., EDC, 1968), p. 13.

22. Peter Dow, "Man: A Course of Study," in *Talks to Teachers,* p. 5.

23. Jerome Bruner, MACOS Position Paper, mimeographed (Cambridge, Mass.: EDC, 1964), p. 24.

24. EDC, ed., *Talks to Teachers,* p. 58.

25. In February 1969, the American Educational Publishers Institute and the American Educators Research Association awarded Bruner a prize for his contribution to the instructional process.

26. Peter Dow, "Publish or Perish," mimeographed (Cambridge, Mass.: EDC, 9 May 1975).

II

THE SCIENCE-TEXTBOOK WATCHERS

I don't know very much, I just know the difference between right and wrong.

—George Bernard Shaw, *Major Barbara*

4

Textbook Watchers and Space-Age Fundamentalism

Forbidden Subjects

Just as perceptions of social and political needs generate curriculum reform, so social and political tensions provoke educational disputes.[1] Indeed, public schools have been an active political arena in curriculum as well as organizational matters as parents, community groups, or self-appointed textbook watchers contest any changes in the substance or methods of teaching that violate their perceptions about the values to be conveyed to young citizens.

Patriotism, educational standards, and morality are three traditional themes of curriculum disputes, emerging in relation to contemporary political and social issues. Waves of immigration, incidents that suggest communist expansion, or U.S. involvement in international affairs have invariably put textbook watchers on guard against what they feel are threats to American values. Classroom discussions of the United Nations, the labor movement, the

New Deal, or socialism have provoked calls for censorship. Textbooks, claimed a patriotic group called America's Future, must "reflect appreciation of American sovereignty and the reasons for preserving it." Schools, after all, could become "a breeding ground for alien ideologies."[2]

These conservative themes emerged just prior to World War II as a reaction to the progressive movement in education. Critics labeled progressive schools "anti-intellectual playhouses" and "crime breeders" run by a "liberal establishment." They wrote about "Treason in the Textbooks" and "Lollypops vs. Learning."[3] Fifteen years later, this sentiment converged with cold-war concerns about American technological inadequacy, and the criticism of progressive education grew both more forceful and more widespread. It came from respectable academics as well as from congenital reactionaries. Education was divorced from scholarship, contended the American historian Arthur Bestor; in democratizing the school system educators had forgotten its function of systematic intellectual training. "Where are our standards?" asked the Council for Basic Education, formed in 1956 to protect educational standards. Critics turned against the professional educators, who were blamed for neglecting scholarship and suspected for their "left-wing liberalism."[4] In the late 1950s, concern over Soviet technological competition reached its peak after Sputnik, and the progressive movement in education collapsed.

Among the critics of progressive education were scientists. Their criticism of the weakness of scientific scholarship in the school system had led to the science curriculum reform movement. But just as scientists associated "technological decadence" with the absence of scientific rationality in education, so textbook watchers would later associate "moral decadence" with the dominance of scientific rationality.

The 1963 Supreme Court decision on the unconstitutionality of forcing children to read prayers in school inspired special vigilance against the influence of secular and scientific values. Rapidly changing life styles among young people in the 1960s and their rejection of tradition confirmed conservatives' worst fears about the moral implications of declining religious influence.

The decadence of scientism is provoking the resurrection of bacchanals and orgies. One can observe a thirst for ritual . . . the monolithic stranglehold which scientism has on education has issued in the contamination of minds. . . . the erosion of sensibility, the corruption of imagination, and ultimately the explosion of hate.[5]

Thus, by the time the NSF education projects were well under way in public schools, textbook watchers had found another theme—the erosion of religious and moral values implicit in biological- and social-science courses. The denial that nature was subordinated to a transcendent purpose was, they argued, a primary source of the damaging material culture and the decline in morality that they witnessed.

The popular reaction against scientific rationality in the late 1960s was evident in the wide interest in Eastern mysticism, occultism, astrology, and the pop cosmologies of Velikovsky and Von Däniken. Less visible, but perhaps of more political importance in the long run, has been the reaction among an entirely different group of people, expressed in a revival of interest in traditional religion and educational fundamentalism, and in an outcry against "secular humanism."[6]

The Conservative Ministries

Changing patterns of church membership in the 1960s reflected a renewed interest in conservative religions. Memberships in established Protestant churches began to level off around 1964 and to decline by 1967, but during this same period conservative ministries, often holding very traditional beliefs and making strict demands on their members concerning appropriate behavior, began to grow. Among Lutherans, only the Missouri Synod—the most conservative denomination—expanded its membership. Similarly, the Assemblies of God, the Pentecostal and Holiness groups, Mormons, and Jehovah's Witnesses began to grow steadily around 1960.[7] (See Table 4.1 and Figure 4.1.)

Pentecostal faith healers (such as Oral Roberts) who started their careers in the 1940s began to build universities and Bible

Figure 4.1. Changing Church Membership in Twelve Protestant Groups (1958–1974)

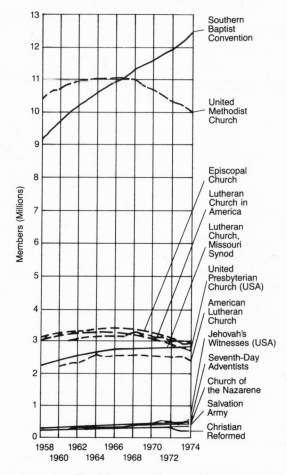

SOURCE: Data compiled from National Council of Churches, *Yearbook of American Churches* (annual statistics). Graph from Dorothy Nelkin, "The Science Textbook Controversies," *Scientific American,* 234 (April 1976): 36. *Note:* Membership of groups with a fundamentalist viewpoint (solid line) has increased steadily, while membership of nonfundamentalist groups (dotted line) peaked in the mid-1960s and has declined since then.

TABLE 4.1. Membership Statistics for Conservative Churches

Church	Year	Number of Churches	Church Membership
Assemblies of God	1960	8,233	508,602
	1971	8,734	1,064,631
	1979	9,562	1,629,014
Southern Baptist Convention	1960	32,251	9,731,591
	1970	34,340	11,628,032
	1979	35,552	13,372,757
United Pentecostal Church	1960	1,700	175,000
	1971	2,400	250,000
	1980	2,892	465,000
Seventh-Day Adventists	1960	3,032	317,852
	1970	3,218	420,419
	1979	3,672	553,089
Jehovah's Witnesses (USA)	1960	4,170	250,000
	1970	5,492	388,290
	1979	7,545	526,961
Lutheran Church (Missouri Synod)	1960	5,215	2,391,195
	1970	5,690	2,788,536
	1979	5,689	2,673,181

SOURCE: National Council of Churches, *Yearbook of American Churches* (published annually).

institutes. The radio religions expanded to television. One of the most successful of the 1960s preachers was Herbert W. Armstrong, who organized the World Wide Church of God, based in Southern California. Armstrong runs Ambassador College in Pasadena, devoted to restoring the "missing dimension of moral and spiritual values to education." Some fundamentalists associated their movement with the space program. Carl McIntire developed 300 acres at Cape Canaveral as a "freedom center" for his Twentieth Century Reform Movement. He bought the Cape Kennedy Hilton, a convention center, and several other buildings, calling the multimillion dollar complex "Gateway to the Stars, a place that would be witness to His word and a haven for patriots who put their love for God first."[8] Similarly, several astronauts organized High Flight, an evangelical ministry in Colorado.

The reaction against the dominance of scientific values in education was compatible with fundamentalist views. "Our ministry is very proud of the fact that we hold the creationist viewpoint as related in the Book of Genesis," claims Billy James Hargis, minister of Christian Crusade. "We feel strongly that any school that teaches evolution should also teach creation in an equal and fair manner."[9] Herbert Armstrong publishes antievolution material in his magazine *Plain Truth,* which advocates literal belief in "the simple, factual, logical record of the Bible." The Armstrong Ambassador College catalogue expresses the following view:

> Science, industry, and much of modern education have concentrated on developing the machine rather than the man. The actual bitter fruits of this modern materialist "progress" are increasing unhappiness, discontent, boredom, moral and spiritual decadence . . . the way to peace and happiness is through the Bible . . . the authoritative revelation of the most necessary basic knowledge . . . the foundation of all knowledge and the approach to humanly acquirable knowledge.[10]

This perspective is widely shared in the fundamentalist press, which dwells on "disaster," "lurking evil," "terrible peril," and "threats to survival"—all of these the consequence of scientific secularism.[11]

Fundamentalists criticize scientists for "suppressing" religious views. The Watch Tower Society's Magazine, *Awake* (distribution 7.5 million), has attempted to mobilize its leadership to challenge evolutionary teaching as "the greatest fairytale ever to masquerade under the name of science."[12] In an article entitled "Do I Have to Believe in Evolution?" *Awake* attacks biologists: "Like a religious hierarchy in the dark ages, they declare *ex cathedra* that evolution is a fact and excommunicate into the outer darkness of ignorance anyone who will not embrace their faith."[13] A set of comic books widely disseminated by Jack Chick Publications in Chino, California, conveys similar themes.[14] *Link Lizard Defeats Evolution* portrays the "superscientist" humbled before evidence provided by Little Laurie, who argues that "Any kind of in-between creatures would be a flop, Doc." A more pernicious booklet, *Big Daddy,* depicts a Jewish-looking professor teaching evolution to his class of long-haired hippies, liberated women, and blacks with Afros. A clean-cut, short-haired blond youth politely and cooly challenges the professor with "facts," citing reputable scientific journals. The professor becomes more and more emotional, trying in vain to support his "beliefs" and finally resigns, defeated and humiliated, as the class turns to religious themes.

In the 1920s, the fundamentalist movement mirrored the discontent of marginal people threatened with disintegration of old life styles. It prevailed mostly in small-town rural areas isolated from modern scientific culture. Today, fundamentalism flourishes in the centers of advanced science and technology, and fundamentalists include middle-class suburbanites, often people with technical training. Anxious about the uncertainty caused by rapid social and technological change, they seek new patterns of personal meaning and definitive answers to complex social problems through traditional fundamentalist values. This need for more rigid religious programs has permeated the larger, more liberal Protestant denominations as well as the fundamentalist churches. There is increasing criticism of "secular theology" (the reliance on the ability of man to solve his own problems) and an emphasis on "the need for sound fundamental beliefs and personal faith."[15]

This renewal of fundamentalism is important to our discussion of science textbook politics. Evangelical conservatives, disillusioned with modernism, are the political and financial base for the movement against science curriculum reform. The fundamentalist ministries are a communications network for the textbook watchers; their interest allows some very active individuals to wield significant influence.

The New Censors

In 1963, Mr. and Mrs. Mel Gabler of Longview, Texas, began to scrutinize the textbooks used in Texas schools. Gabler retired from his job as a clerk in an Exxon district office in 1973 to devote full time to textbook review. Mrs. Gabler is a housewife and mother. The Gablers are among the most active of Texas textbook watchers, appearing at hearings and public meetings to warn communities about threats to their children's education. They have had considerable support from their local home town of Longview, Texas (population: 44,000), which in 1973 awarded Mrs. Gabler a prize as the most outstanding citizen of the year. They have also built up a network of contacts throughout the country among people who share their views.

The Gablers are motivated by concerns with morality. "Have you noticed how texts have been systematically eliminating the basic moral and philosophical precepts of Biblical Christianity and good sense?"[16] They believe that textbooks foster anti-American-ism and hatred for the home and family, as well as the "pernicious idea that man is an animal." The only defense, they argue, is community involvement in textbook decisions. "Unless local people take an active voice in assisting the authorized units of government in the program of selecting textbooks, the selection will continue to deteriorate."

The Gablers claim that schools are "government seminars," promoting a godless religion of secular humanism. They want to return to Biblical standards, the teaching of absolute values, and respect for authority and the free-enterprise system. Consistent with this mission, their targets include Robin Hood, Watergate, and Vietnam. They also include the teaching of evolutionary assumptions that may undermine traditional religious beliefs. "Students should be given both sides in order that they may form their own views."

In September 1969, the Gablers' persistent campaign in Texas began to pay off when the board of education did not put the BSCS textbooks on the state-approved list. This gave them encouragement:

> Over the years we have often questioned whether we should continue the textbook work; but this hearing alone justifies the tedious, time-consuming work and budget-drawing expenses for which so few have shown a concern, yet which are vitally important because our nation moves in the exact direction the children are taught.[17]

The Gablers then formed Educational Research Analysts, a non-profit, tax-exempt organization whose assets are described as "wide experience in textbook evaluation, speakers and materials on request, wide recognition, prayer, support, Christian as well as civic ministry, and gains in the battle for the minds of millions of American students." They have enlisted sympathetic scientists to serve as "expert" witnesses at public hearings: T. G. Barnes, professor of physics at the University of Texas at El Paso; John J. Grebe, a retired chemist from Dow Chemical Company; and Richard Le-Tourneau, an industrialist and engineer.

In November 1973, the Gablers asked the state board of education to offer courses in both evolution and creation as electives, neither to be taught as part of the required curriculum. Failing this, they proposed guidelines requiring textbooks to identify evolution as only one of several explanations of origins, and to clarify that the treatment is theoretical rather than factually verifiable. This was adopted as an amendment to the Texas Education Policy Act in May 1974. Subsequently, the Gablers took on MACOS as a target and they traveled around the country to organize protests.

The conservatism of the 1980s has greatly expanded their constituency. The Gablers today have a mailing list of 12,000 and a staff of seven people who scrutinize textbooks, respond to at least 200 letters a week, and provide groups of parents with lobbying techniques and material to attack specific books. Because of their national reputation as the most persistent and influential textbook watchers in the country, publishers closely follow their activities.

The Gablers' efforts are reinforced by several national organizations. Some of them watch curriculum innovation because they generally oppose the increased intervention of federal government in local affairs. The inevitable resentment caused by desegregation legislation in the 1960s greatly enhanced the political appeal of questions concerning local control, attracting several national groups to the issue of government influence on curriculum. These included the Heritage Foundation, a tax-exempt policy research organization in Washington, D.C., that supports studies expressing a conservative point of view on current issues (federal spending, energy, foreign policy, educational policy). This foundation was initially supported at about $500,000 a year by Joseph Coors, a well-known contributor to right-wing causes.[18] Coors believes that government is chipping away at individual initiative through too much interference in the lives of citizens, and he combines this belief with his concerns about "atheism, liberalism, and Godless

Communism." Federally funded science textbooks are thus a natural target. By 1980, the Heritage Foundation expanded in size and increased in influence. It is the Reagan administration's "think tank," employing a staff of seventy and maintaining an active network of consultants and advisers from universities, businesses, and government agencies. Its budget has grown to $5 million a year.

Other Washington-based organizations survey the textbook scene to preserve local initiatives in education. Leadership Action, Inc. is a group devoted to "involving citizens in active government participation." This includes increased lay involvement in the selection of textbooks, and decreased federal intervention. NSF-funded courses are one of their targets.

The Council for Basic Education (CBE) was founded in 1956 to preserve the standards of education against the liberalizing trends of progressive education (interestingly, the same issue that motivated the science curriculum reform movement). CBE's original membership of 158 grew to 4,500 by 1974 as it began to take an active position against some NSF-supported curriculum, especially concerning the teaching of social science in public schools. Its director, George Weber, argues that schools must avoid controversial topics. These include morality, religion, and politics, all of which he sees permeating the social sciences. Moreover, he feels that by promoting method (inquiry-oriented instruction) over substance (facts), the federally supported courses perpetuate the same neglect of basic skills that characterized the progressive education movement. The general permissiveness and lack of authority in the new curriculum fosters "rampant illiteracy." "Students are getting diplomas for warming their seats and not striking the teacher."

CBE spreads its views through speeches and publications, and by responding to inquiries from educators, journalists, and congressmen. Weber claims that the *CBE Bulletin* is increasingly in demand. "Educators who once asked that it be sent in a plain brown wrapper are now ordering multiple copies."[19]

The growing influence of textbook watchers mirrors the emergence of the New Right. Frances FitzGerald has aptly described the New Right as a direct-mail movement. The Moral Majority, the Christian Broadcasting Network, Phyllis Schlafly's Eagle

Forum, and a variety of other Evangelical political groups raise funds and mobilize constituencies among conservative single-issue groups through skillful manipulation of computerized mailing lists.[20] The constituent support behind the New Right has been variously estimated at 30 million to 65 million Americans. But the number is less significant than the mood of political activism among groups with religious intent. Richard Viguerie, the direct-mail expert for the movement, describes this activism as an " 'ideological war' against the Godless minority of treacherous individuals who have been permitted to formulate national policy."[21] The war focuses on diverse issues—among them are reinstating prayer in the schools, blocking the Equal Rights Amendment, prohibiting abortion, banning books, influencing elections, and removing the civil rights of homosexuals. The educational system, as a source of values, is a critical target.

Like their fundamentalist ancestors, New Right activists fear cultural diversity and the secular trends implied by a scientific world view. Their target is "secular humanism," a term loosely used to describe a world view that is human-centered and secular, and that emphasizes a human being's ability to achieve self-realization through the use of reason and scientific method rather than through belief in a spiritual and moral order. For the Moral Majority, secular humanism is a "civil religion," implying that ethical standards should be determined by human interests without reference to traditional religious belief. The term is a shorthand for the forces of evil.[22]

The New Right encompasses hundreds of local groups organized to prevent the circulation of books that threaten Christian values —"to put God back into the classroom." Some of the groups active in textbook disputes (such as Citizens for Decency through Law) were first organized to deal with obscenity issues. The Supreme Court ruling on pornography and obscenity allowed local communities to prevail in setting standards for questionable films. While this ruling was certainly not intended for school textbooks, it did stimulate demands for local control over educational material, which, after all, claimed textbook watchers, also infringed on local values. By 1980, local groups had formed throughout the country with such names as Young Parents Alert, Pro-Family

Forum, and Guardians of Education. They circulate pamphlets and leaflets: "Humanism Is Molesting Your Child," "Weep for Your Children," "Anti-God Humanists Are Conditioning Our Children." And they try to cleanse the schools and libraries of objectionable books.

Library and public-school administrators report greatly increased pressures from such groups. The America⹈ Library Association Office for Intellectual Freedom had received about 100 censorship complaints a year during the early 1970s; they received 1,000 in 1981. An estimated 300 communities reported incidents of censorship pressure on the public schools in 1979; 1,200 reported incidents in 1980.

Textbook watchers are antiliberal, often anti-intellectual, and certainly antiestablishment. They are not necessarily antiscience, but they object profoundly to the prevailing dominance of scientific values. Their vision of science is strangely skewed with religious and personal values, yet they will argue the importance of increased public understanding of science in terms that on the surface would be quite acceptable to scientists themselves.

> Science has innumerable social implications and applications. Solutions to social problems require real understanding of the origin of the physical processes which affect them (e.g., nuclear energy, fossil fuels, ecology, genetic engineering, hallucinogenic drugs, etc.). Each person needs, more than anything, a sense of his own identity and personal goals, and this is impossible without some sense of his origin. . . . Lack of a sound scientific understanding of origins and meanings among modern young people has impelled them to seek help in such anti-scientific solutions as "mind-expanding" drugs, witchcraft, astrology, and the like.[23]

However, the textbook watchers conclude from this argument that scientific understanding requires a religious perspective, that secular scientific theories based entirely on naturalistic explanations have drastic implications for social and personal behavior. These views are dramatically evident among the "scientific creationists," a group of textbook watchers with scientific training who initiated much of the recent opposition to the teaching of evolution theory.

Notes

1. Mary Anne Raywid, *The Axe-Grinders* (New York: Macmillan, 1962), is a useful history of curriculum disputes. Michael W. Kirst and Decker Walker, "An Analysis of Curriculum Policy-Making," *Review of Educational Research* 41, no. 5: 479–501, emphasizes the need to analyze curriculum policy in political terms as "a scene of conflict and uneasy accommodation."

2. Raywid, *Axe-Grinders,* p. 51. See also Jack Nelson and Gene Roberts, Jr., *The Censors and the Schools* (Boston: Little, Brown, 1963).

3. Lawrence A. Cremin, *The Transformation of the Schools* (New York: Alfred A. Knopf, 1962).

4. *Ibid.*

5. Letter to the Editor in the *Medford Mall Tribune,* 15 December 1972.

6. Louis Dupree, "Has the Secularist Crisis Come to an End?" *Listening* 9 (Autumn 1974).

7. Dean M. Kelly, *Why Conservative Churches Are Growing* (New York: Harper & Row, 1972). Kelly claims that this growth pattern is due to the rigid commitments required of the membership.

Kelly's statistics are from the National Council of Churches, *Yearbook of American Churches.* These statistics are questionable, and some studies suggest that much of the impressive increase in membership is due to reaffiliation of people after a period of inactivity. See R. W. Bibby and M. Brinkerhoff, "Circulation of the Saints: A Study of People Who Join Conservative Churches," *Journal for the Scientific Study of Religion* 12 (September 1973): 273–284. Rodney Stark and Charles Glick, *American Piety* (Berkeley: University of California Press, 1968), attribute the growing membership of conservative churches to the social mobility of people from lower classes with fundamentalist leanings into the middle class. They predicted the decline of supernatural and religious faith; as their middle-class status crystallized, members of conservative churches would move into more liberal denominations. This has failed to occur; on the contrary, there is a remarkable increase in conservatism within mainline churches as well as growth among the charismatic and Pentecostal sects.

8. James Morris, *The Preachers* (New York: St. Martin's Press, 1973).

9. Billy James Hargis, personal communication.

10. Ambassador College General Catalog, Pasadena, California, 1974–1975, pp. 21–22.

11. James H. Jauncey, *Science Returns to God* (Grand Rapids, Mich.: Zondervan Books, 1973), *passim.*

12. Jehovah's Witness, *Awake* (March 1974). Note that the 7.5 million

copies are distributed free, often to unwilling recipients. Actual membership in the sect is about 400,000 in the United States, and 2 million worldwide, doubling between 1965 and 1975.

13. *Awake* (September 1974). See also the Jehovah's Witness publication *Did Man Get Here by Evolution or by Creation?* (Brooklyn, N.Y.: Watchtower Bible and Tract Society, 1967).

14. Chick runs what he calls a new kind of evangelism based on house-to-house outreach by laymen trained in modern Saul Alinsky–type organizing techniques.

15. See, for example, discussion at the 1975 Hartford Theological Foundation. (Conference reported in the *New York Times,* 9 March 1975.)

16. Mel Gabler, "Have You Read Your Child's Textbooks?" *Faith* (March/April 1975): 10.

17. Educational Research Analysts, *Newsheet,* No. T-110, n.d.

18. See series on Joseph Coors by Stephen Isaacs in the *Washington Post,* 4–7 May 1975. Coors Beer is one of the largest family-owned firms in the United States, with sales of $440 million in 1973.

19. George Weber, personal interview. The *CBE Bulletin* is published monthly, and has a circulation of about 6,700.

20. Frances FitzGerald, "The Triumphs of the New Right," *New York Review of Books,* 19 November 1981.

21. Richard Viguerie, *The New Right: We're Ready to Lead* (Ottowa, Ill.: Caroline House, 1981).

22. On 12 May 1976, the House of Representatives passed an amendment to the National Defense Education Act (vote: 222–174) that "no preference be granted to the religion of secular humanism over the Judaic-Christian viewpoint" in government-supported curriculum.

23. Institute for Creation Research, "Scientific Creationism for Public Schools" (San Diego, Cal.: ICR, November 1973), Summary.

5

The Scientific Creationists

All religions, nearly all philosophies, and even a part of science testify
to the unwearying, heroic effort of mankind desperately denying its
own contingency. . . . The ideas having the highest invading potential
are those that *explain* man by assigning him his place in an immanent
destiny, in whose bosom his anxiety dissolves.[1]

During the 1960s, a group of scientifically trained fundamentalists
began to re-evaluate fossil evidence from the perspective of special
creation as described in the Biblical record. These creationists,
much like their fundamentalist predecessors in the 1920s, accepted
the Biblical doctrine of creation as literal: "All basic types of living
things, including man, were made by direct creative act of God
during the creation week described in *Genesis.* "[2] They believe that
creation theory is the most basic of all Christian beliefs, "at the
very center of the warfare . . . against Satan," and the fact that
many churches fail to emphasize special creation is a "tragic oversight that has resulted in defection . . . to the evolutionary world
view, and then inevitably later to liberalism."[3] They choose to
reinterpret organic evolution according to Biblical authority.

Some creationists accept aspects of evolution theory but set
limits to scientific explanations, rejecting, for example, natural

selection as a causal explanation of evolutionary change. The more extreme creationists deny all evolutionary processes, arguing that evolution and creation are mutually exclusive theories: "You choose to accept the statements of Scripture, or you choose to accept the claims of evolutionists. You cannot believe in both."[4] Still others accept the common compromise—that there are two levels of reality—but they are concerned that the teaching of evolution denies and obscures all religious explanation and that failure to teach alternative hypotheses implies that science provides a complete and sufficient understanding of ultimate causes.

Among those who identify themselves as creationists are some fanatics (a botanist who claims that evolution theory is "a special argument of the devil"), disciples of traditional fundamentalist sects, some wealthy industrialists and hotel keepers, several astronauts, and many solid, middle-class, technically trained people working in high-technology professions in centers of science-based industry. These modern-day creationists share many of the moral and religious concerns expressed in the twenties, but their style is strikingly different from that of their flamboyant ancestors. Arthur Hays described the circus atmosphere in Dayton, Tennessee, in 1925.

> Thither swarmed ballyhoo artists, hotdog vendors, lemonade merchants, preachers, professional atheists, college students, Greenwich Village radicals, out-of-work coal miners, IWW's, single taxers, libertarians, revivalists of all shapes and sects, hinterland soothsayers, holy-rollers, an army of newspaper men, scientists, editors, and lawyers.[5]

In comparison, creationist confrontations are more like debates within professional societies. Indeed, creationists try to present their views at the annual meetings of professional organizations such as the National Association of Biology Teachers and the American Association for the Advancement of Science. Even during the California public hearings on textbook selection, creationists presented brief technical papers, and the only placard to be seen was a chart of the hydrogen atom intended to demonstrate the scientific validity of creation theory.[6] For creationists argue that Genesis is not religious dogma but an alternative scientific hypothesis capable of evaluation by scientific procedures. They present themselves not as believers but as scientists engaged in a scholarly debate about the methodological validity of two scientific theories.

The Bible as Science

The creationist world view rejects the theory that animals and plants have descended from a single line of ancestors, evolving over billions of years through random mutation. Creationists cannot accept the implication that natural selection is opportunistic and undirected, that selection pressures act to cause genetic change only because of immediate reproductive advantage. According to creation theory, biological life began during a primeval period only six thousand to ten thousand years ago, when all things were created by God's design into "permanent basic forms." Like the pre-Darwinian Charles Lyell, creationists believe that all subsequent variation has occurred within the genetic limits built into "fixed kinds" by the Creator. "Kinds" is a word that appears in Genesis but not in the scientific literature. Creationists use it in different ways. However, they all believe that change is a directed and purposeful process and present variety among animals is merely part of a blueprint to accomodate a variety of environmental conditions,[7] or "simply an expression of the Creator's desire to show as much beauty of a flower, variety of song in birds, or interesting types of behavior in animals as possible."[8] Change would not modify the original design, for nature is static, secure, and predictable, each species containing its full potentiality.

The creationists thus differ from evolutionists in their explanations of the origin of life, the transmission of characteristics, the nature of variation and complexity, and the character of the fossil record. (See Table 5.1.)

Clearly, creationists are faced with a formidable amount of evidence that supports the theory of evolution. This poses a cruel dilemma; they must either admit exceptions to their beliefs that would raise doubts among their constituents, or they must maintain consistency at the risk of public ridicule. They have chosen the

TABLE 5.1. Alternative Models: Creation versus Evolution

	Creation Model	Evolution Model
Theory of origins	All living things brought about by the acts of a Creator.	All living things brought about by naturalistic processes due to properties inherent in inanimate matter.
Transmission of characteristics of living things	Creation of basic plant and animal kinds with ordinal characteristics was complete in the first representatives.	All living things originated from a single living source which itself arose from inanimate matter. Origin of each kind from an ancestral form by slow, gradual change.
Variation	Variation and speciation are limited within each kind.	There is unlimited variation. All forms are genetically related.
Complexity	Sudden appearance in great variety of highly complex forms. Net present decrease in complexity.	Gradual change of simplest forms into more complex forms.
The fossil record	Sudden appearance of each created kind with ordinal characteristics complete. Sharp boundaries separate major taxonomic groups. No transitional forms between higher categories.	Transitional series linking all categories. No systematic gaps.

SOURCE: Adapted by the author from Duane Gish, "Creation, Evolution and the Historical Evidence," *American Biology Teacher* 35 (March 1973): 135. Used by permission.

latter alternative and spend their energies trying to demonstrate that evidence supporting evolution is biased and incomplete, or that it can be reinterpreted to fit whatever conceptual system is convenient. For example, creationist theoreticians argue that the fossil record is far from conclusive and fails to provide the transitional forms or linkages between diverse living groups that would suggest evolution from a common ancestor. While fossils from the Cambrian period indicate a highly complex form of life, it does not necessarily follow that this life had evolved for over a billion years. There is no fossil record in the Precambrian period to sustain this view.

Creationists also deny the evidence from techniques of radioisotope dating, for these techniques are based on assumptions that no uranium or lead has been lost throughout the years and that the rate at which uranium changes has remained constant over time. Rejecting the uniformitarian hypotheses that allow evolutionists to extrapolate events in the ancient past from present evidence, they argue that if a Supreme Being created the world, and a catastrophe like the Flood altered it, then the evidence for radioisotope dating is simply irrelevant.[9]

Creationists also reject the genetic data used to support hypotheses about random mutation, arguing that the same data can be used to deny the theory of evolution; mutations, after all, are usually detrimental and unlikely to contribute to the continuity of life. Similarly, they claim that insights into phylogenetic relationships provided by analysis of protein structure and chromosomal arrangements are based on "dubious assumptions" about the similarity between major plant and animal groups. If one assumed that such groups are unrelated and reexamined the same data according to "polyphylogenetic" assumptions, one would reach different conclusions.[10]

For creationists, the law of conservation of energy (that energy cannot be created or destroyed) and the second law of thermodynamics (that energy approaches increasingly random distribution) are additional proof of an initial ordering of natural processes. Similarly, the laws of quantum mechanics—that individual events (the decay of K-mesons) are not predictable—suggest that theories of origin and change are "fundamentally unprovable" but that change is more likely to have occurred by design than by random mutation.[11]

Creationists' "scientific" arguments, which they claim to develop through concurrent studies of Scripture and nature, touch on floods, on heredity and genetics, on chemical and radioisotope dating techniques, on the blood circulation system, and on the earth's magnetic field, just to name several of the enormous range of topics covered in their writings. Their "facts" are highly selected and suggest a limited understanding of science. For example, in using the second law of thermodynamics to argue that the world began with an orderly design, they ignore that the law is based on the premise of a closed system.

Their own "research" is also limited, devoted mainly to producing evidence that might contradict evolution theory. For example, they conduct expeditions to the Paluxy River in Texas, a site where scientists have found dinosaur tracks. There they claim to have found human footprints of a "Paluxy Man"—a sort of creationist Piltdown—who existed at the same time as the dinosaurs. They say that they have discovered that dinosaurs and humans lived together, and that this proves the existence of a young earth.

Their understanding of scientific method is limited as well. Like Darwin's contemporaries, they view science as an inductive and descriptive process and poorly comprehend the function of theories and models as useful instruments for prediction. Believing that rival hypotheses and debates among evolutionists are evidence of weakness, they use such debates to suggest disagreement about the basic premises of evolution theory, when in fact they are about the processes or the mechanisms involved.[12] Believing that open questions reveal fundamental problems, they buttress their case by citing philosophical expressions of doubt: Freeman Dyson—"We are still at the very beginning of the quest for understanding the origin of life"; Garrett Hardin—"Unsolved puzzles face biologists"; and Stephen Jay Gould—"The fossil record contains precious little in the way of intermediate forms."

When pressed, creationists argue that design in nature exists simply because of the will of the Creator. They are aware of the problems in this argument, but then they claim that evolution theory is but today's creation myth, based also on faith, although it excludes consideration of a supernatural force. If one accepts a different set of assumptions, then creation theory becomes fully as workable and fruitful a hypothesis as evolution.

Scientists try in vain to refute creationists' arguments. They note the practical and historical problems in a literal interpretation of Genesis and the many facts that contradict creationist theories. They accuse creationists of repeating their arguments, as if repetition could establish verity. Factual arguments and criticism, however, are not likely to change creationist beliefs. Groups committed to particular assumptions tend to suppress dissonant evidence, and criticism only encourages increasing activity in support of existing beliefs.[13] For those who believe in creationism, it is a distinct and coherent logical system that fully explains the world. "Studying the facts of physics and chemistry, I find that the only way I could truly understand the present world is by the word of God and the inspiration of the Holy Spirit."[14] It is evolution theory that is the "scientific fairy tale."

While creationists' ideas may appear irrational to a modern biologist, so the ideas of evolutionists are irrational to a creationist. But the accuracy and rationality of creation beliefs are of less interest here than their political efforts to impose these beliefs on the educational establishment. These efforts come from the "research centers" where scientific creationists work.

Creationist Organizations

THE AMERICAN SCIENTIFIC AFFILIATION

The American Scientific Affiliation (ASA), formed in 1941, is an "evangelical organization of men and women of science who share a common fidelity to the Word of God and to Christian Faith." Founded by five scientists concerned about "the sweeping tide of scientific materialism and waning faith of modern youth subjected to its influence," the ASA investigates problems bearing upon the relation between Christian faith and science. Most of its 3,000 members carefully distinguish themselves from scientific creationists, whom they would prefer to label "antievolutionists."[15] However, like the scientific creationists, they believe that evolutionary concepts are misleading and have serious moral and social as well as theological implications.

Because of diverse opinions among its membership, the organization has avoided taking a position that advocates teaching creation theory in public schools. ASA does, however, criticize the evolutionary emphasis in textbooks, arguing that evolution is taught in a far too dogmatic way, that the theory is extended beyond what is scientifically appropriate, and that it unnecessarily excludes consideration of alternative theories. "For the great mass of people, acceptance of evolution is not a personal judgment rising from evidence any more than scientific beliefs generally are; rather, popular acceptance represents a deference to scientific authority."[16] Their proposed solution is to compromise; students should learn to appreciate creation and design as complementary to evolution but not necessarily as part of the biology curriculum. Biology teachers, however, must avoid implying that evolution is the only acceptable theory. This view was to be of considerable political importance, for ASA members have been influential in mediating textbook controversies, especially in California. But their moderation also brought dissension within the organization. Some members argued that the ASA leadership had capitulated to the mainstream of scientific thought. In fact, it was this group of disaffected ASA members who formed the first organization for "scientific creationism."

THE CREATION RESEARCH SOCIETY

In 1963, ten men formed the Creation Research Society (CRS) in Ann Arbor, Michigan. Some of them had been members of the ASA, but left that organization when it refused to take a firm position on the teaching of evolution. Their objective in founding the CRS was "to publish research evidence supporting the thesis that the material universe, including plants, animals, and man are the result of direct creative acts by a personal God."[17]

The founders of CRS call themselves "scientific creationists." To attain the status of voting membership in the organization, members must meet two requirements: a postgraduate degree in science and belief in the literal truth of the Bible. Applicants for membership must sign a statement of belief: that the Bible is the written word of God and that its assertions are historically and scientifically true; that all basic types of living things, including man, were made by direct creative acts of God as described in Genesis; and that the Noachian Deluge was a historical event. CRS has about 500 voting members, plus several thousand associates. Its activities are supported mainly through membership dues of $7 per year and tax-deductible contributions. About 50 members contribute articles to the organization's quarterly journal (circulation: 2,000). Active members include a retired chemist who had been a director of research at Dow Chemical, the president and a professor from Concordia Lutheran College, and a professor of natural science at Michigan State University.

Religious groups concerned with doctrinal purity are characterized by schisms. Creationists are no exception, and CRS soon split into several factions. In 1970, several members formed the Creation Science Research Center (CSRC) in San Diego, California.

THE CREATION SCIENCE RESEARCH CENTER

CSRC is a small, tax-exempt, research and publishing organization formed "to take advantage of the tremendous opportunity that God has given us. . . . to reach the 63 million children in the United States with the scientific teaching of Biblical creationism."[18] Its research projects, which include investigation of the physical aspects of the Flood, are intended to "clarify problems in the field of geophysics, oceanography and structural geology as well as Biblical and geological chronology."[19] The organization also engages in legal activities to undermine what they claim is illegitimate federal funding of school curriculum. CSRC has accused the California State Board of Education of illegally accepting federal programs, and it has filed injunctions in several California counties to delay the expenditure of funds for "biased" textbooks. Meanwhile, the organization offers publishers its services to "neutralize" textbook material.

CSRC is engaged primarily in its own "curriculum reform pro-

gram," devoted to the popular dissemination of creationist literature. It publishes a magazine called *Science and Scripture,* a textbook series, film strips, and cassettes all colorfully packaged, and
an "action kit," including the legal, organizational, and technical
information necessary to implement the teaching of creation theory
in public schools.[20] Finally, the organization runs a tourist service:
"Visit the mountains of Ararat with the world's foremost authority
on the search for Noah's ark—cost, $1,397 from New York."

In the early 1970s, CSRC tried to reach 210,000 people through
a computerized direct-mail campaign. By 1975, their mailing list
was greatly reduced. However, distribution of CSRC material is
facilitated by the group's association with the Southern California
branch of the Bible Science Association, which runs a radio ministry and an active extension service. Together the two organizations
have a mailing list of about 200,000 individuals and many schools,
churches, and textbook committees. In 1972, the CSRC was divided in a conflict over copyright questions, and some of its members formed a new group, the Institute for Creation Research,
which soon became the dominant creationist organization.

THE INSTITUTE FOR CREATION RESEARCH

The Institute for Creation Research (ICR) is the research division
of Christian Heritage College, founded in 1970 with the sponsorship of the Scott Memorial Baptist Church, an independent Baptist
organization. In 1972, this church purchased a monastery on thirty
acres east of San Diego, California, for its parochial high school
and shared the site with the college and institute. It is an old,
attractive, Spanish-style campus set against the dry but scenic hills
of southern California. The corridors of the Spanish-style buildings
are bare, decorated with only a few nature scenes. One office door
carries the label "Noah's Ark," another, a cartoon: Smidgeon asks
a computer, "If you're so smart, how did the world start?" and the
computer replies, "Read Chapter 1 of Genesis."

The college, with about four hundred students, has undergradu-
ate and graduate school programs in "The Study of Christian
Evidence and Scientific Creationism." The college catalog de-

scribes its introductory biology course as "a survey of the life sciences; general and molecular biology; human physiology; creationism in biological origins." Its psychology course includes a section on "the unique nature of man." Its ten-man science faculty (all members of the ICR) is involved in an open campaign against evolution theory. To teach at the college, they must swear, at the time of appointment and annually, that they agree with the following philosophical and doctrinal position:

> We believe in the absolute integrity of Holy Scripture and its plenary verbal inspiration by the Holy Spirit as originally written by men prepared for God for this purpose. The scriptures, both Old and New Testament, are inerrant in relation to any subject with which they deal, and are to be accepted in their natural and intended sense . . . all things in the universe were created and made by God in the six days of special creation described in Genesis. The creationist account is accepted as factual, historical and perspicuous and is thus fundamental in the understanding of every fact and phenomenon in the created universe.[21]

Creationists are able to sustain their beliefs in the face of considerable criticism because they have strong social support. This is evident at Christian Heritage College and at its research institute, where faculty and staff are mostly kin. Tim LaHaye was the college president and pastor of the Baptist church. He is a radio minister known in fundamentalist circles for his series of family life seminars which dwell upon the destruction of family life in modern technological society. LaHaye became the president of a national steering committee for the New Right called the Council on National Policy. His wife, as well as his sister and brother-in-law, works at the college, as do her brother and daughter-in-law. The ICR's senior faculty members are Duane Gish and Henry Morris. Gish's wife is a librarian, and four members of the Morris family are also on the ICR staff.

Besides Gish and Morris, six other scientists and a lawyer work on the ICR faculty. At least one of the scientists uses a pseudonym because he worries that identification with creationism will ruin his academic career. However, ICR works to develop a reputation as the "scholarly arm of the creationist movement," debunking the CSRC as "a promotional and sales organization" and its director as a man with "an honorary doctorate from Los Angeles Christian University—a college with no telephone listing and no campus." The use of "false titles," it is feared, reflects badly on the "real scientific creationists." ICR identifies its own primary activity as research devoted to developing an empirical base for creation theory and claims to leave political, legal, and lobbying activities to other organizations.

The institute runs radio programs, conferences, workshops, and summer institutes, and publishes a monthly magazine called *Acts and Facts,* containing both technical articles and current news of creationists' activities. It is circulated to 60,000 people. The ICR also runs Creation-Life Publishers, the main source of creationist books.

By 1980, the ICR staff had written 55 books (some of which were translated into 10 languages), prepared filmstrips and slides, participated in 100 public debates, lectured in 400 college campuses and 400 churches, given seminars in 350 cities and 35 summer institutes, appeared on hundreds of radio and television programs and lectured to hundreds of secular groups (including professional golfers, military officers, and dermatologists)—all in addition to teaching at Christian Heritage College.[22]

ICR projects include expeditions to find geological evidence that the earth is young and archaeological investigations of Mount Ararat to prove the validity of the Noachian myth. These expeditions are led by John Morris, who is the director of field research for the institute. There have been many attempts by religious groups to find Noah's Ark, but Morris claims that ICR is the only serious scientific organization that is capable of interpreting the scientific evidence of the Ark's existence. ICR expeditions, however, have been catastrophic. During the first attempt in August 1972, "The men were robbed and beaten by Kurdish outlaws, victimized by city officials, and fired on in an ambush. And three of them were temporarily incapacitated by the body-rending blows of lightening."[23] These events might have been taken as ill omens, but the group planned further trips in 1973, 1974, and 1975, all of which were blocked by the Turkish government. However, Morris claims to have seen enough evidence of the Ark to conclude that its capacity was equal to 567 railroad stock cars that could hold 50,000 animals.

Despite the small size of each organization and the obvious advantage of coordination, creationist groups are competitive and highly critical of each other. However, their combined activity has brought attention from state legislatures and school boards as well as angry criticism from biologists. News about their activities has appeared in the national media, and publicity, even if negative, encourages creationists to feel that they are finally being taken seriously.

OTHER ORGANIZATIONS

California is a major center for creationist activity, but similar organizations can be found in other states. The Genesis School of Graduate Studies in Gainesville, Florida, is advertised as the "first known postgraduate level college stressing scientific creationism." It offers a Ph.D. in science-creation research, and its curriculum emphasizes "special creation and the young earth model." Its president is the pastor of the Gainesville University Baptist Church. Other Bible schools, such as Bob Jones University in South Carolina, teach courses presenting both evolution theory and special creation.

An occasional creationist course appears in the catalogs of major universities. A professor of chemistry at Southern Illinois University has taught a course called The Creation Alternative, which includes lectures such as "Principles of Geology Revisited." At Michigan State University, creationist John N. Moore teaches a course called Science, Beliefs, and Values, presenting creation theory as an alternative to evolution.

Creationists work with various publishing organizations, such as the Bible Science Association of Caldwell, Idaho, formed by the Lutheran minister Walter Lang, to "set forth the scientific value of the creationists' position." Lang claims that the Bible is scientific and "because of the miracle of inspiration, is also infallible in its scientific statements." This organization distributes the *Bible Science Newsletter* to 27,000 subscribers, and sponsors seminars, radio programs, and films "for those who have been misled into accepting evolution theory." The Bible Science Association models itself after a scientific society, holding annual conventions in which speakers are identified primarily by their professional degrees and academic positions. In 1973, a new chapter was organized called the Scientific Creationism Association of Southern New Jersey. Other supportive organizations include Educational Research Analysts in Texas, the Creation Research Science Education Foundation Inc. in Ohio, the Triangle Association for Scientific Creationism in the Research Triangle near Raleigh, North Carolina, and the Missouri Association for Creation, to name just a few.

A British equivalent, called the Evolution Protest Movement (EPM), founded in 1932, is a "scientific, educational, religious, nonsectarian, non-political and non-profit-making" organization with over eight hundred members devoted to demonstrating that the theory of evolution is not in accordance with fact and causes a decline in morality. EPM has published more than two hundred pamphlets and several books. It was financed by Captain Ackworth, a submarine commander, and its presidents have included Douglas Deward (once an auditor-general of India), Sir J. Ambrose Fleming (the physicist who devised an electron tube in 1904), and Sir Cecil Wakely (a one-time biologist and president of the Royal College of Surgeons).[24] A second British group, The Newton Scientific Organization, was formed in 1973 to distribute creationist literature and to advance the scientific study of creation.

The Activists

Who are these dedicated individuals who have presumed to question one of the scientific community's more strongly held concepts?[25] Henry Morris, director of the ICR and vice-president for academic affairs at Christian Heritage College, has a Ph.D. in hydraulics from the University of Minnesota (1950), and served at one time as a professor of hydraulic engineering and chairman of the department of civil engineering at Virginia Polytechnic Institute (1957–1970). Now in his fifties, Morris has been an active creationist for some thirty years. During his college training at Rice, he accepted evolution theory despite his religious upbringing. But during his graduate years, he began to read the Bible and to take a more active role in Christian affairs. "In trying to lead others to Christ, I needed answers and this led me to research. And being an engineer, I looked for solid evidence." Morris had a hard time with his colleagues at VPI, where he claims there are at least thirty-five creationists who are quiet about their beliefs in order to protect their professional standing. Collegial pressures eventually convinced him to leave the secular university setting. He continues to do some work in applied hydraulics, but most of his work is on "Biblical subjects."

Duane T. Gish, associate director of ICR, received a Ph.D. from the University of California, Berkeley (1953), in biochemistry and held a postdoctoral fellowship at Cornell University Medical School for several years. He spent most of his career as a member of the research staff at Upjohn and Company; he studied scientific evidence related to creation theory as an avocation. In 1971, in his mid-fifties, he began to devote full time to this work, encouraged by the "growing evidence that special creation was valid scientifically." Gish voiced his concern about the "appalling ignorance on the subject of science both within the academic community and among the public." If people understood the nature of scientific evidence, he claimed, they would be more sympathetic to creation theory.

Lane Lester joined the ICR in 1974. He has a Ph.D. in genetics from Purdue University, has taught high school, and was an assistant professor at the University of Tennessee. Lester had been brought up as a devout Southern Baptist. For years he reconciled his religious upbringing with science by believing in theistic evolution (that God set in motion the process of natural selection). Then, in 1972, he heard Gish talk and he plunged into creationist literature, discovering that he could interpret scientific data within a creationist framework. He was gratified that he no longer had to compromise his religious beliefs and joined the CRS. He then took a job at the Biology Science Curriculum Study (BSCS) for a year to learn about methods of developing educational materials—of course, he did not reveal that he was a creationist. In 1974, he left BSCS to join ICR.

Many of the activists in the creationist movement are people who, like Gish and Lester, once made an uncomfortable accommodation between their religious beliefs and their scientific training. Creationism appealed to them as a means to resolve contradictions. An ex-evolutionist and professor of science education, Gary Parker, describes his conversion in "a personal testimony." Evolution, he claims, had been his God, but it gave him no basis to respond to his problems or those of his students. However, "the Lord did change my heart and opened doors of blessings I never dreamed of."[26]

Many of the creationists are from the applied physical sciences and engineering. The creationists claim that applied scientists are interested in creationism because "they have their feet on the ground and are heavily committed to test out theories." Most biologists, they feel, are too "brainwashed" with evolution theory to think flexibly about the evidence. They also argue that people in technical professions, working in highly structured and ordered contexts, are inclined to think in terms of order and design.[27] Another explanation came from Wernher von Braun, the famous NASA rocket engineer, who declared his personal support for the "case for design" as a viable scientific theory: "One cannot be exposed to the law and order of the universe without concluding that there must be design and purpose behind it all . . . I endorse the presentation of alternative theories for the origin of the universe, life, and man in the science classroom."[28]

Perhaps this sense of order explains why several of the astronauts have also endorsed the creationist view. For example, the astronaut James Irwin is a creationist. After his experience on the moon ("I feel the power of God as I'd never felt it before"), he founded an evangelical foundation called High Flight. Astronauts Frank Borman and Edgar Mitchell have also indicated that they feel the Genesis account of creation to be an appropriate explanation. Mitchell wrote to Vernon Grose:

I strongly favor the presentation of both points of view with the added hope that such duality will ultimately lead to one of two eventualities. First, the scientific community may modify our model of living organisms. . . . The second alternative might be that scientists will postulate a new unified field concept that will allow predictive incorporation of a distinct, energetic mechanism which interacts with the field of matter to produce a higher order functioning of life which we call "consiousness"—a view distinctly different from that of a chance origin in evolution of life.[29]

Clearly, the scientists and engineers active in creation movements are not against science and technology. Many of them earn their living in technical industries. (See Table 5.2.) Indeed, when questioned on specific contemporary issues, creationist leaders were generally favorable to technology. Some supported development of the SST and the Alaska pipeline. Others expressed ambivalence about the development of civilian nuclear power, but only because the techniques for the disposal of nuclear waste were based on evolutionary assumptions. Far from being against science, the creationists spend much of their energy legitimizing their beliefs in scientific terms, firmly convinced that failure to do so would trivialize them. Their main objection to evolution theory is that it "incorporates all the attributes of a religion"; it is "a doctrine of origin" that replaces God with eternal matter and creation by random mutation; it is a doctrine of salvation not through faith but through foresight and the manipulation of nature. Thus, claim the creationists, it violates traditional religious assumptions and endorses its own system of ethics.[30]

It was in the context of this ambivalence toward science that the new precollege curriculum in biology and the social sciences, both based on evolutionary assumptions, became targets for textbook watchers. In addition to their persistent concern with patriotism and the standards of education, textbook watchers became alerted to religious and moral issues as creationists organized to fight what they perceived to be efforts to "indoctrinate" their children with the dangerous values of "secular humanism."

TABLE 5.2.
Advisory Board and Staff of the Institute for
Creation Research (1973–1980)

Name	Discipline, Degree	Present Position
A. Technical Advisory Board		
Thomas G. Barnes	Physicist, D.Sc. (Hardin-Simmons U.)	Prof. of Physics, U. of Texas, El Paso; Pres. of CRS
Edward F. Blick	Nuclear Engineering, Ph.D. (Oklahoma)	Prof. of Aerospace, Mech. and Nuclear Engineering, U. of Oklahoma
David R. Boylan	Engineering, Ph.D. (Iowa State)	Dean of College of Engineering, Iowa State U.
Larry G. Butler	Biochemist, Ph.D. (UCLA)	Prof. of Biochemistry, Purdue U.
Malcolm A. Cutchins	Engineering Mechanics, Ph.D. (VPI)	Prof. of Aerospace Engineering, Auburn U., Alabama
Carl B. Fliermans	Microbiology, Ph.D. (Indiana U.)	Microbiologist, Dupont
Donald D. Hamann	Food Technology, Ph.D. (VPI)	Prof. of Food Technology, N. Carolina State U.
Charles W. Harrison	Electrical Engineering & Applied Physics, Ph.D. (Harvard)	Sandia Laboratories, Albuquerque, N.M.
Harold R. Henry	Fluid Mechanics, Ph.D. (Columbia)	Chairman, Dept. Civil and Mining Engineering, U. of Alabama
Joseph L. Henson	Entomology, Ph.D. (Clemson)	Chairman, Science Division, Bob Jones U.

David Menton	Anatomy, Ph.D. (Indiana U.)	Prof., Washington U. (St. Louis)
John R. Meyer	Biology, Ph.D. (U. of Iowa)	Prof. of Biology, Los Angeles Baptist College
John N. Moore	Science Education, Ed.D. (Mich. State)	Prof. of Natural Science, Michigan State
Jean Sloat Morton	Biology, Ph.D. (George Washington U.)	Biology Writer, Alpha-Omega Publications
John W. Oller	Linguistics, Ph.D. (U. of Rochester)	Prof. of Linguistics, U. of New Mexico
Charles C. Ryrie	Theologian, Th.D. (Dallas Theol. Seminary) Ph.D. (U. of Edinburgh)	Prof. of Systematic Theology, Dallas Theological Seminary
John C. Whitcomb, Jr.	Old Testament Scholar, Th.D. (Grace Theol. Seminary)	Prof. of Theology, Dr. of Post-Grad. Studies, Grace Theological Seminary

B. Staff of ICR and Christian Heritage College

Steven Austin	Geology, Ph.D. (Penn. State)	Research Associate Geosciences, ICR; Prof., Christian Heritage College
William A. Beckman	Chemistry, Ph.D. (Western Reserve College)	Prof. Physical Sciences, Christian Heritage College
Wendell Bird	Law, J.D. (Yale Law School)	Attorney, ICR
Richard Bliss	Science Education, Ed.D. (U. of Sarasota, Florida)	Dir. of Curriculum Development, Christian Heritage College
Kenneth B. Cumming	Biologist, Ph.D. (Harvard)	Prof., Christian Heritage College
Robert Franks	M.D. (UCLA)	Prof. of Biological Science, Christian Heritage College

TABLE 5.2.
Advisory Board and Staff of the Institute for
Creation Research (1973–1980) . . . continued

Duane T. Gish	Biochemistry, Ph.D. (Berkeley)	Prof. Natural Science, Christian Heritage College; Assoc. Dir., ICR
Lane Lester	Genetics, Ph.D. (Purdue)	Prof., Christian Heritage College
Henry M. Morris	Hydraulics, Ph.D. (U. of Minn.)	Dir., ICR; VP Acad. Affairs, Christian Heritage College
John D. Morris	Biology, Ph.D. (Christian Heritage College)	Field Research Scientist, ICR
Maurice Nelles	Engineering Physics, Ph.D. (Harvard)	Lecturer, Christian Heritage College
Stuart Nevins	Geology, M.S. (San Jose State)	Prof. Earth Science, Christian Heritage College
Theodore W. Rybka	Physics, Ph.D. (U. of Oklahoma)	Prof. of Physics, Christian Heritage College
Harold S. Slusher	Geophysics, M.S. (U. of Oklahoma)	Dir. Planetary Science Program, Christian Heritage College
Gary Parker	Education, Ed.D. (Georgia State)	Prof. of Biology, Christian Heritage College, ICR Museum Director

Notes

1. Jacques Monod, *Chance and Necessity* (New York: Vintage Books, 1972), pp. 44, 166.

2. Creation Research Society brochure.

3. Richard Bube, "Science Teaching in California," *Reformed Journal* (April 1973): 3–4.

4. Joseph L. Henson, "Theistic Evolution," *Faith* (March/April 1973): 23.

5. Arthur Garfield Hays, "The Scopes Trial," in *Evolution and Religion,* ed. Gail Kennedy (New York: D. C. Health, 1957), p. 35.

6. The ironies of the California hearings were described by Calvin Trillin, "U.S. Journal: Sacramento, California," *The New Yorker,* 6 January 1973, pp. 55 ff.

7. John N. Moore and Harold Slusher, *Biology: A Search for Order in Complexity* (Grand Rapids: Zondervan, 1970), p. 422.

8. *Ibid;* see review by Wyatt Anderson, Rossiter Crozier, and Ronald Simpson, *The Georgia Science Teacher* 13 (1974): 15–18.

9. Duane Gish, "Creation, Evolution, and the Historical Evidence," *American Biology Teacher* 35 (March 1973): 132–141.

10. John N. Moore, "Evolution, Creation and the Scientific Method," *American Biology Teacher* 35 (January 1973): 23–27.

11. Ronald S. Remmel, "Randomness in Quantum Mechanics and Its Implications for Evolutionary Theory," testimony to the California State Board of Education, 19 November 1972.

12. These recent debates involve rival hypotheses concerning the process of evolutionary change. Stephen Jay Gould and Niles Eldridge have challenged the notion that evolution proceeds by gradual change with a theory of "punctuated equilibrium" by which periods of stability are punctuated by sudden changes. This in no way challenges the fact of genealogical relationship among organisms that is fundamental to evolution.

13. See the work on cognitive dissonance by Leon Festinger, *A Theory of Cognitive Dissonance* (Evanston, Ill.: Row Peterson, 1957). The relationship between beliefs and the interpretation of scientific information is discussed by S. B. Barnes, "On the Reception of Scientific Belief," in *Sociology of Science,* ed. Barry Barnes (Harmondsworth: Penguin Books, 1972), pp. 269–291.

14. Letter in *Acts and Facts* (November/December 1973).

15. Some scientific creationists have, however, retained their ASA membership.

16. Carl F. H. Henry, "Theology and Evolution," in *Evolution and Christian Thought Today,* ed. Russell L. Mixter (Grand Rapids, Mich.: Eerdmans Publishers, 1959), p. 202.

17. Creation Research Society, Articles of Incorporation, Lansing, Mich.

18. In 1974 the CSRC employed eighteen people and used twelve outside technical consultants. They claimed to have over 10,000 regular donors who could be counted on for small gifts at every fund-raising appeal.

Quoted material is from Creation Science Research Center, *Report* (October 1973).

19. Creation Science Research Center brochure.

20. CSRC claims that the science and creation textbook series sold about 30,000 copies to each grade level and that one of their most popular books sold 70,000 hardbacks.

21. Christian Heritage College Catalog (San Diego, 1974).

22. A description of ICR activities appears in *The Decade of Creation,* ed. Henry Morris and Donald Rohrer, (San Diego, Calif.: Creation-Life Publishers, 1981).

23. *San Diego Union,* 23 February 1974, p. B-8.

24. The Evolution Protest Movement has branches in England, Australia, New Zealand, Canada, and Johannesburg, South Africa. It has published several hundred pamphlets intended to demonstrate that the theory of evolution contradicts scientific fact; titles include "Ape Men Are Fakes or Fiction," "Man from Monkey Myth," "How the British Museum Chooses Our Ancestors," "God Is Science Plus," "Evolution: The Great Delusion," "An Atheist Kicks against the Pricks," "God Took Risks in Making Men and Monkeys," and "Evolutionary Magic or Creative Miracle." See *Nature* 241 (February 1974): 360.

25. Most of the following information was obtained from personal interviews, from brochures published by creationist organizations, and from *curricula vitae.*

26. Gary Parker, *From Evolution to Creation: A Personal Testimony* (San Diego: Creation-Life Publishers, 1977), p. 12.

27. A study of the religious orientation of scientists finds that those in applied fields who work outside major universities are more orthodox in their religious beliefs than other scientists. Chemical engineers, for example, are much more likely than other scientists to attend church regularly and to avow their belief in life after death. This persists regardless of educational level. Ted R. Vaughan et al., "The Religious Commitment of Natural Scientists," *Social Forces* 44 (June 1966): 519–526.

28. Wernher von Braun, letter to John Ford, published in *Science and Scripture* (March/April 1973): 4. Von Braun later qualified his position, stating that he believed there was "divine intent" behind the processes of nature, but did not believe that all living species were created in their final form 5,000 years ago.

29. *New York Times,* 26 April 1974, p. 18-C.

30. Institute for Creation Research, *Acts and Facts* (June 1975).

6

Political Tactics

Textbook watchers use a variety of political tactics to translate their concerns into administrative decisions; they adjust these tactics according to the educational policy-making structure in different states and to their own access to power within that structure. Where policy decisions concerning textbooks are made by centralized school boards and statewide textbook commissions, these administrative organizations become the target for political pressure. Elsewhere, efforts are directed toward local school boards, and if administrative action seems unlikely to yield change, textbook watchers go to the legislatures, to the courts, and sometimes to the streets.

In School Boards and Commissions

Twenty-two states, including Texas and California (the largest consumers of textbooks), make major educational decisions through centralized state school boards and textbook commissions. These are composed of teachers and laymen, often political appointees. The commissions meet every five to six years to select textbooks in various subject areas for the state board of education. While local school districts can use textbooks that do not appear on the list, there are financial incentives to order state-approved textbooks, for these are usually the only books that are subsidized. Thus it becomes extremely important for publishers to have their books on these lists, especially in the more populous states. State recommendations also influence the general policies of textbook publishers, who normally do not print separate editions for each state. A decision in California or Texas may have repercussions throughout the industry, affecting the character of books available in the whole country. Thus, textbook watchers direct much of their energy toward the state boards of education and curriculum committees, hoping to influence the state-approved textbook lists.

They have had some success. Creationists in California convinced the state textbook commission to recommend that creation theory be taught as an alternative viable theory of origins (see Chapter 7). While California provided the most dramatic and well-publicized case of political pressure to influence textbook selection, similar activities continue quietly in other states. For example, in September 1973 the Oregon School Board ruled that school libraries must have creationist resource materials and that teachers must encourage students to "weigh the information and arrive at their own conclusions." A creationist in New York State has been indirectly working to influence the selection of textbooks by trying to include questions on scientific creationism on the statewide Board of Regents exam. Textbook commissions in Mississippi, Georgia, and Indiana have included creationist textbooks on their state-approved lists.

Textbook critics have their greatest leverage when they attempt to influence local school districts or even individual schools. In Ohio, for example, an organization called the Creation Research Science Education Foundation, Inc., was formed in 1973 to bring creation material to libraries and schools. This organization established local chapters, called Boosters of True Education, throughout the state to lobby with local school boards. They convinced the Columbus School Board to pass a resolution encouraging teachers to present creation theory along with evolution theory "so that students may choose." Local school authorities in Dallas, Chicago, and Atlanta have also opted to present both views and to purchase creationist books.

In most parts of the country, local or community values are

reflected in the teaching of science, and the matter never becomes a policy issue. The science coordinator for a school system in southern California organized a service course for high-school teachers to explore diverse points of view on questions of evolution versus creation. "Since scientists do deal with questions of origin, there is a place for creation theory in our curriculum." He hoped there would be a "better balance" in future textbooks. Well aware of current scientific thinking, this man was concerned about the "fairness" of presenting alternative beliefs and values threatened by science education.

One way in which local textbook watchers deal with educational trends that they find disturbing is to form "fundamental" or "alternative" schools.[1] The alternative school movement first developed in the 1960s as liberal groups sought less structured educational programs than were offered in the public schools. In the 1970s, however, such schools were formed by conservatives who resent the "liberalization" of public education. These new "fundamental" schools emphasize basic skills, moral and religious values, and discipline. Their traditional curricula often includes Bible studies and excludes the new math, new science curricula, and other "liberal innovations" that are felt to threaten local values, reduce achievement, or contribute to disciplinary problems. In areas where such efforts cannot be easily organized, textbook watchers sometimes bring their concerns to the streets.

In the Streets

In April 1974, the citizens of Kanawha County, West Virginia, started a long and violent protest against "godless teaching" in the public schools. The conflict began when the board of education tried to develop a modern English Language Arts Program in the school district of 46,000 students, the largest in the state. This included textbooks identified as "dirty," "antireligious," and generally threatening to local values. During the following months there were pickets, strikes, the closing of mines employing 5,000 workers, shootings, beatings, and the firebombing of school buildings. The civil strife was concerned variously with "dirty books," "secular humanism," and "federal influence on local education." The militancy was abetted by national organizations such as the Heritage Foundation, whose attorney represented the protesters.

Religious fundamentalists dominate the rural hollows of Kanawha County, the heart of the Appalachian coal district; but if Kanawha is poor, it is by no means the poorest or most isolated part of Appalachia. Less than 25 percent of the rural labor force still works in the mines, and the county has become a commercial and industrial center, providing diversified employment and a median income of $7,381 for rural households.[2] Kanawha has experienced rapid social and economic change, and its rural population has not been assimilated into the new social structure. The county is polarized between the relatively sophisticated urban and educated people of Charleston and those in the hollows who resent the domination of the city and take seriously West Virginia's striking motto *Montani Semper Libri*. Fundamentalist religion persists and is even strengthened by having to serve as a cushion for the stresses of social change; indeed the textbook conflict became a religious and cultural war, as parents saw their beliefs ignored by the educated and the powerful urbanites who dominate the school system. The leading textbook critic was the wife of a Church of Christ minister; she confronted a teacher with a doctorate from Yale. As a reporter described the meeting, it was "a war between people who depend on books and people who depend on The Book."[3]

Textbooks teaching evolution were one of many concerns in the Kanawha dispute. Schoolbooks were perceived as advocating sex and crime as well as anti-Christian and anti-American values. The conservative Pentecostal churches, believing in literal interpretation of the Bible, felt their beliefs were violated by both the scientific and the literary texts recommended for schools. They opposed any curriculum that encouraged disbelief. "We don't teach this at home, we don't want this at school."[4]

One family, assisted by a lawyer from the Heritage Foundation, sued the Kanawha County Board of Education for "encouraging disbelief in a supreme being."[5] The family sought an injunction against the offensive material, but the court found no violation of constitutional rights and recommended administrative remedies through the Board of Education.

The Kanawha County Board of Education compromised; it voted to return most books to the classroom but approved a district-wide adoption of creation science textbook material, and stipulated that no student would be required to read any book objectionable to parents on religious or moral grounds. Protest continued, however, with renewed violence. Finally the board adopted new guidelines for textbook selection that excluded many of the disputed books and set up screening committees of laymen to review books for controversial content. Meanwhile, the Kanawha schools reopened, and the most violent protesters were brought to court. But the issues remained unresolved. Should parents or professionals decide on school curriculum? What should be done when modern scholarly thinking infringes on morality as perceived by local communities? Kanawha raised fears of violent resistance to educational decisions—fears that were already an important factor in educational policy following civil rights and busing disruptions. The incident thus led to increased caution concerning the development and distribution of new curricula.

In State Legislatures

The repeal of Tennessee's "monkey laws" in 1967 reflected more a change in the alignment of voting districts than a change in attitudes. Antievolution sentiments persisted; in some areas teachers attempting to teach evolution have been reprimanded or dismissed. According to a public-opinion poll in September 1972, three-quarters of the high-school students in Dayton, Tennessee, still believed in creation: "Darwinian evolution breeds corruption, lust, immorality, greed and such acts of criminal depravity as drug addiction, war, and atrocious acts of genocide."[6] And in 1973, less than six years after repealing its antievolution legislation, the Tennessee General Assembly passed a new statute requiring that

Any biology textbook used for teaching in the public schools which expresses an opinion of, or relates to a theory about origins or creation of man and his world shall be prohibited from being used as a textbook in such system unless it specifically states that it is a theory as to the origin and creation of man and his world and is not represented to be scientific fact. Any textbook so used in the public education system which expresses an opinion or relates to a theory or theories shall give in the same textbook and under the same subject commensurate attention to, and an equal amount of emphasis on, the origins and creation of man and his world as the same is recorded in other theories including, but not limited to, the Genesis account in the Bible.[7]

This law, essentially declaring the Bible a reference book for biology, passed the Tennessee House of Representatives by a vote of 69 to 15, and the Senate by 28 to 1.

The National Association of Biology Teachers (NABT) challenged the constitutionality of the legislation, contending in a federal district court that it interfered with free speech, free exercise of religion, and freedom of the press as guaranteed by the First and Fourteenth Amendments.[8] One month later, unknown to the NABT, an organization called America United for the Separation of Church and State, Inc., filed a similar suit in a state chancery court in Nashville. As a result, the district court abstained from considering NABT's suit until the constitutional issues were resolved by the state court. NABT attorney Frederic LeClercq then appealed to the United States Supreme Court, both on the jurisdictional issues and on whether the Tennessee act violated constitutional amendments. The Supreme Court refused to accept the case, but finally on April 10, 1975, a court of appeals in Tennessee overruled the equal-time legislation, claiming that it showed

a clearly defined preferential position for the Biblical version of creation as opposed to any account of the development of man based on scientific research and reasoning. For a state to seek to enforce such preference by law is to seek to accomplish the very establishment of religion which the First Amendment to the Constitution of the United States squarely forbids.[9]

This decision was an important precedent, for similar bills were being introduced in other state legislatures. In 1973, textbook watchers in Michigan, the home base of the Creation Research Society, introduced several bills for "equal time."

In Georgia, the home of an estimated 2 million fundamentalists, the state Senate did pass equal time legislation in 1973, but it was tabled while the Divine Creation Committee of Georgia House held hearings. The committee reported the prevailing public view that information on all theories of creation should be available in public schools. It recommended, however, that the state Board of Education deal with the problem through selection of textbooks rather than legislation. Subsequently, the board approved the Science and Creation Series for state adoption. Georgia creationists reintroduced their equal-time bill in 1979 and again in 1980, when it was approved by the House (139 to 30) and by the Senate (46 to 7). However, the compromise bill did not come up for vote before the end of the legislative session. Two new creationist bills will be presented in Georgia in 1982. One allows school districts to exempt themselves from teaching creationism by a referendum; the other permits districts to adopt creationism by referendum. By incorporating some possibilities of choice at the district level, the bill's proponents expect success.

A powerful fundamentalist group in Huntsville, Alabama, where the primary industry is technical work for NASA and the U.S. Army, successfully passed a creationist resolution in the Madison County School Board in 1980 and lobbied in the legislature for a creationist bill. After six hours of open hearings involving some sixty speakers, the state Senate passed a bill to encourage equitable treatment and to train teachers on scientific creationism. The bill met sufficient opposition in the House that it was withdrawn without a vote. However, it is expected to reappear in 1982.

By 1981, creationists had introduced bills into the legislatures of about twenty states and prepared a bill for the U.S. Congress.[10] Learning from the failure of early legislative efforts, their strategy gradually changed. Two men were responsible for this change: Wendell Bird and Paul Ellwanger. Bird, a graduate of the Yale Law School, affiliated with the Institute for Creation Research, is a specialist on constitutional law. He believes that creationists can develop legislation that will not violate the First Amendment.[11] To demonstrate this, he wrote a model resolution that he felt would

"neutralize" the teaching of scientific creationism by sharply distinguishing it from religious creationism. The former would focus
on scientific evidence, the latter on Biblical doctrine. The ICR
began to publish two versions of their textbooks, one for the public,
the other for Christian schools. The versions are identical except
for the avoidance of specific references to God, the Bible, and Noah
in the public-school edition: God becomes the "Master Designer";
the "creative work of God" becomes simply "Creation."

Paul Ellwanger, from Anderson, South Carolina, is a respiratory
therapist, a Biblical literalist, and the president of Citizens for
Fairness in Education. He took Bird's model resolution and, with
some change in its organization, created a bill that was specifically
designed to avoid conflict with the First Amendment. This bill was
signed into law in 1981 by the governors of Arkansas and Louisiana. (See Chapter 9.)

In the Courts

The legislative initiatives of the creationists inevitably brought
them to court. In December 1981, the American Civil Liberties
Union and twenty-three plaintiffs went to a federal district court
to challenge the Arkansas law (Act 590) requiring balanced treatment of creation science. Act 590 was a model for similar statutes
under consideration in the legislatures of twenty other states. The
ACLU had to show that, despite all claims to the contrary, scientific creationism could not be dissociated from its religious base. As
a judicial test of the act, the case was important and will be discussed in detail in Chapter 9. However, this was not the first time
that creationists were in court, for legal battles are an increasingly
important tactic as creationists seek to expand their constituency
and advance their cause.

In August 1972, William Willoughby, religion editor of the
Washington Evening Star, filed suit ("in the interest of forty million
evangelistic Christians in the United States") against H. Guyford
Stever, director of the National Science Foundation, and the Board
of Regents of the University of Colorado. The NSF had supported

the development of the BSCS textbooks at Colorado, and Willoughby wanted the foundation to spend an equal amount "for the promulgation of the creationist theory of the origin of man." Willoughby, who called himself "a liberal evangelist," claimed that citizens are coerced to pay taxes to support educational activities that violate their religious beliefs. Supporting educational programs that are "one-sided, biased and damaging" to religious views is an improper use of governmental monies.[12]

Willoughby tried to distinguish himself from other creationists. He was "as embarrassed as anyone else" by the excessive zeal of fundamentalists with "hard core, doctrinal demands." He expressed his concern for "impartiality" and "fair play" for those with evangelical convictions and his resentment of the "intellectual snobbery" of scientists, who present their ideas as "Truth." He received many supportive letters from people who were not religious but only concerned with fairness and tolerance for minority beliefs.[13]

Willoughby's formal complaint alleged that the NSF violated the First Amendment: "The government is establishing as the official religion of the United States, secular humanism." The U.S. District Court in Washington, D.C., dismissed the case in May 1973, claiming that the First Amendment does not allow the state to require that teaching be tailored to particular religious beliefs and that the BSCS books were secular. Willoughby then went to the U.S. Supreme Court, which dismissed the case in February 1975.

Another federal case occurred in 1978, when creationists sued the Smithsonian Institute in a U.S. District Court. They wanted the courts to block an exhibit called "The Emergence of Man." The court ruled against the creationists and in 1980 the U.S. Court of Appeals upheld the district court.

Creationists also lost a case in Tennessee when the NABT challenged the constitutionality of the 1973 legislation requiring the teaching of the Genesis account of creation. Undaunted, however, creationists took the initiative in California. This time, instead of defending legislation, they sued the California Board of Education for violating the religious rights of children.

The trial was touted as a "rerun of the Scopes trial," "the trial of the century," and a "test of religious freedom." The plaintiffs lined up school children to plead that kids should not be told their religious beliefs are wrong. The thirteen-year-old son of a creationist solemnly testified that his teacher told him he had descended from an ape. In defense, the state attorney general mobilized eminent scientists as expert witnesses to vouch for the validity of evolution theory. However, during the trial, the creationists reduced their complaint to an administrative detail concerning the wording of the guidelines in the *Science Framework.* The trial concluded with a recommendation by Judge Irving Perluss that the Board of Education circulate a policy statement emphasizing the need to reduce dogmatism and include conditional statements whenever textbooks speculate on the origins of life. This was hardly a major victory, but the event brought publicity and media attention to the creationists and helped to legitimate their cause.

Interpreting the judge's administrative recommendation as a major victory, creationists prepared to defend the Arkansas legislation with some optimism. Unlike in Tennessee, the Arkansas law avoided references to religion, defining creationism as a science. They hoped thereby to avoid the inevitable challenge to the constitutionality of their demands. However, by defining creationism as a science, creationists walk a tightrope between their religious followers and the pragmatic constraints of the First Amendment. This is a source of schisms and strains within their ranks as they use legal tactics to support their goals.

Notes

1. The Pasadena School Board, for example, is advocating fundamentalist schools as a reaction against breakdown in discipline and declining scholastic achievement (*New York Times,* 26 November 1975). See Council for Basic Education, *Bulletin,* for monthly reports on the alternative school movement.

2. National Education Association, *Kanawha County, West Virginia: A Textbook Study in Cultural Conflict* (Washington, D.C.: NEA Teachers Rights Division, February 1975).

3. Paul Cowan, "Holy War in West Virginia," *Village Voice,* 9 December 1974.

4. *Washington Post,* 13 September 1974.

5. *Williams* v. *Kanawha Board of Education,* 74-378-CH (Decision 30, January 1975).

6. *New York Times,* 1 October 1972.

7. Amendment to the Tennessee Code, Annotated Section 49–2008, passed 30 April 1973.

8. There were three coplaintiffs from Tennessee: Joseph Daniels, Jr., and Arthur Jones (professors at the University of Tennessee), and Larry Wilder (a public-school teacher). They contended that the legislation violated their academic freedom.

9. National Association of Biology Teachers, *News and Views* 19 (April 1975).

10. The federal bill, known as the Academic Freedom in Scientific Inquiry without Federal Censorship Act, focuses on the use of federal funds for research, curriculum development, and museum exhibitions that deal with the origin of life. It calls for hearings on the scientific evidence for the creation-science model and for equal dispensation of research funds to scientific creationists.

11. Wendell Bird, "Freedom of Religion and Science Instruction in Public Schools," *Yale Law Journal* 87 (January 1978): 515 ff.

12. *William Willoughby* v. *H. Guyford Stever;* U.S. District Court for the District of Columbia; brief filed August 7, 1972; civil action 1574–1572.

13. Telephone interview with Willoughby.

III

DISPUTES

SOCRATES:	Did you say you believe in the separation of church and state?
BRYAN:	I did. It is a fundamental principle.
SOCRATES:	Is the right of the majority to rule a fundamental principle?
BRYAN:	It is.
SOCRATES:	Is freedom of thought a fundamental principle, Mr. Jefferson?
JEFFERSON:	It is.
SOCRATES:	Well, how would you gentlemen compose your fundamental principles, if a majority, exercising its fundamental right to rule, ordained that only Buddhism should be taught in public schools?
BRYAN:	I'd move to a Christian country.
JEFFERSON:	I'd exercise the sacred right of revolution. What would you do, Socrates?
SOCRATES:	I'd re-examine my fundamental principles.

—Walter Lippmann, *Four Dialogues*

7

Creation versus Evolution: The California Controversy

In 1963, two women from Orange County, California, Nell Se-graves and Jean Sumrall, decided to "seek justice for the Christian child." They justified their demand on the basis of the 1963 Supreme Court decision *(Abington School District* v. *Schempp)* that it was unconstitutional to force nonbelieving children to read prayers in school. Segraves and Sumrall argued that if it is unconstitutional "to teach God in the school," it is equally unconstitutional "to teach the absence of God." They cited the majority opinion of Justice Clark: "We agree, of course, that the state may not establish a 'religion of secularism' in the sense of affirmatively opposing or showing hostility to religion, thus 'preferring those who believe in no religion over those who do believe.' "[1]

In 1963, assisted by Walter Lammerts, a geneticist and one of the founders of the Creation Research Society, they petitioned the state Board of Education to require that textbooks clearly specify that evolution is a theory rather than truth. Arguing that Christian children must have equal protection under the law, they sought a legal opinion from the Department of Justice concerning the teaching of theories believed by atheists. If religious persons cannot teach their doctrines in public schools, why should atheists and agnostics be allowed to do so? Assistant Attorney General Norbert A. Schlei agreed that it would be unconstitutional for a state to prescribe atheism, agnosticism, or irreligious teaching. Max Rafferty, then California Superintendent of Public Instruction, promptly ruled that all California texts dealing with evolution must clearly label evolution as a theory.

Rafferty was notoriously sympathetic to conservative and fundamentalist causes. In a California Department of Education booklet called *Guidelines for Moral Instruction in California Schools*, he unequivocally expressed his concern with "protecting the child's morality from attack by secular humanists."

> I always think that America was built on the Bible. . . . The teaching of evolution as a part of the religion of Humanism, therefore, is yet another area of concern. . . . If the origins of man were taught from the point of view of both evolution and creation, the purpose of education would be satisfied.[2]

In 1966, Rafferty encouraged creationists to demand that creation theory be given equal time in biology classes, claiming it was consistent with the education code of the 1964 Civil Rights Act prohibiting teaching that reflects adversely on any persons because of race, color, or creed. This code states that references to religion are not prohibited as long as they do not constitute instruction in religious principles. Creationists interpreted this as a sanction for the teaching of creation theory as an alternate scientific hypothesis.

The state Board of Education denied the creationists' 1966 proposal for equal time. Then, in 1969, the California State Advisory Committee on Science Education prepared a set of curriculum guidelines for its public-school science programs called *The Science Framework for California Schools*, intended to be the model for science curriculum development in California.[3] The committee is an advisory group appointed by the Board of Education. Its fourteen members consist of scientists and teachers, and they are advised by distinguished consultants. Their advice is implemented by the State Curriculum Commission, a group of sixteen laymen and scientists, thirteen of whom are appointed by the Board of Education and one each by the California Assembly, Senate, and Governor. This commission advises the board on specific textbooks that are appropriate within the guidelines of the *Science Framework.* Textbook decisions are made every six years. Local school districts are not required to abide by state selections, but they lose state subsidies for textbooks outside the state-approved list. The state Department of Education works closely with publishers to make any changes that are required by the curriculum commission.

Creationist Demands

In October 1969, the state advisory committee presented a draft of the *Science Framework* to the Board of Education. It contained two paragraphs on evolution, and several of the nine members of the board objected. These included Howard Day, president of the board and a Mormon; John Ford, M.D., a physician and Seventh-Day Adventist; David Hubbard, president of Fuller Theological Seminary in Pasadena; Thomas Harward, M.D., a Mormon and personal physician to Max Rafferty; and Eugene Ragle, a Baptist.[4] Their objections were described in the *Los Angeles Times* and read by Vernon Grose, an aerospace engineer and expert on systems safety who works for a consulting firm in Los Angeles. Grose belongs to the American Scientific Affiliation and to the Assemblies of God, a Pentecostal denomination. He is a "commission-sitter" serving on fourteen state commissions, and a writer of numerous archconservative tracts on the decline of American morality. He was "called" to action by the discussion of evolution theory in the *Science Framework.* Grose's motivation and his qualifications are suggested by his own statement:

> My citizenship really is in heaven. And even though I wasn't trained in biology, when I got into the issue I believe I must have felt something like Jesus did when he overthrew the tables and the money changers in the temple . . . the odds were extremely high against success. Yet I believe, because my trust was in the Lord, and because the issue was a significant one, that He honored the effort.[5]

Thus Grose decided to fight the evolutionary bias that was "threatening our national heritage."

> Can you imagine the impact on the logic required for justice in our courts if we were forced to amend the Declaration of Independence to read: we hold these truths to be self-evident, that all men arose as equals from a soup of amino-like molecules, and that they, by virtue of this common molecular ancestry, are endowed with certain inalienable rights.[6]

On November 13, 1969, Grose presented a thirteen-page memorandum to the Board of Education, arguing that the theory of creation be included in textbooks as an alternative explanation for the origin of life. He reduced this to a brief statement for the *Science Framework.*

> All scientific evidence to date concerning the origin of life implies at least a dualism or the necessity to use several theories to fully explain relationships. . . . While the Bible and other philosophical treatises also mention creation, science has independently postulated the various theories of creation. Therefore, creation in scientific terms is not a religious or philosophical belief. Also note that creation and evolutionary theories are not necessarily mutual exclusives. Some of the scientific data (e.g., the regular absence of transitional forms) may be best explained by a creation theory, while other data (e.g., transmutation of species) substantiate a process of evolution.[7]

The Board of Education unanimously accepted the statement and printed it in the *Science Framework.* Thus, forty-five years after the Scopes trial, the guidelines for a state educational system that serves 1 million children included a formal recommendation to teach creation theory.

The California State Advisory Committee on Science was horrified by the revision. "The changes, though small in extent, have the effect of entirely undercutting the thrust of the 205-page document . . . offend[ing] the very essence of science, if not religion."[8] The committee publicly repudiated the document, and the panel of science advisers appointed by the Curriculum Commission to advise on the choice of textbooks resigned.

The implications began to be evident in 1971, when the Curriculum Commission selected specific biology textbooks to be used in the schools. No creationist texts were among the books submitted to the Board of Education. Dr. Ford, vice-president of the board, reminded his colleagues on the commission that "No textbook should be considered for adoption . . . that has not clearly discussed at least two major contrasting theories of origin."[9] In May 1972, the board restored the omitted texts and reorganized the commission, changing its name to the Curriculum Development and Supplemental Materials Commission. Creationists, including Vernon Grose, were well represented; the new commission included only one professional scientist, Junji Kumamoto, a chemist, who for several years was to engage in a one-man defense of evolution in California.

California buys 10 percent of the nation's textbooks. Grose was responsible for negotiating with publishers, and in June 1972, he called publisher's representatives to ask them how they intended to include creation theory. He found some quite willing to adapt to the new *Science Framework.* One proposed replacing a section about Leakey's archeological discoveries of primitive man with a reproduction of Michelangelo's Sistine Chapel painting of the Creation and a drawing of Moses. Another submitted a fourth-grade science text that claimed that science had nothing to say about who made the world and why. One chapter had as an exercise an investigation of the Biblical account of creation.[10] One fifth-grade text on "concepts in science" mentioned that George Darwin was the son of a famous English scientist, Charles Darwin; this is the book's only reference to Darwin.[11]

To prepare for the final adoption of the textbooks, the Board of Education called a hearing on November 9, 1972, in order to assess public opinion. The hearing became a confrontation between creationists and evolutionists. It promised to be a circus—Dayton 1972 —but bureaucratic procedures (five-minute limitations on speeches) and the creationists' efforts to present themselves as scientists set a tone of sober debate. Engineers appointed to curriculum development commissions somehow lack the fire of fundamentalist preachers. Yet the ironies were striking. "Witnesses from each side appeared in each other's clothing," observed a journalist amused by the spectacle of scientists speaking for creation theory and theologians supporting science.[12] The twenty-three witnesses for Genesis included only three Baptist ministers, but twelve scientists and engineers. The evolutionists, on the other hand, called forth only four scientists. Other witnesses included Presbyterian, Episcopalian, and Mormon ministers, Catholic and Buddhist priests, and a rabbi; all testified for the need to separate science and religion.

The California Solution

Educational policy-making bodies are well accustomed to responding to political pressure. Criteria for the selection of textbooks are continually being adjusted to meet the demands of the times. A state board's responsiveness depends on the pressure that various groups can bring to bear on board members. For example, the concerns of ethnic and racial minorities and of women were a source of many textbook changes during the 1960s.

The California education establishment was especially sensitive to issues concerning the teaching of biology, for there had been long legislative debates about the use of live animals for scientific experiments. These had culminated in an ambiguous amendment to the State Education Code limiting the use of vertebrate animals in classrooms, and many science educators, worried that the life-sciences instructional program was jeopardized, were already active in educational politics during the early 1970s.[13] Thus the California State Board of Education was deluged with letters, resolutions, and petitions from educators and scientists, and soon after the November textbook hearings, it began to reexamine its policies.

In December 1972, the Curriculum Committee announced to the board that its members had agreed unanimously on guidelines that would ensure the neutrality of science textbooks. They proposed to eliminate all scientific dogmatism by changing offending statements in textbooks to indicate their conditional nature. Books should discuss *how* things occur and avoid questions of ultimate causes; unresolved questions should be presented as such to students, with an emphasis on the tentative nature of evolution theory.

The Board of Education accepted these recommendations, voting 7 to 1 to treat evolution as a speculative theory, a decision described in the *Los Angeles Times* as "A Victory for Adam & Eve." The board appointed a committee to implement the recommendations; two of its members, Richard Bube and Robert Fischer, were members of the American Scientific Affiliation; the other two were Dr. John Ford and David Hubbard, state Board of Education members who had revised the *Science Framework.* None of these men was a biologist, and all identified themselves as creationists who accepted the teaching of evolution *if* it remained neutral on the subject of ultimate causes. Fischer, for example, defined the issue as "neither creation vs. evolution, nor design vs. chance, but the existence of a Supreme Being, an issue that lies beyond the limits of science."[14] The committee edited the textbooks to clarify both the potentialities and the limitations of science, intending to guard against the "religion of science" as well as "other" religious positions.

The committee prepared a statement, to be printed in all textbooks dealing with evolution, that science cannot answer questions about "where the first matter and energy come from," for scientific methods can only deal with the "physical mechanisms involved." The statement declares that, while the term *evolution* can be used to describe observable processes, the accuracy of the theory of evolution in reconstructing life in the past "depends largely upon the validity of the assumptions on which it is based."

The committee screened thirty textbooks, proposing many changes, and taking particular care to replace specific words that implied acceptance of evolution theory. They changed "developed" or "evolved" to "appeared" and "unfolded" to "occurred." They deleted some words ("ancestors," "descendents," "origins"), and they added qualifying phrases ("according to one particular point of view"; "It is believed, in the theory of evolution"; "The evidence is not clear, but"). Pictures were relabeled: "This is an artist's conception of what might have been," or "Some people think that plants might have looked like this: What do you think?" And they prefaced each section discussing evolution with a statement indicating that "science has no way of knowing how life began." Some specific changes are listed in Table 7.1.

TABLE 7.1.
Changes in Biology Textbooks Recommended by the
California Board of Education

Original Version	Changed Version
Changes in Definitions	
Science is the total knowledge of facts and principles that govern our lives, the world, and everything in it, and the universe of which the world is just a part.	Science is one way of discovering and interpreting the facts and principles that govern our lives, the world and everything in it, and the universe of which the world is just a part. The scientific way limits itself to natural causes and to descriptions that can be contradicted, at least in principle, by experimental investigation.
Evolution is a central explanatory hypothesis in the biological sciences. Students who have taken a biology course without learning about evolution probably have not been adequately or honestly educated.	Evolution is a central explanatory hypothesis in the biological sciences. Therefore, students need some knowledge of its assumptions and basic concepts.
Qualifications to "Reduce Dogmatism"	
Scientists can reconstruct the (prehistoric) animal.	Scientists do their best to reconstruct the (prehistoric) animal.
Scientists believe that these species were ancestors.	According to the evolutionary view, these species were ancestors.
A short description . . .	A short approximate description . . .
Modern animals that are descendents . . .	Modern animals that seem to be direct descendents . . .
Some fish began to change.	Some fish began to change although we don't know why.
The earth had spore-bearing plants long before the first seed plants appeared.	There is evidence that the earth had spore-bearing green plants long before the first seed plants appeared.

Paleontologists . . . have reconstructed past history . . .	Paleontologists . . . have done their best to reconstruct the past history . . .
How do we know . . .	On what basis has it been concluded that . . .
The evidence that shows how . . .	Evidence that is often interpreted to mean . . .
They would have to change.	They would have to be different.
Fishes adapted . . .	Fishes were adapted . . .
Paleontologists have been able to date the geological history of North America.	Paleontologists have assembled a tentative outline of the geological history of North America.

Changes to Avoid Evolutionary Assumptions

Slowly, over millions of years, the dinosaurs died out.	Slowly, the dinosaurs died out.
As reptiles evolved from fishlike ancestors, they developed a thicker scaly surface.	If reptiles evolved from fishlike ancestors, as proposed in the theory of evolution, they must have developed a thick scaly surface.
Many scientists believe that the universe had a beginning similar to that of a snow fort. They believe that the stars and the galaxies of the entire universe in the beginning were in the form of very small scattered particles.	Science, by definition, cannot say anything about where the first matter and energy of which our universe is made came from. That is because there cannot be any science without matter and energy to deal with. When scientists speak of the beginning of the universe, therefore, they mean the first interactions of matter and energy. Many scientists believe that these first interactions were like those in making a snow fort . . .
Shortly after the flying reptiles took to the air, the early birds developed.	Birds appear in the fossil record shortly after flying reptiles.

The constant rate at which radioactive elements give off particles enables scientists to determine how long it will take for one ball of any sample of a radioactive element to form another element.

Scientists know that radioactive elements give off particles today at a constant rate. If they assume that this rate has remained constant back in time to the date of interest, they can determine how long a . . .

Scientists believe life may have begun from amino acids or viruses, neither of which is usually considered living. Scientists believe life may have been transported from another planet.

Scientists do not know how life began on earth. Some suggest that life began from non-living material. Others suggest that life may have been transported . . .

Plants took to the land and conquered it.

Plants appeared on the land.

SOURCE: From a notebook distributed by the California Board of Education containing single pages from textbooks with changes typed on slips of paper that were superimposed on the original passages.

Most changes were basically unobjectionable and, indeed, a few did correct some unnecessarily dogmatic statements. The board accepted the revision committee's recommended changes by a vote of 5 to 3. Since the publishers submitted their bids for basic texts after the *Science Framework* was published, the revisions were considered "technical," that is, based on criteria agreed upon prior to the contract, and they were forced to comply.

Scientists accepted the changes with relief. While they felt the qualifications did injustice to the great body of scientific expertise, the changes were far less disturbing than anticipated. Furthermore, two biologists, Garrett Hardin and Barbara Hopper, wrote a new page 106 for the *Science Framework*, and their revision, focusing on evolution, was accepted by the Board of Education in March 1974.

The scientific creationists felt "sold out" by what they viewed as minimal changes that neglected their demand for equal time—but by no means did they give up. They began to gather survey material to prove the extent of public support for their views. The Seventh-Day Adventist Church of Crescent City, California, polled 1,500 adults, about 57 percent of whom attended church. They claimed that 91 percent of church attenders and 85 percent of nonchurch attenders favored teaching creation in the public schools. Fifty-four percent of church attenders and 65 percent of nonattenders also favored the teaching of evolution. They respectfully submitted their findings in support of "equal time" to the Board of Education as a form of "public service" in order to help the board "represent our community." Creationists continued their speaking engagements, particularly in California, and they remained highly visible, as newspapers played up their colorful speeches. On college campuses, they often received a favorable press that stimulated months of controversy in the student newspapers.[15]

In February 1973, the creationists presented a new motion for "equal time." They nearly won, for the board upheld its earlier decision by only a one-vote margin. However, a motion by John Ford to place creation in social-science books passed unanimously, and a social-science framework committee was formed in April to develop the necessary guidelines required by the board. The committee's proposed framework provided that "various views of human origins together with various approaches to the relationship of religious beliefs to scientific theory, must be seen as part of the intellectual and cultural diversity of our society."[16] Thus it required that the analysis of belief systems in social-science courses include discussion of creation theory. In these discussions, teachers would help students review the evidence for the various theories or myths of creation.

The creationists continued to gather evidence of public support, polling the Cupertino Union school district near San Jose, California, one of the largest elementary school districts in the state. A survey of a random sample of 2,000 residents, conducted by Citizens for Scientific Creation, asked, "Should scientific evidence of creation be presented in the schools along with evolution?" The survey found that 84.3 percent of the respondents agreed. The poll also questioned respondents about their personal convictions, to find that 44.3 percent believed in creation, 23.3 percent in evolution, 18.3 percent were undecided, 10.6 percent believed in neither, and 3.5 percent in both. Among those claiming to be evolutionists, 75 percent favored the inclusion of both theories, evidently influenced by the assertion that scientific evidence for creation does in fact exist.

Despite the polls and a swarm of letters and petitions to the state

Board of Education, creationists began to lose their influence in 1974, when the board initiated a new method of evaluating educational materials that would include many more civic organizations and lay-interest groups in the textbook evaluation committee. Creation-science books were eliminated, as this broader participatory base gave extremist positions less influence. On May 8, 1974, the board reversed the decision to include creation theory in social science classes. The vote of 5–5 left creationists complaining bitterly about injustice and educational tyranny. "The public schools are not controlled by the public nor does the public have any say in the educational process. It seems that the public through taxes simply pays for that which they do not want."[17]

The creationists were, however, able to delay the publication and distribution of the social science framework until January 1976. The final version did not require discussion of human origins in social studies classrooms or the presentation of creation as an alternative to evolution, but the board of education did advise that both evolution and creation theory be discussed as examples of the intellectual and cultural diversity of society. As a further concession to creationists, the board sent a memo to school districts to remind teachers that whenever human origins were discussed, alternative theories should be presented.

Indefatigable, the creationists accelerated their campaign in order to influence the 1976 revisions of the *Science Framework*. Once again they argued that "theistic and materialistic philosophies are equally religious and/or anti-religious and . . . equally inaccessible to falsification by experimental test." Therefore, they concluded, "both should be studied in the light of the scientific data."[18] (See Appendix 3.)

Failing to gain substantial changes in the guidelines, the creationists in California concentrated on building a constituency and developing the legal expertise to confront state legislatures and the courts. Encouraged by the changing political mood of the 1980s, the Segraves family of the Creation Science Research Center took their complaints to court. Kelly Segraves sued the California Board of Education, charging that it had violated the "religious rights of his children." (See Chapter 6.)

While the California events focused on biology textbooks, textbook watchers were expressing their concerns about evolution in other ways. A vulnerable target had appeared in a new NSF social-science curriculum that explicitly raised several controversial issues only implied by the evolutionary assumptions of biology textbooks.

Notes

1. Nell Segraves and Jean Sumrall, *A Legal Premise for Moral and Spiritual Guidelines for California Public Schools* (San Diego: Creation Science Research Center, n.d.).

2. Max Rafferty, *Guidelines for Moral Instruction in California, a Report Accepted by the State Board of Education* (Sacramento: California State Department of Education, May 1969), pp. 7, 64.

3. For a review of the work of this committee and the background to the creationist controversy, see John A. Moore, "Creationism in California," *Daedalus* (Summer 1974): 173–190.

4. Board of Education members were appointed by Governor Ronald Reagan, and the selection clearly reflected his personal piety.

5. Cited in Frederic S. LeClercq, "The Monkey Laws and the Public Schools: A Second Consumption?" *Vanderbilt Law Review* 27 (March 1974): 242.

6. Vernon Grose, statement to California Board of Education, 1969 (mimeographed).

7. California State Department of Education, *Science Framework for California Public Schools* (Sacramento: 1970), p. 106.

8. Paul DeHart Hurd, a spokesman for the committee, cited by Walter G. Peter III, "Fundamental Scientists Oppose Darwinian Evolution," *Bioscience* 20 (July 1970): 1069.

9. Board of Education, minutes of meeting, 8 July 1971.

10. Texts considered were a creationist book by Leswing, *Science, Environment and Man,* and a Macmillan science series. Both were later omitted from the California textbooks screening process.

11. John E. Summers, M.D., "Letter to Editor," *Science,* 9 November 1973, p. 535.

12. Nicholas Wade, "Creationists and Evolutionists: Confrontation in California," *Science,* 17 November 1972, pp. 724–729.

13. Clifford Frederickson, "Use of Live Vertebrate Animals in Science Instruction in California Schools," *California Science Teachers Journal*

(October 1974). The amendment was an addition to the California Education Code, Article 2, Section 1, cl. 8 in Senate Bill 112, signed 1 June 1973.

14. Cited in Richard Bube, "Science Teaching in California," *The Reformed Journal* (April 1973): 4.

15. See exchange of letters in the UCSD, *Triton Times,* 16, 23, 30 January; 2, 6, 20 February; and 19 March 1973.

16. Quoted in *San Diego Union,* 14 April 1974.

17. This is from a report mailed to 75,000 people from the director of CSRC (Kelly Segraves) in May 1974.

18. Robert E. Kofahl, "Position Paper: The Science Framework Should Be Revised with Respect to Evolution and Creation," submitted to California Science Committee of Curriculum Development and Supplemental Materials Commission, by CSRC, October 1975. (See Appendix 3.)

8

The Proper Study of Mankind . . . : Evolution and the MACOS Dispute

Education is a major industry in Corinth, a small city in an agricultural region of upstate New York.[1] Corinth is both a university town and a commercial center for the surrounding region, and it has experienced typical "town-gown" strains. The Corinth school district was one of the earliest in the country to adopt MACOS and, not surprisingly, the first school to request the course was Lakeview, located in the upper middle-class university suburb where most of the students were faculty offspring. MACOS was implemented at Lakeview School just as intended by its developers; a university team of educators and scientists arrived to train teachers to use the materials. The principal informed parents about the course prior to its implementation. It was enthusiastically received.

In September 1973, the principal of the Springbrook School in Corinth also ordered MACOS for its fourth-, fifth-, and sixth-grade

classes. The Springbrook School, less than a mile away from Lakeview, is in a quite different neighborhood; its residents are employed in local civil service and technical jobs, and few have more
than a high-school education. In implementing MACOS the school
administration did not consult with parents or seek local approval.
The two teachers responsible for MACOS received no special training; and they were not warned that the course material might be
controversial.

For four months, there was, in fact, no hint of a problem. One
teacher was enthusiastic about the pedagogical value of MACOS;
the other was ambivalent, concerned about the lack of traditional
factual and historical content. In January 1974, one of the teachers
discussed some of the evolutionary assumptions of MACOS.
Knowing the conservative religious feelings of some of her students, she carefully prefaced her discussion with remarks on the
existence of diverse beliefs on the question of origins. But the
discussion led to an argument, and several children brought to
school religious tracts that specifically condemned evolution theory. The children also brought MACOS booklets home, and in a
few days a group of mothers "stormed the school." They came to
observe classrooms, to question students and teachers, and they
argued that the school must give equal time to traditional religious
beliefs if it was "preaching" evolution.

"We're all animals, kids are taught here"

One hundred twelve students were taking the MACOS course in
Springbrook School; the parents of twenty-five of these children
protested. The principal set up a series of meetings with parents to
explain the course and its intentions, hoping that parental concerns
could be aired in a rational context. By this time, however, opinions
were well formed, and the conflict escalated; according to one of
the teachers, "Parents were rude; they questioned my credentials
during class period, leafed through the materials on my desk, and
recorded my replies to their questions." They also petitioned the
Board of Education to have the principal fired. While the discussion of evolution triggered the protest, other issues soon entered:

We're all animals, kids are taught here.

The children are thinking too much about values; they are too young to be exposed to this type of thing.

Their morals must be shaped at home.

If we cannot sing Christmas carols, then we are not going to let you teach other kinds of religion.[2]

Parents complained about the "permissive" format of MACOS, and suspected that their children were missing traditional subjects. Above all, the community resented "indoctrination by outside experts," and, reflecting local town-gown tensions, they associated the course with "those experts on the campus." Why, asked the parents, were they not consulted before introducing a course that was so offensive to family values?

MACOS had supporters in the neighborhood, but few cared to get involved in the public controversy. There was some fear, triggered by telephone threats, that open support of MACOS might endanger their children.

The anti-MACOS groups were well organized. Four parents from a local organization called Save Our Schools, concerned with censoring "dirty books in the classroom," served as spokesmen. About seventy-five people from the community regularly attended meetings to discuss how to get rid of the program. Some participants from local fundamentalist churches focused on religious issues, using passages from the Bible to support their opposition. Others had overt political concerns about the "communist" values they perceived in MACOS. Some resources for organizing the protest came from outside the community; local parents had access to duplicating facilities and to Xeroxed materials from the national media. They were knowledgeable about anti-MACOS protests elsewhere. During the dispute, several speakers from the John Birch Society in a nearby city came to town to talk about "educational issues," and focused on MACOS.

Opposition continued throughout the winter at great cost to the students and staff. Students took sides in the controversy, and many found it difficult to handle the conflicting attitudes of their parents, their teachers, and their peers. Finally, in April 1974, the Springbrook School dropped MACOS entirely. This, claimed the principal, was a political, not a curriculum, decision; the tension simply had to be dissipated.

The Politics of Local Protest

MACOS had been acclaimed by teachers, parents, and students throughout the country as a major innovation in science teaching.[3] Yet the Corinth controversy was only one of many; protests spread like an epidemic in 1974, and sales of the curriculum declined by about 70 percent. One of the first MACOS protests took place in Lake City, Florida, in 1970 when the course was being tested. Integration decisions in Florida had left the population tense and suspicious of any changes in educational policy. The liberal assumptions underlying MACOS were an obvious target, and the course could not be taught in Lake City schools.

One year later parents in Phoenix, Arizona, raised such strong objections to MACOS that the state superintendent of public instruction banned purchase of the material throughout the state until the case was settled.[4] Subsequent controversies erupted in New York, Vermont, Tennessee, Florida, Oregon, Alaska, Maryland, Pennsylvania, Idaho, California, and Texas.[5]

Some selected quotations from MACOS critics during these controversies suggest the range of concerns over the course.[6]

1. Teaching that man is an animal violates religious beliefs.
"I will never say I came from an ape."
"I do believe it should be countered or balanced with alternative theories of the origin of life, and obviously what I am getting at is Genesis."
"Teaching that man is an animal and nothing more is denying the existence of God and religion. Should such teaching be banned in the public schools as unconstitutional?"
"Children are warned to distinguish between human-like behavior

and attributing human motives to animals. It seems that children at that age are not able to make the distinction and do tend to overdo the similarity between animals and man."

"I wonder how many parents would be happy to see their son identify with a baboon instead of his father."

2. MACOS teaches disturbing values.

"It teaches that violence and power are necessary for survival."

"It will break down the moral fiber of American youth."

"The course is a steady diet of bloodletting and promiscuity."

"It is violent, unnecessary, and even heretical. The study of Eskimo infanticide has serious implications for abortion practices by students expected to feel that it is up to some authority who or when a baby becomes human."

"It is part of a humanistic cult that claims there is no God or creative force within the universe."

"It perpetuates the humanist idea of one world."

"It openly favors a communal way of life."

"It is used for the political subversion of our children."

3. Educational experts undermine parental authority.

"It alienates the beliefs, values, and allegiances of children, alienating them from their parents."

"The education experts are dictating our values."

"St. Jerome (Bruner) is trying to indoctrinate students."

"The course should be brought up as an election issue or at least judged by a lay curriculum committee."

4. Substitutes for traditional education are not useful.

"There are, after all, no facts."

"Does cultural relativism make better citizens?"

"How does it prepare students for their future experience?"

"It will take the heart out of education."

"The mood of the country is strongly to return to basic education."

These or similar objections were repeated in every community conflict, but the emphasis shifted somewhat in each, depending on immediate local concerns. Thus, in the university community of Corinth the town-gown conflict assumed importance as local groups targeted "those experts on the campus." Religious issues dominated Bible Belt protests; cultural relativism was a concern in isolated rural communities. Complaints about the moral implications of MACOS prevailed in urban disputes. Aspects of the course thus became targets for the expression of local frustrations.

MACOS protests often appeared as isolated incidents, but there was considerable communication among the activists in various disputes. The same few individuals, well-known textbook watchers, appeared at the site of many controversies; for example, the Gablers, who had been monitoring textbooks in Texas, traveled around the country to win their "battle for the minds of American students." The Gablers were instrumental in removing BSCS textbooks from the Texas Board of Education's approved curriculum in 1969, and they have since carried on a continued diatribe against evolution theory and smut. MACOS was on their disapproved list, and they lectured in many of the communities where protests developed. Ona Lee McGraw of Maryland, an officer in the National Coalition for Children and a member of Leadership Action, Inc., of Washington, D.C., was also a ubiquitous MACOS critic. Several of the California creationists included MACOS in their speeches, although they did not fight the adoption of MACOS materials in the California curriculum once it was agreed that all references to evolution would be qualified by the phrase "many scientists believe that . . . ."[7]

A popular California journalist, John Steinbacher, traveled to communities lecturing about "the massive bulldozer operation to convert America's school system into a series of behavioral science classes for reshaping and restructuring children away from the Christian-Judaic tradition."[8] Syndicated columnist James Kilpatrick took a similar line in numerous editorials.[9]

The character of letters published in local papers or sent to congressmen also suggested links between apparently isolated textbook protests. The same Xeroxed articles were cited again and again. An unsigned information sheet about MACOS was widely circulated in the spring of 1975. It presented a list of objectionable points in the course and instructed citizens to write to their congressmen expressing these objections in their own words. Within a period of several weeks, congressmen received many similar letters objecting to the biased presentation of evolution, to the disturbing discussions of Netsilik behavior, and to the "atheistic philosophy" labeled variously "cultural relativism," "situational ethics," or "secular humanism."

As the letters arrived, a further question emerged. What was the federal government doing supporting such a course?

MACOS: A National Debate

"Is the Federal government supporting the subversion of American school children?"

The objections to the content of MACOS converged with the question of federal funding of public-school curriculum to turn the textbook controversy into a national issue. Congressional interest in MACOS can be traced back to to 1971, when citizens groups in Phoenix, Arizona, complained about MACOS to their state senator John Conlan. Conlan, a Harvard Law School graduate and Fulbright scholar, was elected to the U.S. Congress in 1972 and remained interested in these concerns of his constituency. He hired as a staff aid George Archibald, a writer for the *Arizona Republic,* who had focused on educational issues and served on the Arizona Board of Education's commission to develop guidelines for social-studies texts. Archibald's goal is to "get schools out of the business of social engineering and indoctrination. . . . Schools exist for people, not for gurus."[10] He is convinced that the government should not support programs that have "any value orientation."

Congressional interest in MACOS was again apparent in 1973, when Republican representatives Marjorie Holt (Maryland) and John Ashford (Ohio) expressed their objections to "the usurpation by the educational system of what we used to consider parents' rights." Modern educators are competing with families, they claimed, and schools seek to "save children by bringing them into the arms of experts." They pointed to MACOS as one of several culprits.[11]

By late 1974, several Washington, D.C., organizations had begun questioning the federal government's role in developing and implementing MACOS. A Heritage Foundation report argued that MACOS taught a value system that was fundamentally deterministic, behavioristic, and relativistic. The course denied the existence of God and replaced traditional religious beliefs with concepts of Darwinian adaptation. School textbooks, claimed the report, must be either neutral or present alternative values in a more equitable manner. The report cites letters from psychologists and therapists attributing cases of anxiety among children to the value conflicts provoked by MACOS. The government is blamed for MACOS, for without federal support, claims the report, "MACOS would fall on its own lack of merit."[12]

The Council for Basic Education also criticized the NSF for supporting a course that presented "cultural relativism and environmental determination" as a scientific explanation of the place of man in society. The children taking MACOS are shortchanged by its deemphasis on skills and facts: "What is thrown out to make room for MACOS?"[13]

Leadership Action, Inc., mailed copies of selected "lurid" excerpts from MACOS to thousands of congressmen and state legislators. In April 1975, it presented a display of "100 dirty textbooks," in the Capitol, including mostly MACOS materials.[14] During the same month, a Washington, D.C., radio station placed an ad in the *Washington Post* for a brief NBC coverage of the dispute: "Tonight at 6:00: Horror Flicks—Is your 10-year-old watching X-rated films in school?"[15]

It was not, however, these moral objections to MACOS that influenced the largely urban and liberal Congress. Rather, the anti-MACOS campaign appealed to the desire of many congressmen to control "unaccountable executive bureaucracies" such as the NSF; their resentment of scientists, who often tended to disdain congressional politics; and, above all, the concern with secrecy and confidentiality that followed the Watergate affair. The focus on MACOS during the NSF appropriations hearings in the spring of 1975 was more a reflection of post-Watergate morality than of Eskimo morality.

Conlan himself initiated the action against appropriations for

MACOS on the grounds of its "abhorrent, repugnant, vulgar, morally sick content." It is "a godawful course" that was "almost always at variance with the beliefs and values of parents and local communities." It was "an assault on tradition," an attempt to "mold the children's social attitudes and beliefs and set them apart from the beliefs and moral values of their communities." It was, he claimed, the product of an "elite group of scholars" who want to "reform human nature from a behavioral program rather than along classic Judaeo-Christian lines."[16]

Conlan brought these accusations to the House Committee on Science and Technology, seeking an amendment to the NSF appropriations bill that would deny the use of federal funds for the implementation or marketing of course curriculum programs unless the House Committee on Science and Technology and the Senate Committee on Labor and Public Welfare first approved the materials. To counter any such restriction, H. Guyford Stever, NSF director, wrote to the Committee Chairman, Olin Teague, announcing his intention of terminating all funds for MACOS and of placing a moratorium on the NSF implementation program pending the results of an internal review. Despite this letter, Teague initially supported Conlan's proposed amendment. Representatives Symington and Mosher, however, raised questions about the appropriateness of congressional censorship of specific programs. This censorship issue created interesting alignments within the Committee on Science and Technology. Its Democratic chairman (Teague) supported a proposal by its most conservative Republican (Conlan). Both were opposed by the ranking Republican (Mosher), whose position against the amendment was supported by most of the Committee's Democrats. In addition, a number of conservative members who basically agreed with Conlan on the issue of morality were reluctant to engage in censorship. The amendment thus lost within the committee by a vote of 17 to 13.

Conlan changed his tactics when he brought the issue to the House floor on 9 April 1975. Avoiding the question of censorship, he focused on the federal role in implementing MACOS, on the accountability of federal agencies, and on the controversial nature of the social sciences. One must remember that this issue followed on the heels of Senator Proxmire's attack on NSF support of "crazy studies" in the social sciences; it followed the Watergate concern over public accountability and secrecy in federal bureaucracies; and it followed soon after dramatic and violent disruptions over textbook selection in Kanawha County, West Virginia. Thus a single elementary-school course became the focus of national debate.

Several specific aspects of NSF's role upset the Congress. First was the marketing issue—the concern that the NSF used taxpayers' money to interfere with private enterprise. In fact, most publishers stayed out of this dispute, having themselves benefited from NSF programs, but a few had written to their congressmen to complain about "unfair competition" from a federal agency. A letter to the Committee on Science and Technology from Follett Publishers, for example, accused the foundation of supporting a program that would fail to sell if it had to compete directly with the private sector. "Let the program die a natural death." Likewise, Lippincott wrote to Congressman Conlan, accusing the foundation of unfair competition with the private sector when it adjusted the normal royalty arrangements in order to meet the high cost of the professional dissemination program.

A second and related complaint among congressional critics was NSF's use of resources "to set up a network of educator-lobbyists to control education throughout America." The flamboyant arguments of syndicated columnist James Kilpatrick, who attacked NSF's curriculum program as "an ominous echo of the Soviet Union's promulgation of official scientific theory," impressed a number of congressmen.[17] Resentment of the "elitism" of science reinforced concern that the NSF was naively promulgating the liberal values of the scientific community to a reluctant public. The market, it was claimed, was an adequate indicator of local preferences, and the reluctance of experienced publishers to market MACOS suggested what local communities really wanted. For the NSF to override market indicators by providing federal funds to implement MACOS was simply to support experts "who are trying to promulgate their own values." This was "an insidious invasion of local autonomy in education."[18]

MACOS defenders justified NSF support, arguing that the curriculum had been well-tested and acclaimed as a major educational advance. The issue, they argued, involved academic freedom. Can educators' freedom of access to the fruits of scholarship and educational research be limited by the views of a small group of people concerned with "anti-American motives"?[19] For Congress to restrict the NSF would be political censorship; to deny schools access to an existing curriculum would be an even greater restriction on local school board autonomy. What right had Congress to interfere? "The Holy Bible would never pass muster under this kind of demagoguery . . . in the Holy Bible there is murder, adultery, and there is bestiality in Little Red Riding Hood."[20]

A third issue in the congressional discussion of MACOS, having little to do with the course itself, was the desire to extend political control over "faceless, nameless executive agencies." Conlan complained about the difficulties he had encountered obtaining material from the NSF. "Somewhere, sometime, we are going to have to stop and make a stand as to whether the bureaucracy runs us or whether we represent the people and are accountable to them. I say this is a good place to start."[21] The uproar over "crazy" social-science projects had reinforced the concern for accountability among congressmen, who often had to take the blame for decisions made by agencies they did not directly control. One congressman wrote to Stever about "those damn fool projects in the behavioral sciences," complaining that he was "sick and tired of responding to correspondence from citizens who are blaming Congress for some of the idiotic things done by a few unstable people in the executive branch."[22]

These issues converged in the congressional debates on NSF appropriations on 9 April 1975. After three hours of debate, the Conlan amendment was defeated on the House floor by a vote of 215 (182 Democrats, 33 Republicans) to 196 (89 Democrats, 107 Republicans). Funds for MACOS were terminated and further support of science curriculum projects suspended, pending review of the entire NSF educational program. The congressional mood was clear when, on the same day, the House passed the notorious Bauman amendment—a much broader measure that would have involved Congress directly in the NSF grant applications review process, giving it veto power over *all* proposed grant awards. Despite the impracticality of congressional review of some 15,000 often highly technical proposals each year, Congress approved this amendment by a vote of 212 to 199. It was killed by a Senate Conference Committee before reaching a vote in the Senate, but neither NSF nor its congressional critics failed to realize its importance as a sign of political attitudes toward the NSF and its potential threat to the autonomy of science.

The Tip of the Iceberg: MACOS, Accountability, and the NSF

By October 1975, the three committees that had been reviewing the NSF curriculum program had published their reports. NSF's internal review committee concluded that the foundation could not avoid controversy at the expense of educational and scientific values, but that tighter review and evaluation procedures were in order. Procedures must guarantee that programs are funded on the basis of broad solicitation for proposals and competitive review. The committee also recommended review mechanisms that would include participation by public representatives and implementation approaches that would involve local authorities and allow NSF "to remain at arm's length from the process."[23]

A committee appointed by Congressman Olin Teague and chaired by T. M. Moudy, chancellor of Texas Christian University, also reported in October. While reflecting Teague's links to the space program and Texas, it included a spectrum of opinion ranging from a fundamentalist Texas housewife to Gerard Piel, publisher of *Scientific American*. The committee held hearings and conducted a mail inquiry to local school districts in fourteen states, receiving a largely positive response. The letters from school superintendents and principals were enthusiastic, although some noted they had omitted sections of the course as "not in keeping with the mores of their community," while others observed that local pressures had caused the course to be dropped.

Some committee members criticized MACOS as "a venture in applied behavioral psychology without informed consent." They were distressed with the "presentation of evolution as a fact," with "cultural relativism," and with discussions that were "offensive to Judaeo-Christian values." One person wanted NSF out of the curriculum development business entirely; two others proposed that NSF restrict itself to funding only natural science and mathematics. The committee, however, with one formal dissent, recommended that the NSF continue to fund precollege science curriculum activities, advising only that it must avoid the appearance of "exercising such undue influence on local curriculum decisions." "Representative parents . . . innocent of professional or scholarly bias" should be appointed to curriculum review and evaluation groups so that they are involved in decisions that may affect widely observed customs or religious beliefs. The Moudy committee also warned the foundation to caution teachers about their handling of cultural differences; teachers must honor the diverse value systems of the homes from which their pupils come.[24]

The General Accounting Office (GAO) conducted a review of NSF in response to accusations of improper financing. It cleared the foundation, noting only a lack of clarity in its policies concerning royalties. It recommended strengthening NSF's review process, and then added a new wrinkle: children involved in new courses could be regarded as the objects of behavioral experiments, and yet the NSF had no procedures directed to their protection as human subjects.[25]

As the various committees examined MACOS, congressional critics extended their attacks to other NSF policies. In July, the House Science and Technology Committee held oversight hearings on the NSF peer review system. Conlan's frustration over the foundation's refusal to identify MACOS reviewers led to accusations that the NSF had misrepresented the peer review evaluations. Conlan also announced his objections to NSF's funding of "low priority behavioral research and curriculum projects." There was, he claimed at an interview with two members of the National Science Board, no excuse for funding so much social research instead of other work that would help industry create jobs.

Two weeks later, Conlan and Senator Jesse Helms (R.—North Carolina) simultaneously introduced bills to the House and Senate, asking for an amendment to the NSF Act that would require a peer review and grant management system that was "fair, open, and accountable to the scientific community and to Congress."[26] "MACOS is the tip of the iceberg . . . the beginning of what may be a wholesale reform of the massive NSF operation." NSF's policies, claimed Helms, are "contrary to the American democratic spirit, the principles of justice and fairness. . . . At a time when the Congress is embracing openness as an antidote to Watergate, NSF stands firm for confidentiality."[27] Conlan and Helms called for disclosure of proposal reviews. When Stever responded that he would send edited versions of reviews to Congress, they compared his offer with Nixon's providing Congress with edited White House transcripts.

NSF responded with an internal reorganization. Prior to July 1975, all scientific divisions were under the assistant director of research. In July, the biological and social sciences, the two most controversial areas, were placed under a separate directorate. This was done to provide additional senior management attention to these areas, but the move provoked an internal rumor that the foundation was preparing to lop off both controversial areas.

Reviewing its policies for approval of educational programs, NSF preferred to treat them like research proposals, evaluating them through the peer review system, and avoiding further monitoring on the assumption that collegial pressures are sufficient to assure the quality and neutrality of the scholarship. NSF hoped thereby to avoid imposing a federal "mark of approval"; it would simply provide a model curriculum developed by competent scholars, to be adopted as desired at the initiative of local users. Yet members of the National Science Board, as well as external critics, urged NSF itself to control the quality of its educational products. This posed a dilemma. With this responsibility, if the foundation failed to approve a curriculum for dissemination, it could be accused of censorship. If it did sanction a curriculum, this was indeed a mark of federal approval, and NSF could then be accused of imposing federal standards on the educational system.

Later, in the conservative context of the Reagan administration, such contradictions destroyed NSF's educational effort. When Congressman Conlan failed to get reelected, his aide, George Archibald, moved to the Heritage Foundation, where he continued to work on educational policy. Then, as a member of Reagan's transition team, he investigated federal funding of education concluding, not surprisingly, that federal programs were promoting "secular humanism." In 1981, Archibald became deputy assistant secretary for congressional affairs in the Department of Education, where he continues his mission to remove values of "secular humanism" from the schools.

Notes

1. This case study is a report of actual events in a specific school, but names are changed. The discussion is based on interviews with the school principal, teachers, and parents in the district, and on records that were kept of meetings. Unidentified quotations are from interviews.

2. There had been a Christmas-carol dispute in town the year before. The school board had ruled it was not compulsory to sing Christmas carols, and many parents had objected.

3. This was evident in correspondence to Education Development Center and Curriculum Development Associates, and in evaluations as well in national awards.

4. EDC, *Community in Conflict over Curriculum Change* (Cambridge, Mass.: EDC, 1972). This is a record of clippings and letters pertaining to the Phoenix dispute brought together by EDC.

5. Records are available from local newspapers wherever there were disputes (e.g., *Burlington Free Press,* throughout November 1973) and from minutes of meetings held with school-board officials.

6. The quotes that follow are from newspapers, records of disputes, interviews, and minutes of meetings.

7. The state approval in California came about in part because of the fragmentation of the forces that would have opposed the adoption of the series. Legislative changes in the textbook selection process required consideration of racism, sexism, and other issues in textbooks; the board had to contend with many new interest groups, and the concern with evolution had been diffused. In addition, MACOS was already used in fifty-six schools in the state, which had adopted the series through local decisions.

8. Interview with Steinbacher reported in the *Green Mountain Gazette,* 7 November 1973. Steinbacher's philosophy is laid out in *The Conspirators: Men against God* (California: Orange Tree Press, 1972).

9. These appear in local newspapers—for example, *Troy Times Record,* 3 April 1975; *Boston Globe,* 27 March 1975 and 2 April 1975.

10. George Archibald, personal interview.

11. Cited in *Review of the News,* 24 October 1973.

12. Susan Marshner, *Man: A Course of Study—Prototype for Federalized Textbooks?* (Washington, D.C.: The Heritage Foundation, July 1975).

13. Council for Basic Education, *Bulletin* 19 (May 1975): 9.

14. Leadership Action, *Special Textbook Report* (Washington, D.C.: Leadership Action Inc., n.d.).

15. *Washington Post,* 24 April 1975.

16. Congressman Conlan, during a House session authorizing appropriations to NSF, *Congressional Record,* 9 April 1975. H2588.

17. Editorial in *Boston Globe,* 2 April 1975.

18. Congressman Conlan, *Congressional Record,* 9 April 1975, H2588.

19. Peter Dow, "Open Letter from EDC," 4 April 1975 (mimeographed).

20. Congressman Ottinger, *Congressional Record,* 9 April 1975, H2591.

21. Congressman Conlan, *Congressional Record,* 9 April 1975, H2603–4.

22. Reported in *Science,* 4 July 1975, p. 26.

23. National Science Foundation, *Pre-College Science Curriculum Activities of the NSF: Report* (Washington, D.C.: NSF, May 1975).

24. J. M. Moudy, chairman of Science Curriculum Implementation Review Group, *Report to the Committee on Science and Technology.* U.S. House of Representatives, 1 October 1975.

25. General Accounting Office, *Administration of the Science Education Project "MACOS"* Report No. MWD-76-26, 1975.

26. Bills, House of Representatives H.R. 98921, 29 September 1975. Senate S 17003, 29 September 1975.

27. *Congressional Record* 121, no. 144, 29 September 1975.

9

Legislating Science in Arkansas

It took God only six days to create the universe—it's gonna
take the court two weeks to decide if it should be taught.
—An anonymous observer at the Arkansas
creation-evolution trial

On March 19, 1981, the governor of the state of Arkansas, Frank
White, signed into law a statute requiring "balanced treatment of
creation science and evolution science." Act 590 was the model for
legislation being introduced by creationists in at least twenty other
states. It represented the most coherent effort to date to remove the
religious content of creationism and to define it as a scientific
theory. The ACLU took on the case on behalf of twenty-three
plaintiffs, including twelve clergymen and several religious organizations. They challenged the constitutionality of the law in light of
the First Amendment requirement for the separation of church and
state. They won an unambiguous victory—a decision that clearly
defined the legislation as an effort to introduce a religious belief into
the public-school curriculum.

The Legislation

In passing Act 590, the Arkansas legislature reflected its long history of opposition to the teaching of evolution in this state. Arkansas had passed antievolution legislation in 1928, prohibiting the teaching of the subject in the public schools. The law was defended again and again as reflecting the "will of the people." In 1966, a Little Rock high school biology teacher, Susan Epperson, challenged the law, charging that a statute forbidding the teaching of evolution was unconstitutional, conflicting with federal guarantees of free speech. She received support from the Little Rock Ministerial Association, which unequivocally stated that "to use the Bible to support an irrational and an archaic concept of static and undeveloping creation is not only to misunderstand the meaning of the Book of Genesis, but to do God and religion a disservice by making both enemies of scientific advancement and academic freedom."[1] The Chancery Court of Pulaski County decided the case in her favor, finding no compelling reason to prohibit a teacher from presenting the theory "even though the theory may be objectionable to many of our citizens." However, the State Supreme Court upheld the constitutionality of the law forbidding the teaching of evolution. It was not until 1968, when the Supreme Court in *Epperson* v. *Arkansas* declared the law unconstitutional, that Arkansas remove it from the books. Repeal, however, did not necessarily affect the values of many Arkansas citizens, who kept the issue alive.

Act 590, known as the "Balanced Treatment of Creation Science and Evolution Science Act," required that a "two model" approach to the study of origins must be reflected in textbooks, library materials, and lectures. The act specifically prohibited religious instruction, limiting the treatment of both theories to scientific evidence. Its stated purpose was to "protect academic freedom by providing student choice; to ensure freedom of religious exercise, to guarantee freedom of belief and speech; to prevent establishment of religion; to prohibit religious instruction concerning origins; to bar discrimination on the basis of creationist's or evolutionist's belief; to provide definitions and clarifications."

Paul Ellwanger, the president of a group of textbook watchers called Citizens for Fairness in Education, had created the act, adapting a resolution proposed by Wendell Bird, the constitutional lawyer from the Institute for Creation Research. Ellwanger himself was convinced that neither creation nor evolution are scientific, and his purpose, frankly stated in correspondence that was later uncovered during the trial challenging the law, was to "kill evolution instead of playing these debating games that we've been playing for over a decade already."[2] Nevertheless, he used Bird's resolution essentially word for word, although it specifically prohibited religious instruction and claimed to teach creation as a "science."

Ellwanger brought the proposed bill to the Reverend W. A. Blount, chairman of the Greater Little Rock Evangelical Fellowship. This organization adopted a resolution to introduce it into the state legislature. They approached state Senator James L. Holsted, who, without consulting the Department of Education, science educators, or the State Attorney General, agreed to sponsor the bill. Holsted, a "born again" fundamentalist, later explained in court that he could not separate the proposal from his religious beliefs. Nor could many other state senators, who debated the statute for only five minutes and held no hearing. Similarly, the House passed the bill after only a fifteen-minute hearing in which no scientists were called upon to testify. Then, Governor Frank White, also "born again," signed the statute, but as he admitted later, had not even read it. Thirteen years after the Supreme Court had ruled the ban on the teaching of evolution unconstitutional, Arkansas required its public schools to teach the literal interpretation of Genesis as a scientific theory. The issue went once again to the courts.

The Trial

The Arkansas trial, lasting from December 7 through 17, was the first judicial test of an act that was specifically designed to meet the constraints of the First Amendment. Thus, it was closely watched. About fifty journalists from the major networks, newspapers, and magazines were at the federal district court in Little Rock. So, too, was the Reverend Roy McLaughlin, leader of the Arkansas branch of the Moral Majority and, on the pulpit, an ardent and eloquent proponent of the inerrancy of the Bible. Duane Gish from the Institute for Creation Research was there. A group of fundamentalists came in by bus from a church 100 miles away, and a number of teachers showed up with their students. Despite the potential for theatrics, the mood was serious—only occasionally punctuated by incidents such as a man in a gorilla suit, a reference (seriously intended) to "astrophysicism," and a woman praying in tongues.[3]

The ACLU, assisted by three law firms and about twenty lawyers and paralegal aides,[4] challenged the legislation on three grounds: that it violated the First Amendment because it is religious and not scientific in purpose and advances the religious beliefs of fundamentalists; that it would abridge academic freedom of students and teachers by forcing the teaching of a doctrine that has no scientific merit; and that it was unconstitutionally vague, allowing unfettered discretion over its enforcement.

The ACLU first presented expert witnesses from their "religious team," including a bishop of the United Methodist Church of Arkansas, a Roman Catholic priest, a historian of fundamentalism, a theologian, a sociologist, and a philosopher of science.[5] These witnesses argued that, historically, philosophically, and sociologically, creationism is a religious movement of fundamentalists who base their beliefs on the inerrancy of the Bible and that creation science is no more than religious apologetics. To distinguish scientific from Biblical creationism was meaningless and, indeed, deceptive. Without God, creation science is but a "motley assortment of facts and assertions"; with God, it is religion, subject to neither testing nor disproof. They attacked the methodology of the creation scientists: their arguments were simply based on *a priori* belief in the inerrancy of Genesis. They attacked the language of the law; the use of the word "kinds" comes directly from the book of Genesis and has no meaning in science. And they described the activities of the creationists, documenting their religious motivations. In short, the witnesses testified that the questions, the methods, and the assumptions of the scientific creationists as incorporated in Act 590 were religious in nature and that the label of science was simply a means to gain legitimacy.[6] "Even if some of its minor premises look, smell, taste, feel and sound scientific, its major premise—God—is not subject to testing or to disproof and, accordingly, is not scientific."

The ACLU then presented its "scientific team"; a geneticist, a paleontologist, a geologist, and a biophysicist. They documented the absence of scientific evidence for the creationist beliefs, dismissing their specific claims concerning the age of the earth ("off by about 4.5 billion years" and "based on misused and disproved techniques"), the use of the second law of thermodynamics (completely "misinterpreted"), and the denial of fossil evidence for evolution (based on "bald assertions"). They then offered evidence for evolution, observing that the theory provided the intellectual framework necessary for the coherent understanding of nature.

Finally several teachers and school administrators presented their concerns about actually implementing the act in the classroom. They had tried to find usable material to develop a creation-science curriculum guide in compliance with the law, but their efforts were frustrating and unsuccessful. Permeated with religion, the creation-science literature was unacceptable. A literature search failed to unearth scientific articles that would comply with the act. To comply would require the teaching of religion in the science classroom.

State Attorney General Steve Clark organized the defense, partially supported by a Creation Science Legal Defense Fund. His three attorneys emphasized that a two-model approach to biology education did not violate the First Amendment, nor did it restrain freedom of choice—on the contrary, it allowed students to gain a broader perspective. The defense admitted that the creationist theory of origins "may partially coincide with the tenets of some religion," but that this in itself was not the establishment of religion. Creationism is, they claimed, a scientific model that can, and indeed must, under the act, be taught in a nonreligious manner, that diversity in the teaching of scientific theories is a necessary part of academic freedom, and that limiting instruction to one model was in itself a constitutional violation.

The defense's argument hinged on distinguishing between the notion of a creator and a deity. This was expressed in a remarkable (and surely heretical) statement in the defendants' legal brief:

Assuming *arguendo* that a "creator" and "creation" are consistent with some religions, this does not make these inherently religious. The entity which cause the creation hypothesized in creation-science is far, far away from any conception of a god or deity. All that creation-science requires is that the entity which caused creation have power, intelligence, and a sense of design. There are no attributes of the personality generally associated with a deity, nor is there necessarily present in the creator any love, compassion, sense of justice, or concern for any individuals. Indeed, under creation-science as defined in Act 590, there is no requirement that the entity which caused creation still be in existence. Assuming for purposes of argument that teaching creation-science may to some degree advance religion, any such advancement would be purely incidental.[7]

The defense witnesses, a mix of scientific rebels and true believers, mostly from Bible colleges, included seven scientists who presented negative arguments and scientific anomalies intended to discredit evolutionary biology by showing what it could not explain. It also included theologians who supported the argument that God was not necessarily a religious concept and that the concept of a designer could be dealt with simply as philosophy.[8]

Their testimony quickly revealed the difficulties in trying to distinguish science from religion in order to meet constitutional imperatives. While witnesses had to emphasize the scientific nature of creationism, their fundamentalist beliefs prevailed. Balancing their beliefs against the pragmatic realities of the law, inconsistencies were inevitable. Under cross-examination, several witnesses weakened their case by acknowledging that their guidance and indeed their evidence for creation came mainly from Genesis. Norman Geisler, a professor of theology from Dallas Theological Seminary and a key witness brought in to show the "enlightened and scientific attitude of today's creationists," created a stir when he expressed his belief in demonic possession, exorcism, occultism, and UFOs as "a satanic manifestation in the world for the purpose of deception." Chandra W. Wickramasinghe, a well-known astrophysicist from Wales and the state's most credible witness in terms of scientific reputation, presented his theory that interstellar space was sprinkled with genes which, carried by comets, seeded life on earth and provided new sources of genetic material to advance genetic complexity. He, too, created a stir by declaring that insects may be more intelligent than humans, but "they're not letting on." Wickramasinghe is critical of conventional evolutionary hypotheses and believes in a creator, but by no means does he support creationist beliefs. Under cross-examination he admitted that no rational scientist could believe that the earth was less than a million years old, and that belief in a separate ancestry for man and apes was "clap trap."

Most of the scientific witnesses for the defense (five were members of the Creation Research Society) wavered in their defense of creationism as a science, preferring to argue that neither creation nor evolution is a scientific theory and that the vaguer term "model" is more appropriate for both. They offered no positive evidence, provoking the judge at one point to complain to a witness: "I've been sitting here since ten thirty listening to you give me one opinion after another, but I haven't heard you give a solid basis for a single one of them." They mainly accused evolutionary biologists of "censorship," of "country club exclusion," of keeping those theories which were incompatible with their personal or philosophical views "out of the marketplace of ideas."

Several of the state's witnesses failed to appear, discouraged from participation by Wendell Bird of the Institute for Creation Research. Bird was piqued at not being allowed to organize the case, especially since Act 590 had so closely followed his model resolution. Anticipating the decision, he called eleven witnesses to advise them that the state was ill prepared to defend the law.[9]

Judge William R. Overton's decision in favor of the plaintiffs was sharply worded and unambiguous.[10] He based his decision primarily on Judge Hugo Black's famous test of the establishment-of-religion clause of the First Amendment. "Neither a state nor the federal government can pass laws which aid one religion, aid all religions, or prefer one religion over another."[11] Overton especially emphasized the critical importance of keeping public schools free of religious conflict. Then, dissecting the statute, he found "inescapable religiosity," a "hodgepodge of limited assertions many of which are incorrect," "continued dualism which has no scientific factual basis or legitimate educational purpose," "meaningless assertions," and "fallacious pedagogy." He argued that creation science fails to conform to the essential and accepted characteristics of science. "It is not explanatory by reference to natural laws, is not testable, and is not falsifiable . . . they take the literal wording of the book of Genesis and attempt to find scientific support for it." To comply, schools would have to "forgo significant portions of subjects such as biology, world history, geology, zoology, botany, psychology, anthropology, sociology, philosophy, physics and chemistry." Concluding that the act was "simply and purely an effort to introduce the Biblical version of creationism into the public school curriculum," Overton issued a permanent injunction on the law. (See Appendix 1.)

Unlike the California ruling on the guidelines, the Arkansas decision left no possibility of doubt as to who had won. Yet the creationists remain undeterred. Wendell Bird, who will organize the defense of the Louisiana legislation against an ACLU suit, had dissociated himself from the case well before the decision. Others had also laid the groundwork for dismissing the case as biased and therefore meaningless as a test of the constitutionality of creationist legislation. During the trial, television preacher Pat Robertson and Moral Majority leader Jerry Falwell accused the attorney general of collusion with the ACLU. The Creation Science Legal Defense Fund attacked the attorney general for inadquate preparation. Reverand Blount, leader of the Evangelical Fellowship, said he knew from the first day that Clark would lose. Roy McLaughlin questioned the neutrality of the judge and called the decision a form of censorship. Duane Gish of the ICR called the decision a blow to academic and religious freedom. "If anything the creation-scientists' efforts will be intensified." The senator who had introduced the Louisiana bill said that the Arkansas defense was "outgunned and outmaneuvered." He expected that his defense would win.

The decision did not deter the Mississippi state Senate from passing a creationist bill with a vote of 48 to 4. The author of Georgia's creationist bills is continuing his effort. The National Foundation of Fairness in Education and the National Bible Knowledge Association are continuing their case against the federally supported Smithsonian museums for basing their exhibitions on evolutionary assumptions without adequate attention to the alternative of scientific creation.[12]

Jim Holsted, who had introduced the bill, had announced even before the decision that "if we lose it won't matter that much. If the law is unconstitutional it'll be because of something in the language that's wrong. So we'll just change the wording and try again with another bill. . . . We got a lot of time. Eventually we'll get one that's constitutional."[13] Indeed, before the trial was over, Ellwanger was redrafting the act in light of the ACLU challenge. He changed its name from "Balanced Treatment" to "The Unbiased Presentation of Creation-Science and Evolution-Science Bills," believing that it would be difficult to argue against the removal of bias. He modified any statements or references that could be construed as religious or supernatural. He inserted technical language (e.g., referring to the "Chronometric processes" that indicate the age of the earth), specified what was meant by "unbiased presentation" to avoid charges of vagueness, and emphasized the need for a fair, balanced, and unbiased approach. This new draft is circulating in legislatures throughout the country.

Despite their failure in Arkansas, the creationists are encouraged by evidence of public support. In an astonishing editorial on Judge Overton's decision, the prestigious *Wall Street Journal* warned against using the decision to dismiss the "political discontent" that gave birth to the law. While admitting that the Arkansas act was constitutionally questionable, the editorial had little sympathy for those who "run to the courts" every time a teacher uses the word *God* or *church:*

> If caught between the relativists and the fundamentalists, we ourselves might often be tempted to side with the fundamentalists, at least those who are concerned, as we are, about a decline in the moral order. . . . We are not sure the courts have considered what it may be like if they insist on divorcing government entirely from spiritual thought. . . . We hope that the forces who have won this narrow battle in court won't labor too long with the notion that they have scored some major victory against religious belief.[14]

This editorial assessment of public opinion is supported by a 1981 national public-opinion survey conducted by NBC news: 76

percent of the American people feel that public schools should teach both the scientific theory of evolution and the Biblical theory of creation, 8 percent favor teaching only the scientific theory, and 10 percent only the Biblical theory.

With such support, creationists can turn defeat to their advantage, using it to support their image as a beleaguered group, rejected by a scientific establishment bent on protecting itself against "new" ideas. This image and the publicity of judicial actions serves them well as they continue to mobilize public support to bring creationism to the schools.

Notes

1. Quoted in *Christian Century* 83 (January 1966).

2. Correspondence cited in Judge William Overton, U.S. District Court, Eastern Division of Arkansas Western Division, "Memorandum Opinion on Rev. Bill Mclean et al. vs. the Arkansas Board of Education et al.," 3 January 1982, p. 12.

3. The observations in this section were made by the author, who attended the trial as an expert witness.

4. Working with the ACLU were lawyers from one of the largest New York law firms, Skadden, Arps, Slate, Meagher and Flom; and from Arkansas firms Cearley, Gitchel, Mitchell and Roachell, and Kaplan, Hollingsworth, Brewer and Bilheimer. All legal assistance was on a *pro bona* basis. The cost was estimated at about $2 million.

5. Witnesses for plaintiffs were Kenneth Hicks, a bishop of the United Methodist Church of Arkansas; Bruce Vawter, a Roman Catholic Old Testament scholar; George Marsden, a historian of fundamentalism; Dorothy Nelkin, a sociologist of science; Langdon Gilkey, a professor of theology; Michael Ruse, a philosopher of science; Francisco Ayala, a geneticist; Stephen Jay Gould, a paleontologist; Brent Dalrymple, a geologist; Harold Morowitz, a biophysicist; Bill Wood, high-school administrator; Ron Coward, a biology instructor; Marianne Wilson, county supervisor of science curriculum; Dennis Glasgow, science supervisor; William Mayer, BSCS director.

6. The use of the labels of science as a means to advance religious beliefs had recently been tested in the courts when transcendental meditation

groups tried to teach the Science of Creative Intelligence in New Jersey public schools. The court in *Malnak* v. *Yogi,* 440 Supp. 1284 (D.N.J. 1977) ruled it unconstitutional.

7. Quoted from the defendants' pretrial brief at *Rev. Bill Mclean* v. *Arkansas Board of Education,* 7 December 1981, p. 15.

8. Witnesses for the defense were Norman Geisler, theologian; Chandra Wickramasinghe, an astrophysicist from Wales; Robert Gentry, physicist; Wayne Friar, zoologist; the Reverend W. A. Blount, minister; Larry Parker, education specialist; Harold Coffin, geologist; Ariel Roth, biologist; W. Scott Morrow, biologist; Margaret Helder, botanist; Donald Chittick, physical chemist; Jim Don Townley, high-school teacher.

9. *New York Times,* 24 December 1972. Clark, who was running for reelection, wanted to run the case himself and to dissociate it from the Institute for Creation Research. His handling of the case, however, gained him criticism from both creation-science groups and national New Right leaders such as Jerry Falwell.

10. Overton, *op. cit.* The following discussion is from this memorandum.

11. *Everson* v. *Board of Education,* 330 U.S. 1, 15–16 (1947).

12. The targets of the complaint include the Museum of Natural History for its exhibition of evolution and the National Air and Space Museum for alluding to the evolution of the moon and the planets and the age of the universe. The Institute for Creation Research has its own museum exhibiting footprints "proving" that man and dinosaurs lived at the same time, and fossils "proving" the occurrence of a worldwide flood.

13. Interview with Philip J. Hilts, quoted in *Washington Post,* 7 December 1981. Two weeks after the trial Holsted was charged with a felony theft. He pleaded guilty, and the charge was dropped in exchange for his resignation from the Senate.

14. Editorial, *Wall Street Journal,* 8 January 1982.

IV

SCIENCE AND THE RESISTANCE IDEOLOGY

Today's American ideologue is a middle-class man who objects to his dependence on science even when he accepts its norms. He is resentful of the superiority of the educated and antagonistic to knowledge. His ideology is characteristically not of the left but of the right. It . . . looks back to a more bucolic age of individuality and localism, in which parochial qualities of mind were precisely those most esteemed—to a simple democracy, in fact . . . it is the resistance ideology of all those who hitherto were the "staid" figures of our society in an earlier day; the models of once sober, industrious, and responsible citizens.

—David Apter, *Ideology and Discontent*

10

Censorship
by Surrender

Although less than successful in their legislative quest, creation scientists have gained considerable ground through community pressure and national publicity. The media, attracted by the ironies of the disputes, provide extraordinary coverage of creationist actions. Most textbook publishers, seeking the widest possible market for their product, watch the creationists with care. Many teachers, hoping to avoid conflict, try to avoid the issue. And most scientists, buried in the details of their research, give little thought to the implications of resistance to scientific ideas.

Manipulated Media

The creation-evolution controversy is a "newspeg," a lively, weird, and often funny affair. Journalists can easily write an interesting and readable story about creationist events. In an often turgid political environment, creationism offers occasions for humor and irony. A reporter from the *Dallas Times Herald* described the 1975 school-board debate:

"The School Board proposes to offer most of us a choice of believing that life forms crawled from the seas, sprouted limbs and dwelled in the trees until they became men . . . or believing that man walked from the heavenly Garden of Eden full of wisdom and knowledge, to degenerate into school board trustees."[1]

The issue is a natural one for cartoonists, who draw lizardlike primordial forms or "expert" apes in court. Headlines are catchy: "Bryan's Ghost Rides Again," "Monkey Trials," "Darwin on the Rocks," "And God Created Ape," "The Creationists' Second Coming," "Monkeying with Evolution."

The creationists make it easy for the press. They are always willing and eager to talk to journalists. They write books with provocative titles: *Evolution: The Fossils Say No, The Handy Dandy Evolution Refuter.* They produce television documentary films directed to a wide audience: "In Search of Noah's Flood." Their museum is called Bones of Contention.

They also organize their activities to attract maximum media attention. The Segraves publicized their 1980 lawsuit against the California Board of Education as "the trial of the century," a "rerun of the Scopes trial." When creationists challenge scientists to public debates, they assure maximum publicity. The 1981 television debate between Russell Doolittle, a professor of biochemistry at the University of California, San Diego, and Duane Gish of the Institute for Creation Research demonstrated their media skill. Gish was experienced and prepared. He understood the timing and the cadence of a television event.

Like many other protest movements, creationists have learned to use the media to mobilize groups that are basically receptive to their goals. Their own literature turns critical coverage into support. A *Wall Street Journal* article was "unusually insightful and fair." A *Scientific American* writeup showed its "increasingly sympathetic view." *Science,* "though admittedly on the side of evolution," is "increasingly objective." Creationists claim that the press is beginning to treat them "respectfully and seriously," that even when reports are clearly negative, national media coverage indicates the significant impact that the case for creation science is making in the nation's schools.[2]

Publishers and Profits

The textbook industry is highly competitive. The top ten publishers dominate 50 percent of the sales in the United States, and conglomerates such as CBS and the Bell-Howard Empire are increasingly in control. There are also hundreds of smaller publishers competing for state textbook approval. These include the creationist press. Gross sales in the textbook industry are over $1 billion annually. Large publishers rely on market surveys and records of past sales to estimate demands; they normally write for a national readership, and few are likely to take major risks on ideological grounds.

The "adoption states," those with state textbook commissions that determine the books to be used in the public schools, are vital to publishers, who covet the guaranteed sales. The stakes in winning a place on a state-approved list are high. Texas alone has an annual textbook budget of $45 million, $3 million of which is for biology textbooks alone. When the BSCS refused to concede to creationist demands, their books disappeared from the Texas list.

Dominated by the economics of potential markets in the large and conservative sunbelt states, publishers have been ready to accommodate creationist pressures by adding qualifications to statements about evolution theory or by simply avoiding sensitive issues. Some avoid the word "evolution" altogether by substituting "change." Some delete references to fossil formations, geological eras, the age of the earth, and Cro-Magnon man. Some include material on divine creation. Most banish the discussion of evolution to a single chapter than can be avoided or simply plucked out.

The new editions of several major textbooks have significantly reduced the discussion of the origin of life and the treatment of Darwin's view of nature. One book introduces a study of geology with the statement that "present ideas about the Earth's history include many speculations about the meaning of the relatively few facts that have been discovered." And another timidly states that "Darwin asked some interesting questions and set forth a thought-provoking hypothesis about which people are seeking new clues in the light of modern science."[3] A psychology textbook has removed all discussion of evolution theory in its section on the development of the brain. A new American-history book mentions neither Darrow nor the Scopes trial.

Textbook publishers are accustomed to social and political pressure and have made it their business to adapt. In the 1960s, they discovered ethnic pluralism and minority groups. In the 1970s, they discovered women. In the 1980s, they face challenges from the New Right. As one publisher of a forthcoming biology textbook put it:

> We are very, very aware of the concern of scientific creationism, which is what the moral majority wants. We reviewed the coverage of evolution and reproduction. We looked at the competitive data. We can't publish a book in 1983 that doesn't recognize another point of view.[4]

And another admits:

> Creation has no place in biology books, but after all we are in the business of selling textbooks.[5]

The NSF science curriculum reform movement had originally developed to counteract such problems: that is, to prepare materials in keeping with modern scientific knowledge when the textbook industry was unwilling to take financial risks. However, partly in response to textbook critics, the NSF Science Education Division has been destroyed, its staff reduced from 105 in 1980 to 60 in 1981. In 1982 it lost its remaining budget (except for a graduate fellowship program). Ironically, the educational programs initially developed to promote scientific and technical competence have been eliminated just at a time when our national competence in the face of economic competition is once again in question.

Conflict Avoidance in the Schools

Just as important as the changes in textbooks is the vulnerability of teachers to the creationists' demands. Many teachers are convinced that the plea for "fairness" in the presentation of scientific alternatives is reasonable. In November 1972, the National Science Teachers Association polled 1,200 teachers participating in its western area convention. Only 147 teachers responded (30 percent from biology, 21 percent from chemistry, 26 percent from general science, and 18 percent from physics), but the response suggests a perception of science that requires "fairness" in the presentation of scientific material. Fifty-seven percent agreed that alternative theories should be taught in public schools, and 39 percent agreed that it was acceptable to present creation theory in science classes. Fifty-three percent disagreed with the statement that evolution theory and creation theory are mutually exclusive and that, therefore, only evolution theory should be included in science curriculum.

While some teachers are willing to teach creationism on grounds of "fairness," many others simply hope to avoid conflict in the classroom. One survey of a cross section of grade-school teachers found that 92 percent of the 2,000 respondents would not initiate a discussion of controversial issues in the classroom; 89 percent would not participate in discussing controversial issues, and 79 percent believed they should not be discussed in the classroom at all.[6]

Teachers are often intimidated by the pressures from the creationists and their New Right supporters, who are bent on removing "secular humanism" from the classrooms. Fearing the growing willingness of parents and local citizen groups to challenge their authority, they have chosen to avoid the subject of evolution in their classroom rather than risk confrontation.

For example, in a high school in Appleton, Wisconsin, topics such as evolution are simply avoided. In this conservative, middle-class community, the home of many fundamentalists, the local people still decorate the grave of Joseph McCarthy annually in a formal public ceremony. One of the high-school science teachers and at least one of the school board members are creationists. Teaching the contemporary scientific perspective is hardly a high priority. A biology teacher who wanted to present the theory of evolution to his class had to present Genesis as well, allowing students to choose what made most sense to them.

Arkansas teachers expressed a sense of panic about the pressure to teach creation theory. Some want to resist but fear they will be fired. They also expect the state to seek teachers from Bible colleges

—teachers unprepared to deal with science at all. In some cases, teachers have begun to organize, forming coalitions with parents and clergymen to resist the creationist demands. Among these groups is the Georgia Ontological Association for the Protection of Evolution (the acronym is GO APE). These efforts have been effective but they are isolated and uncoordinated, resting on the initiative and organizing ability of local activists.

The Scientists' Response

Evolutionists were incredulous that creationists could have any influence. "It just does not make sense in this day and age." Incredulity led to amused disdain. The British journal *Nature* confidently offered free subscriptions to the first ten biologists who could claim that their present observations are inconsistent with the commonly accepted views of evolution.[7] A Stanford biochemist placed the creationists' argument "in the same arena as those advanced by the Flat Earth Society."[8] Facetious remarks were abundant. It was proposed that Bible publishers insert a sentence in Genesis to indicate that "scientific method rejects the supernatural approach to explaining the universe."[9] A biologist and member of the state advisory committee inquired whether a scientific course on reproduction should mention the stork theory.[10]

John A. Moore, a biologist (who, to his dismay, is often mistaken for creationist John N. Moore), satirized creation theory by examining it critically as a serious scientific hypothesis. In a masterful exercise in Biblical exegesis that reminds one of Darrow's cross-examination of Bryan, he pointed out problems of accuracy revealed by scholarly disagreement about different versions of the Scripture. He noted internal contradictions in the account of creation in Genesis and practical impossibilities involved in literal interpretation of the Bible. How can one explain in rigorous scientific terms the practical difficulties involved in the Noachian myth: the migration of animals, the necessary size of the Ark, the coexistence of species?[11]

The creationists' public claims of scientific verity were especially embarrassing to biologists. Until recently, scientists have rarely aired their disputes in public. Mindful of their public image and eager to avoid political interference, they usually try to avoid public exposés of arguments among themselves. Control is maintained through informal internal communications and through a peer review system that determines research funding and the acceptance of papers by journals. Creationists claim publicly to be scientists, and they adopt the language and the forms of science. Yet by seeking external political approval of the validity and justice of their arguments, they ignore the constraints imposed by the norms of the scientific community.

As creationists persisted in their efforts to influence textbook selection, the biologists' amusement and disdain gave way to defensiveness. They became concerned about external control over the definition of science as it would be taught in the schools. "The State Board's repudiation of its own committee in favor of a lay opinion from the audience should ultimately become a classic example in textbooks on school administration of how *not* to proceed with the development of standards," claimed an evolutionist.[12] "Why are comments related to science made by high-priced technicians such as medical doctors and by persons in related fields of technology more readily acceptable as statements of science than those made by scientists themselves?" complained another.[13] This response to external pressure differed little from the response in the 1930s, when scientists feared that "What is taught as science would be determined by . . . shopgirls and farm hands, ignorant alike of science." (See Chapter 2.) Scientists also worried that if creation theory was placed on an equal footing with Darwinism, it would further confuse school children's understanding of what science was about. Thus, scientists countered creationists' demands with legal and political strategies, and they attempted to discredit the movement by refusing to acknowledge the creationists' claim to scientific status.

The National Association of Biology Teachers (NABT) organized the political and legal opposition. NABT is a national organization devoted to the improvement of biology teaching. It has about 8,000 members, mostly high-school and junior-college teachers, and it distributes its journal, *The American Biology Teacher*,

to about 13,000 subscribers. Increasingly dismayed by the California events, in March 1972 NABT organized a committee to plan
legal action and retained legal counsel in California, hoping to
prevent the Board of Education from implementing the *Science
Framework.* During the following spring and summer, NABT
tried to arouse the interest of the scientific community. It set up
a Fund for Freedom in Science Teaching, receiving contributions
of about $12,000 to support its legal and organizational activities,
and it organized a response from professional societies.

NABT soon discovered that its own membership included creationists. Letters poured into the Washington, D.C., office. "I do not
support your editorial position and the vicious scientific attacks on
the creationists." "I feel the fund is being misused to try to force
everyone into one mold. It is worse to block false approaches than
to tolerate them." One writer suggested that the fund would be
used to "promote atheism and agnosticism in the schools." "It
should be called a HUSH fund ('Help Us to Silence Him')." "It is
a campaign to close the mouths of those who espouse theories other
than those of evolution."

NABT also found itself caught in the middle of a debate over
editorial policy. Should its journal consider publishing creationist
articles? Should it print letters from creationists? For several years,
the journal had included occasional creationist articles qualified to
indicate that they did not reflect the NABT view. The editor felt
that their bias and lack of logic would be obvious and self-defeat-
ing. In 1972, this editorial policy received a deluge of criticism
from scientists, who complained about the journal's lack of discretion. "Creationists' goals are obviously to discredit science and
scientists." The journal should not present such "trash." By November 1972, as the California situation reached its climax, the
journal stopped publishing creationist articles, although it continued to include a few letters.

A similar discussion took place when NABT organized its 1972
convention. Should creationists be allowed to hold a formal session
at this meeting? Some scientists felt that it was necessary and
appropriate to include creationists. Biologist Claude Welch was
dismayed at the "persecution" of creationists, whom he felt would
only make fools of themselves. "Creationists will prosper and mul-

tiply on martyrdom, but will perish on exposure. Are we so insecure? Will we let our exasperation with the creationists' irrationality provoke us to become irrational ourselves?"[14] Welch felt the controversy excelled as "soil for nurturing the education process," an opportunity to clarify evolution to an uninformed public. From a different perspective, an NABT regional director felt that creationism should be discussed as an important social issue that bears on science teaching.[15] Other scientists, however, strongly opposed a creationist panel; to allow creationists a voice at the association's meeting would imply some acceptance of their legitimacy. William Mayer of the BSCS, the science curriculum most vulnerable to creationist attacks, argued that creationists were using the NABT meeting as a stage on which to present their religious ideas. He condemned them as "religious missionaries, concerned primarily with converting classrooms by . . . smuggling religious dogma into classrooms in a Trojan horse."[16] Mayer criticized NABT as "schizoid," fighting the inclusion of creationists' material through legal means while at the same time providing them a forum at meetings.

Creationists eventually held their panel, and 1,500 biology teachers attended. Later, BSCS itself would be criticized as having "sold out" to creationists, after it developed a sound-slide program called, "An Inquiry into the Origin of Man: Science and Religion." Intended to "end the debate that has engaged the Western world for well over a century," the slides present cosmological sciences from Hindu, Hebrew, Greek, and Roman myths. It then describes evolution theory, emphasizing the conflict with religion. Biologists quickly accused BSCS of trying to profit from the conflict; the film, they felt, would only prove to creationists that biologists were concerned with religious ideas after all.

As events in California revealed the increasing influence of creationists, the prestigious National Academy of Sciences was moved for the first time to interfere in an issue involving a state decision. In October 1972, the academy issued a strongly worded but vague resolution.

Whereas the essential procedural foundations of science exclude appeal to supernatural causes as a concept not susceptible to validation by objective criteria; and

Whereas religion and science are, therefore, separate and mutually exclusive realms of human thought whose presentation in the same context leads to misunderstanding of both scientific theory and religious belief; and

Whereas, further, the proposed action would almost certainly impair the proper segregation of the teaching and understanding of science and religion nationwide, therefore

We . . . urge that textbooks of the sciences, utilized in the public schools of the nation, be limited to the exposition of scientific matter.[17]

The American Association for the Advancement of Science also "vigorously opposed" the inclusion of creation theory in science textbooks.

Scientists have built up the body of knowledge known as the biological theory of origin and evolution of life. There is no currently accepted alternative to scientific theory to explain the phenomena. The various accounts of creation that are part of the religion and heritage of many people are not scientific statements or theories. They have no place in the domain of science and should not be regarded as reasonable alternatives to scientific explanation for the origin and evolution of life.[18]

The American Anthropological Association was less vigorous, for some members argued that it would be absurd to offer any response to the creationists' demands. The Association eventually urged legislative and administrative bodies "to reject all efforts for the compulsory introduction . . . of statements reflecting religious and philosophical beliefs subject to different orders of verification into biology textbooks."[19]

The Academic Senate of the University of California condemned the creationists' statement in the *Science Framework* as a "gross misunderstanding" of the nature of scientific inquiry. Finally, nineteen California Nobel Laureate scientists petitioned the state board to leave the teaching of evolution, the only theory based on scientific evidence, intact.[20]

After November 1972, biologists were increasingly reluctant to acknowledge the creationist movement. The 1973 NABT convention did not mention the controversy. Biologists, with some exceptions, refused to debate creationists in hopes of avoiding any activity that would suggest the scientific legitimacy of the movement.

Many tried to discredit the movement by questioning the credentials and competence of those who claimed to be scientists. They were, claimed the biologists, only "engineers." "They are educated at Bible colleges." "Who are these people?" "They are false authorities." "Dullards." "Rejects from the space age." "Is it legal to misuse professional titles?" "Creationists get their doctorates in a box of crackerjacks." "It is a publishers' racket." "As phony as a $3 bill." "A way to subsidize religion." Biologists attacked textbook publishers for responding to such pressure groups. "We should have a fund for protection of prostitution of publishers."

Despite the formal response from scientific societies and a general dismay at the revival of creationism, most scientists were extremely reluctant to become involved. Some were sensitive to political accusations from school boards and preferred to stay insulated from the controversy in order to avoid interference in their own work. Others had never been interested in political issues and were simply uncomfortable with any public activity such as talking to reporters, writing letters to editors, or appearing at hearings. Some were disturbed at the idea of opposing a minority group. One biologist, for example, called the NABT fund "the fund for suppression of incorrect theories." Although far from believing in creation theory, this scientist had no desire to outlaw a controversial point of view from the public-school system. "Darwin by this time is quite immune to overthrow from fundamentalist attacks, and it isn't going to harm a single child to be made aware that there are divergent opinions available on the subject." He supported an open comparison of creationist and Darwinian arguments. "I am not in favor of the suppression of dissenting opinions."[21]

By 1981, the creationists' legislative efforts, backed by the New Right and considerable public support, presented a more imminent threat, and biologists began to show a greater interest.[22] Scientific societies again issued statements. The AAAS urged "citizens, educational authorities and legislators to oppose the compulsory inclusion in science education curriculum of beliefs that are not amenable to the process of scrutiny and testing that is indispensable to science." A National Academy of Sciences panel agreed that scientists were to avoid debates, but give more attention to the public understanding of science and to science literacy. The panel recommended that the academy produce, under its prestigious name, a booklet in a popular style that systematically refuted the creationists' arguments—a sort of "Handy-Dandy Creationist Refuter." The panel also encouraged scientists to engage in grass-roots activities, reaching science teachers and local communities.[23] So, too, did the NABT, which puts out a newsletter on the controversy called *Scientific Integrity* and compiles information for teachers.

The Iowa Academy of Sciences reacted to their state dispute by appointing a Panel on Controversial Issues to assist teachers and parent groups. They also organized a network of scientists to generate proevolution publicity called the Committees of Correspondence, after the groups of colonists that organized during the American Revolution to warn each other of imminent threats. The committees are a national network of autonomous groups of scientists in forty-two states who are willing to speak to parent and teacher groups and to engage in appropriate defensive actions.[24] The idea is to use the same tactics as the creationists in a battle for public opinion in local communities and schools. However, their task is a difficult one. Public opinion in many communities has crystallized on the issue. Scientists often speak to the convinced. Furthermore, the committees face administrative hassles. One committee, the Minnesota Association for Improvement of Science Education, applied to the Internal Revenue Service for exemption from federal income tax as a nonprofit educational group. The reply from an IRS agent requested further information before the application could be considered:

> When you advocate that "evolution" should be taught in the schools, state specifically what you mean by "evolution" or what "theory of evolution" should be taught.
>
> Are you primarily engaged in improving the quality of science education in general or advocating that a "theory of evolution" should be taught in the schools? Please explain your position.
>
> What do you consider to be the pseudo-scientific versions of the origin of life on earth? What gives you the standing or the prerogative to deem certain versions of the origin of life on earth as pseudo-scientific?

Why are you opposed to permitting the granting of equal time in school curricula to the teaching of the theory of creationism?[24]

Finally, mobilizing scientists for political action is difficult. While scientists are willing to issue statements, they remain reluctant to become engaged in the grass-roots activities that have so effectively served the creationists' cause.

Notes

1. Bronson Havard, quoted in *Christian Century* 94, 2 March 1977, p. 189.

2. "Creation and the Media," in *The Decade of Creation,* ed. Henry Morris and Donald Rohrer (San Diego: Creation-Life Publishers, 1981), ch. VII.

3. See a report of textbook changes in *Time,* 16 March 1981, pp. 80–81; *Christianity Today,* 7 November 1980, pp. 64–67; and Henry Zuidema, "Genetics and Genesis: The New Biology Textbooks," *Creation/Evolution* 5 (Summer 1981): 17 ff.

4. Robert Dahlin, "A Tough Time for Textbooks," *Publishers Weekly,* 7 August 1981, pp. 27–32.

5. Zuidema, *op. cit.,* p. 19.

6. Lawrence A. Cremin, *The Transformation of the School* (New York: Alfred A. Knopf, 1962).

7. *Nature* 239 (October 1972): 420. Two scientists immediately responded to the challenge.

8. David S. Hogness, statement at a meeting of the California State Board of Education, 6 November 1972 (mimeographed).

9. John E. Summers, M.D., statement at hearing of the California State Board of Education, 9 November 1972 (mimeographed).

10. Ralph Gerard, statement at hearing of the California State Board of Education, 9 November 1972 (mimeographed).

11. John A. Moore, "On Giving Time to the Teaching of Evolution and Creation," *Perspectives in Biology and Medicine* 18 (Spring 1975): 405–417. Delivered at AAAS annual meeting, San Francisco, March 1974.

12. William Mayer, "The Nineteenth Century Revisited," *BSCS Newsletter* (November 1972).

13. David Ost, "Statement," *American Biology Teacher* 34 (October 1972): 413–414.

14. Memo to NABT, 28 November 1972.

15. Letter from Wendell McBurney to Jerry Lightner, 22 December 1972.

16. *American Biology Teachers Journal* (April 1974): 246.

17. National Academy of Sciences Resolution, 17 October 1972. Note that this was approved by only thirty-five of sixty members attending the October meeting.

18. Resolution printed in the *BSCS Newsletter* (November 1972).

19. *BSCS Newsletter* (November 1972).

20. *Ibid.*

21. These quotes and the following are from correspondence to the NABT in late 1972.

22. In part, the greater interest among evolutionary biologists reflected their own stakes. Federal funding for evolutionary studies is becoming controversial. The abstracts of research proposals make no mention of evolution in the fear that they may be monitored by congressmen.

23. Summary Report of Meeting on Creationism/Evolution, National Academy of Sciences, 19 October 1981 (mimeographed).

24. Stanley L. Weinberg, "Reactions to Creationism in Iowa: Two Prototype Defense Strategies," 1981 (mimeographed).

11

Social Sources of Textbook Disputes

Recourse to religion is to the promise of science as recourse to the Roman courts was to the promise of Christianity. The older institution in either case was expected to pass away as a great promise was fulfilled. Neither promise was fulfilled and both institutions survived.[1]

In the very center of the most advanced technological societies there has emerged a resistance to science: an ideological resistance to the rationality and reductionism epitomized by science and a political resistance to its pervasive influence as a leading social institution.[2] While the origins of textbook disputes may lie in the regressive and often obscure demands of religious fundamentalists, this analysis suggests that they are manifestations of a much broader social phenomenon—widespread concern with the social implications of technology, and a hostility toward public institutions and expertise that pervades American society. Creationists and other textbook watchers are not numerous, but they are politically effective to the extent that they express social dissatisfactions that dispose people to seek alternative explanations of the human condition. Like antifluoridation disputes or protests against the siting of nuclear power plants or airports, textbook controversies reflect a resistance to impersonal, expertise-dominated bureaucracies that fail to respond to public priorities.[3] Furthermore, the textbook watchers, like many of the people preoccupied with mysticism, astrology, or various pop cosmologies and Eastern religions, question the image of science as an infallible source of truth.[4]

Resistance to science assumes different forms: some groups seek new consciousness through meditation or mysticism. In 1973, the National Opinion Research Center ran a national survey, asking 1,467 people if they had ever "felt very close to a powerful spiritual force." Of these, 35 percent, mostly college-educated, Protestant, over forty, and male, had had what they described as a mystical experience. Mysticism, the authors conclude, was not a property of a maniacal fringe: it suggests the limits of modernization and rationality.[5] Others resist science through traditional values. According to a 1976 Gallup survey, 38 percent of the American people believe that the Bible is the actual word of God and is to be taken literally word for word.

Nevertheless, science has become the language, the label, and the source of legitimacy for many religious and mystical beliefs. Just as creationists set theology in a context of scientific method, research monographs, and professional societies, so do yogis use electroencephalographs to assist in meditation; *The Exorcist* shows doctors using sophisticated scientific medicine to exorcise spirits from a child possessed by voodoo; Scientism and UFO cults use scientific apparatus; and even occultists seek scientific validation for their beliefs.[6] The resistance to science is thus imbued with science. While rejecting its institutional and philosophical implications, which seem to deny man a sense of place and priority, people use science to support their beliefs.

In order to understand the creationists and the attacks on science education programs, therefore, one must go beyond the pejorative labels of antiscience and irrationality to analyze the social and political tensions that sustain the resistance to science. These tensions are expressed in three themes that pervade many disputes over science and, in particular, the textbooks disputes described in this volume:

1. disillusion with science and technology as threats to traditional values;

2. resentment of the authority represented by scientific expertise as it is reflected in public-school curriculum decisions;
3. defense of the pluralist and egalitarian values that appear threatened by modern science.

Disaffected with the scientific approach to nature as taught in the new science curriculum, both creationists and the anti-MACOS groups sought to incorporate traditional values into education, rejecting decisions by experts (the university scholars who created the curriculum), and applying an egalitarian ethos to educational decisions.

Disillusion with Science and Technology

It seems to me that man is not getting better, but is developing more diabolical ways of hurting his fellow man. Moreover because of his ineptness and his inability to see all the implications of his actions, he misuses many of his scientific accomplishments. He is hardly in a position to guide evolution.[7]

The textbook movement has been most active in southern California, Texas, and several western states that have experienced extraordinary population growth and economic fluctuations associated largely with science-based industry. Indeed, many textbook watchers are engineers employed in the aerospace industry, people who have personally experienced the discrepancy between technological expansion and the ability to deal with the social and economic problems induced by rapid change. They are particularly distressed with the uncertainties and disruptions of modern society, and they associate a "decline in moral and religious values" with the dominance of scientific and secular perspectives. Hippies, campus revolts, veneral disease, drugs, and environmental problems, they argue, all reflect "the liberalism of a scientific age."

Vernon Grose, the systems engineer who revised part of the California *Science Framework* to include creation theory in biology textbooks, associates evolution theory with a campaign of secularization in a scientific-materialistic society—a campaign to totally neutralize religious convictions, to destroy any concept of absolute moral values, to deny any racial differences, to mix all ethnic groups in cookbook proportions, and finally the latest —the destruction of the distinction between male and female.[8]

All this, he claims, is nonsense. Differences were created by design; the source of our problems is the secularization of religious beliefs. Similarly, Congressman Conlan argues that a philosophy that assumes all values and moral issues to be open and relative should be blamed for the nation's most pressing social problems.[9]

Three aspects of the biology and social-science curricula appear to be especially distressing for their social implications: the biological determinism that is implicit in the relationship drawn between animals and man; the implication that values are relative to situational factors; and the denial of an omnipotent and omniscient force that determines human behavior. Creationists argued that an emphasis on the genetic similarities between man and animals is a socially dangerous concept that encourages animallike behavior:

> If man is an evolved animal, then the morals of the barnyard and jungle are more natural . . . than the artificially imposed restrictions of premarital chastity and marital fidelity. Instead of monogamy, why not promiscuity and polygamy? . . . Self-preservation is the first law of nature; only the fittest will survive. Be the cock-of-the-walk and the king-of-the-mountain. Eat, drink and be merry, for life is short and that's the end. So says evolution.[10]

According to Judge Braswell Deen of Atlanta, Georgia, a creationist and judge of the State Court of Appeals:

> This monkey mythology of Darwin is the cause of permissiveness, promiscuity, pills, prophylactics, perversions, pregnancies, abortions, pornotherapy, pollution, poisoning and proliferation of crimes of all types.[11]

One woman blamed the "streaking" craze on the theory of evolution. "If young people are taught they are animals long enough, they'll soon begin to act like them."[12]

The evolutionary assumptions so explicit in MACOS as it used examples of animal behavior to develop concepts about the nature of man raised vociferous objections. Why should an explanation of man concentrate in such detail on animals? Was this not a pernicious attempt to spread a religion of "secular humanism"? Studies of how a difficult environment influenced Netsilik values reinforced this concern. To deny absolute standards by emphasizing adaptation to environmental pressures was, to the creationists, socially irresponsible and morally and politically destructive.

> It can be documented that the evolutionary philosophy has served as the pseudo-scientific basis and justification for racism, modern imperialism, Nazism, anarchism, communism, behaviorism, animalistic amoralism, humanism and practically all the other anti-Christian and anti-theistic social philosophies and movements of the past century and more.[13]

Unlike the nineteenth-century fundamentalists, most modern-day creationists are willing to compromise by balancing the "pernicious influence" of modern science with a presentation of alternative theories. "Let the students take their choice." But the direct denial of absolute values in MACOS met the worst expectations of the textbook watchers. Their children were taught that in some societies senilicide and infanticide were functional, that their own values were only relative, based on specific environmental and situational factors in an indeterminate universe. These evolutionary assumptions had profound implications for belief in the omnipotence of a God who determines human behavior. Thus the creationists saw MACOS as a direct threat to their religious beliefs, a threat that would undermine the faith of their children and pull them away from the Bible and the Church.

Both creationists and anti-MACOS groups express their own sense of disillusion with science, but they also touch on popular anxieties about science and technology. Picking up on contemporary issues, they argue that "the denial of the existence of a designer serves as a license to destroy nature, fostering the self-centered behavior that is responsible for environmental problems." Recognizing man as God's steward would help man to understand and live in harmony with nature—to preserve given forms.[14] However, these textbook watchers are not necessarily against technology: on the contrary, most of them earn their livelihood in technological industries.[15]

Probed for their opinions on currently controversial technologies, such as nuclear power or fluoridation, creationists welcome technological growth as evidence of social progress. Yet their arguments capture widely held concerns about the social implications of modern science and technology, and especially about the role of authority and expertise in a democratic society.[16]

Challenges to Authority

An elite corps of unelected professional academics and their government friends run things in the schools.[17]

Schools exist for people, not for gurus.[18]

Modern science developed as a revolt against the authority of "sacred tradition"; yet it has become, for the science-textbook critics, a symbol of an authoritarian ideology that suppresses such tradition. They express extraordinary resentment of "scientific dogmatism," of the "arrogance" and "absence of humility" among scientists. A sympathetic journalist writes of his great joy in "seeing science humbled," of seeing a blow to scientists' "monopoly of truth."[19] In a speech to the California State Board of Education, a creationist observes, "After all, scientists put on their trousers in the morning one leg at a time, just like the rest of the world."[20] And a Jehovah's Witness writes about the "arrogant authoritarianism required by evolutionists to sustain what they cannot prove."[21] These concerns are not unique to textbook watchers. The resentment of professional arrogance is widespread; citizens at a public meeting of the American Nuclear Society complained of "the arrogance of scientists from the nuclear industry."[22] The condescension of medical professionals appeared to have influenced jurors at the Edelin abortion trial.[23] Thus, like the general concern with the impact of science and technology, this theme, too, reaches a receptive audience.

The resentment of authority appears in criticism of the academics who determine the content of school texts, and in the demands for local control of school curriculum. This was the basis of textbook revisions imposed by the California State Board of Education, revisions that guard against what creationists perceive as the imposition of scientific authority beyond its appropriate limits. "They want absolute control over the *Science Framework*—absolute control, mind you—total dictatorial control over the teaching of our children."[24] Particularly irritating to textbook watchers was the role of NSF, a "federal authority," in supporting the development of textbooks. It was this "federal takeover of education" that provoked the Willoughby lawsuit against NSF for funding BSCS materials, and it aroused congressional indignation in the MACOS dispute about

> the insidious attempt to impose particular school courses . . . on local school districts, using the power and financial resources of the Federal government to set up a network of educator lobbyists to control education throughout America. . . . We Americans place a high value on local autonomy. Local school boards, reflecting the prevailing social norms of the community, should be the final arbiter of curriculum development.[25]

The desire to preserve parental control over textbooks motivated the two women who launched the creationist textbook movement in California. Increased parental participation in the selection of textbooks is the theme of the Gablers' organization in Texas. "Unless people take an active voice in assisting the authorized units of government in the process of selecting textbooks, the selection will continue to deteriorate."[26] The coordinator for the National Coalition for Children resents the "elitist groups of educators" that have usurped power from parents. Those opposing MACOS demanded that new curriculum be opened to public referendum, or at least review, a goal reflected in the congressional amendment to the 1975 NSF authorization act, requiring that all NSF-supported educational material be open to parental examination.[27] The Moudy Committee, appointed by Congressman Teague, also emphasized participation when it recommended that "representative parents" with no professional bias be involved in curriculum decisions that impinge upon widely respected customs and long-held religious beliefs.[28]

Similar feelings about "professional and scholarly bias" appeared in Kanawha County, where the local people wanted to "get the government down to where they'll listen to us little old hillbillies."[29] Education was a community issue, and powerful professionals were not to be trusted. When a National Education Association panel investigated the issue, the Kanawha County Board of Education questioned the right of a Washington-based organization to judge the mentality and intelligence of Kanawha County parents, especially with regard to moral and spiritual values.[30]

The Supreme Court decision on pornography stating that definitions of obscenity are a matter for local determination stimulated and sanctioned demands for local control. The textbook watchers, concerned with "smut" in the schools as well as with science, had watched this case with interest and delight, using it to back their argument that, indeed, any program at all that impinged on local values should likewise be judged within the community.

The public education system is one of the last grass-roots institutions in America. School systems have traditionally been decentralized, run by local school boards composed of elected citizens (nonprofessionals). There has been, however, a gradual erosion of local control through court decisions, reliance on nonlocal funds, merging of school districts, and the general trend toward professionalism in education. School curriculum is guided more by national testing standards geared to college entrance requirements than to local values. Those who retain the expectation of local control over educational policy are threatened by the growing power and increasing professionalization of statewide curriculum committees and departments of education. The federally funded programs created by academics who were isolated from local values and who were attempting to develop a "teacher-proof" curriculum were a further insult.

Centralization of curriculum decisions involves some assumptions concerning public choice. Public-school policy is binding on the individual. Once a curriculum is established, every student is involved. Statewide policies are developed either on the assumption that the knowledge in question is objective and indisputable, or that a given policy is of broad social benefit, reflecting dominant values and shared objectives regarding the purpose of education. The objection to evolution as "dogma" suggests that, in science as well as other subjects, unresolvable value differences may preclude consensus.

Insofar as local values influence curriculum decisions, they often do so through watchdog citizens groups. Such groups have several axes to grind: some claim that professionalization and standardization of education favors only middle-class, college-bound students; others are concerned with increased taxes; and still others, like the creationists, have ideological or religious concerns. The declining role of local control is often a source of tension more in matters of ethnic balance and busing than in curriculum and textbooks, but the textbook protest parallels other developments. Thus, it holds appeal not only to fundamentalists but also to people concerned with increasing government activity in education and more broadly with the lack of public discussion of issues vitally affecting community interests.

Textbook critics were quick to use the lessons learned from Watergate: "After the Watergate experience, this country is sensitized to those who appear to decline to open up an issue for full discussion. Neither presidents nor scientists can expect to avoid an issue by virtue of the dignity of their office or profession."[31] They thrive in the political climate of the Reagan administration, bent on reducing the role of the federal government. In this context, any effort to challenge government or scientific authority, or to seek greater representation of community values can count on a wide base of support.[32]

The Ideology of Equal Time

Let us present as many theories as possible and give the child the right to choose the one that seems most logical to him. We are working to have students receive a fair shake.[33]

I don't recall the government ever granting $7 million to scholars for the writing of textbooks reflecting a religious view of man and his destiny.[34]

In January 1973, Henry Morris, president of the Institute for Creation Research, wrote to the director of the BSCS and challenged him to a public debate on the scientific aspects of the creation-evolution controversy. He proposed the following topic: "RESOLVED that the special creation model of the history of the earth and its inhabitants is more effective in the correlation and prediction of scientific data than is the evolution model."[35] Morris proposed that newspapers, telecasters, and the general public be invited, permitting large audiences "to hear both sides and decide for themselves." The outcome, essentially would be determined by audience applause. The issues, claimed the creationist, are free public choice, equality, fairness. Creationists argue that since the Biblical theory of origins is scientifically valid, it deserves "equal time." When there are two "equally valid hypotheses," it is only "fair" that students be exposed to both theories and be allowed to choose for themselves. "We are working to have students receive a fair shake."

Those who deny the right to equal time are accused by creationists of closed-mindedness ("those narrow men, like people standing in the sunlight who argue there is no evidence for the existence of the sun")[36] or exclusiveness (maintaining their "privileged position . . . not by scientific evidence, but by authoritarian proscription").[37] "A young professor could never admit he was a creationist without losing his chances for tenure," claimed a scientist at the Institute for Creation Research.

> In all the history of science, never has dogmatism had such a firm grip on science as it does today with reference to evolution theory. Evolutionists control our schools, the universities, and the means of publication. It would be almost as surprising to find an antievolutionist holding an important professorship at one of our major universities, as it would be to find a capitalist occupying a chair at Moscow University.[38]

The concept of equal time originated with the FCC Fairness Doctrine, confirming the responsibility of broadcasters to afford "reasonable opportunity for the presentation of contrasting viewpoints on controversial issues of public importance."[39] Its basis lay in the idea that power in a knowledge society is controlled by those who can communicate and that there is inequality in the power to communicate ideas just as there is inequality in economic bargaining power.[40] But the concept of equal time has been extraordinarily difficult to define and implement. With limited broadcasting resources, it has proved impossible to evaluate what issues are "of public importance" and who is entitled to present their viewpoints. In fact, the doctrine has tended to inhibit the presentation of controversial ideas. Nevertheless, equated with fairness and justice, and rooted in the democratic impulse, it has had enormous appeal in American society, especially in the almost "evangelically egalitarian educational system."[41]

The concept of pluralism allows that minority groups have a right to maintain cultural and religious traditions in the face of pressures for conformity. In the last decade, for example, we have seen textbook changes instituted by minority groups and by women, who see the presentation of history as biased. Since education is perceived as a condition for equality, such groups seek to have their interests more equally represented to students. Their demands formed a model for those who see bias in science curriculum—the struggle against cultural hegemony is paralleled by the struggle against scientific conformity, as textbook watchers insist that science education must respect beliefs that are outside the dominant scientific culture.[42]

Demands for equal representation of diverse interest groups in the selection of curricula are encouraged by the broadly conceived intentions of modern education. The goal of education, clearly expressed in the teacher materials of the new curricula, is to prepare students for their role as citizens in a democratic society. The BSCS stated that the purpose of improving biology education was to better train students to cope with the problems they will face as individuals, as parents, and as citizens. The architects of MACOS were not simply communicating information: they saw the social sciences as a means of developing the understanding of human nature necessary for citizenship. Unfortunately, they expressed this purpose in terms that were bound to provoke the ire of traditionalists.

It will not do to dream nostalgically of simpler times when children presumably grew up believing in the love of God, the virtue of hard work, the sanctity of the family, and the nobility of the Western historical tradition. . . . We must understand . . . what causes people to love and trust rather than to fear and hate each other, how patterns of mutual support can be fostered without destroying individual initiative and how we can learn to shape competing loyalties to common ends.[43]

The sense of fairness implied by demands for equal time buttressed the antiauthority appeal of the creationist movement. When William Willoughby sued the NSF for its support of textbooks teaching evolution, he reported receiving letters from non-religious people sympathizing with his desire for equality. It is simply not fair, argued his correspondents, that the views of some groups are dismissed in this way. The creationists also convinced many people that they were speaking in the name of open-minded academic inquiry and intellectual honesty. "It is in the highest tradition of science to allow opposing viewpoints to be heard."[44]

Just as creationists appealed for the fairness of including Biblical explanations in biology books, MACOS critics wanted equal time for alternative world views in social-science books. The Heritage Foundation Report, for example, demanded either a value-free social science *or* equal time for the presentation of alternative values.[45] James McKenna of the Heritage Foundation, legal counsel in several textbook protests, asserted:

Under the banner of science, value systems are being marched into the schoolroom with a shameless disregard of the will of the polity. . . . The truth dawning on parents, be they creekers and rednecks from West Virginia or goldcoasters from Connecticut, is that education is a sectarian occupation. . . . The single most perfect example of this in our lifetime is the allegedly scientific disquisition into the roots of man. It has in its time gone by the name of Darwinism, evolutionism, or transformism. It is the most sectarian operation of the allegedly scientific community in the history of man.[46]

According to the Moudy Committee, MACOS is open to allegations that it is promoting "an evolutionary and relativistic humanism," because it "allows no hints of patriotism, theism, creationism, or other explicit values." The applications of science,

especially social science, are "inseparable from people's beliefs, from their theology, from their morality." The committee concludes that input from "representative parents" should be included in every "value-laden" curriculum.[47]

These demands bring questions normally resolved by professional consensus directly into the political arena. From a professional perspective, science education is an enterprise best organized by experts, for it is intended to provide students with the best available information; what is taught or how it is taught is considered a technical matter. For those concerned with the values conveyed to their children in the schools, however, questions of personal beliefs, theology, and morality may enter into all educational decisions; choice of curriculum then becomes a matter of public participation. Scientific merit does not reduce political turmoil; on the contrary, the persistence of textbook conflicts reflects the continuing tension between professional assumptions about uniformity in the teaching of certain subjects and the expectations of pluralism in an educational system that is directed to doing far more than simply providing factual knowledge to students.

The tensions expressed in the science-textbook disputes represent a reaction mostly from a politically conservative population. But criticism of the dominance of scientific values and the role of expertise, as well as demands for increased local participation, can be found among people of a wide spectrum of political ideologies. Indeed, similar tensions generated the "advocacy politics" that emerged during the late 1960s, as planners, health care and consumer advocates, and environmentalists mobilized around their diverse causes. All these groups express disillusion with technology and expertise; their slogans are "accountability," "lay participation," and "demystification of expertise." (See Table 11.1.) However, creationists turn such slogans—the buzz words of the progressive left—upside down, for the rhetoric of participation, accountability, and local control becomes a way to bring authoritarian religious values back into the public schools.

The demands of textbook critics for increased participation and the representation of their religious interests in science curriculum decisions leaves us with difficult questions: How can one determine if textbook material is antireligious or in some way biased? What

TABLE 11.1.

Parallel Concerns among Diverse Critics of Science and Technology

Environmentalists	Medical Critics	Science Textbook Critics
Disillusion		
"With technology's gifts to improve man's environment has come an awesome potential for destruction."	"Psychiatry and psychology are used as direct instruments of coercion against individuals. Under the guise of 'medical methods' people are pacified, punished, or incarcerated."	"Man is developing more diabolical ways of hurting his fellow man. Moreover, because of his ineptness and his inability to see all the implications of his actions, he misuses many of his scientific accomplishments."
Critiques of Expertise		
"The technologist's training can stand in his way. There is a growing awareness that civilized man has blindly followed the technologists into a mess."	"Professionals often regard themselves as more capable of making decisions than other people, even when their technical knowledge does not contribute to a particular decision. . . . Professionalism is not a guarantor of humane, quality services. Rather it is a codeword for a distinct political posture."	"Never has dogmatism had such a firm grip on sciences as it does today with reference to evolution theory." "An elite corps of unelected professional academics and their government friends run things in the schools."
Demands for Increased Participation		
"It doesn't require special training to keep a broad perspective and to apply common sense. Thus, for every technically knowledgeable [person] there is a lay-	"Medicine should be demystified. When possible, patients should be permitted to choose among alternative methods of treatment based upon their needs. Health	"Let us present as many theories as possible and give the child the right to choose the one that seems most logical to him." "Local school boards reflecting pre-

man activist. . . . Any group which has interests at stake in the planning process should have those interests articulated."

care should be deprofessionalized. Health care skills should be transferred to worker and patient alike."

vailing social norms of the community should be the final arbiter of curriculum development."

SOURCE: Editorials and the popular literature circulated by various Earth Day groups, the Health Policy Advisory Center, and science textbook critics.

kind of constraints or standards can be imposed to balance academic judgments with local and individual religious or personal concerns? How, in fact, do the personal beliefs and political values of free choice and fairness affect the communication and evaluation of science?

Notes

1. John A. Miles "Jacques Monod and the Cure of Souls," *Zygon* 9 (March 1974): 41.

2. John Passmore talks of a revolt against science and emphasizes its powerful emotional force. John Passmore. "The Revolt against Science," *Search* 3 (November 1972). See also Theodore Roszak, *Where the Wasteland Ends* (New York: Doubleday, 1972). There is now an extensive literature on current concerns with science. See, for example, J. Ellul, *The Technological Society* (New York: Alfred A. Knopf, 1956); V. Ferkiss, *Technological Man* (New York: Braziller, 1969).

3. See, for example, Dorothy Nelkin, *Nuclear Power and Its Critics* (Ithaca, N.Y.: Cornell University Press, 1971), and *Jetport* (New Brunswick, N.J.: Transaction Books, 1974).

4. Christopher Evans, *Cults of Unreason* (New York: Farrar, Strauss & Giroux, 1973), discusses some of these cults and their relationships to science. There has been little work on the social origins of participants in various cults.

5. W. McCready, "A Survey of Mystical Experience," *Listening* 9 (Autumn 1974).

6. See M. Truzzi, "Towards a Sociology of the Occult," in *Religious Movements in Contemporary America,* eds. I. Zaretsky and M. Leone (Princeton, N.J.: Princeton University Press, 1974).

7. John Klotz, Letter to the Editor, *Christian Century,* 1 March 1967, p. 279.

8. Vernon Grose, "Second Thoughts about Textbooks on Sexism," *Science and Scripture* 4 (January 1974): 14 ff. With respect to the increasing concern about secularization, the editor of *Christian Century* suggests that this reflects a "protestant paranoia" developed as America has been transformed from Protestant domination to a much more diverse outlook. See discussion in Will Herberg's "Religion in a Secularized Society," in *Religion, Culture and Society,* ed. Louis Schneider (New York: Wiley, 1964), p. 596.

9. John Conlan, "The MACOS Controversy," *Social Education* 39 (October 1975): 391.

10. *Acts and Facts* (a publication of the Institute for Creation Research) (April 1974).

11. Quoted in *Time,* 16 March 1981, p. 82.

12. *New York Times,* 10 March 1974, p. 49. "Streaking" was an obscure, short-lived craze in American universities during 1974, when students were running naked across public thoroughfares.

13. "Battle for Creation," *Acts and Facts* (Impacts) 2 (1976): 1–2.

14. The relationship between religion and environmental values has provoked much discussion. Some scholars attribute the environmental crisis to the Judaeo-Christian tradition that assumes that nature exists to serve man. They argue that Western science and technology is "cast in a matrix of Christian theology," that the creation story in Genesis justifies man's subjugation of nature. See Lynn White, Jr. "The Historical Roots of Our Ecological Crisis," *Science* 19 March 1967, pp. 1203 ff. The idea that Christian belief necessarily accepts the exploitation of nature, however, must be challenged by many counterexamples. The Southern Agrarians, while often fundamental Christians, saw the "Gospel of Progress" as an "unrelenting war on nature—well beyond reason," and advocated harmony with nature. See John Crowe Ransom, "Reconstructed but Unregenerated," in *I'll Take My Stand: The South and the Agrarian Tradition, Twelve Southerners* (New York: Harper & Row, 1930), p. 8. Others argue that the creation story implies responsibility and stewardship. See C. F. D. Moule, *Man and Nature in the New Testament* (Philadelphia: Fortress Press, 1967). Moule claims that in Genesis the land belongs ultimately to God, and man is its trustee. The created order is valuable in itself—to be cared for by man.

15. The ambivalence among professionals working in high-technology industries became apparent during the California Initiative on nuclear power, in which an organization called Creative Initiatives Foundation

took an active role. This is a religious sect, and most of its members are upper-middle-class professionals disaffected with the values of modern society. They seek new meaning in a life based on Biblical teaching and in efforts to change the value system of technology-based society. The three nuclear engineers who, with much publicity, left their jobs at General Electric to play an active role in the antinuclear campaign are members of this sect.

16. Disillusion with science and technology also reflects a loss of confidence in leadership and a general alienation and discontent. A Harris poll suggested that "general discontent factors" increased from 29 percent in 1966 to 55 percent in 1973. See discussion in A. Etzioni and C. Nunn, "The Public Appreciation of Science in Contemporary America," *Daedalus* (Summer 1974): 200–201.

17. John Conlan, "MACOS Controversy," 391.

18. Personal interview with George Archibald, congressional aide to Conlan.

19. Ron Kanigel, *San Francisco Examiner,* 16 September 1973.

20. Vernon Grose, *Statement to Board of Education,* in which he suggested revisions of the *Science Framework,* 1969, p. 4.

21. *Awake,* 22 September 1974.

22. *Nuclear News,* May 1975, p. 83.

23. See articles by Barbara Culliton in *Science,* 31 January and 7 March 1975.

24. Creation Science Research Center, "Dear Friend Letter," March 1980.

25. *Congressional Record,* 9 April 1975, H 2585–2587.

26. Educational Research Analysts, Florida (mimeographed brochure).

27. *Congressional Record,* 9 April 1975.

28. T. M. Moudy, chairman of Science Curriculum Implementation Review Group, *Report to the Committee on Science and Technology,* U.S. House of Representatives, 1 October 1975.

29. A speaker at a demonstration in Kanawha, cited by Calvin Trillin, "U.S. Journal," *The New Yorker,* 30 September 1974, p. 121. While these protest groups challenge centralized professional authority, they are often strikingly authoritarian in their own ideas regarding appropriate educational style. For example, a prevalent objection to MACOS was its developmental, nonauthoritarian method of teaching, involving discussion and group participation. Its critics preferred a much more authoritarian approach to education.

30. National Education Association, *Kanawha County, West Virginia:*

A Textbook Study in Cultural Conflict (Washington, D.C.: NEA, February 1975).

31. From a letter to the author in response to an article on textbook controversies.

32. Luther Gerlach and Virginia Hine, *People, Power, and Change* (Indianapolis: Bobbs-Merrill, 1970), attribute the increase in protests to "power deprivation." The reaction against professionals evident in our discussion suggests that these protests do tend to enhance the sense of social power among protesting groups. For a general discussion of the reaction to centralization and the appeal of local control, see Leonard Fein, *The Ecology of the Public Schools* (New York: Pegasus, 1971), and Alan Altshuler, *Community Control* (New York: Pegasus, 1970).

33. Personal interview with Henry Morris.

34. Ronald Reagan, cited in *Science,* 12 September 1980, p. 1214.

35. Letters from Henry Morris to William Mayer, 1 January 1973 through 15 April 1973. See *Acts and Facts* (June 1973).

36. George Howe, statement at hearing before the California State Board of Education, 9 November 1972.

37. Letter from Henry Morris to William Mayer, 1 January 1973.

38. Duane Gish, "A Challenge to Neo-Darwinism," *American Biology Teacher* 32 (February 1973): 495.

39. *Federal Register,* 10406, 1 July 1964.

40. Jerome Barron, "Access to the Press—a New First Amendment Right," *Harvard Law Review* 80 (1967): 1647. Proponents of the fairness doctrine claim that the First Amendment was written without the knowledge that communication could be dominated by a few private interests capable of practicing their own form of censorship over free expression.

41. This term was used to describe some sources of anti-intellectualism by Richard Hofstader, *Anti-Intellectualism in American Life* (New York: Vintage Books, 1962), p. 23.

42. That the teaching of biology poses a distinct problem for minority religious groups whose belief systems are incompatible with science has been recognized in court rulings exempting Amish children from school requirements. These decisions recognized that "the values of parental direction of the religious upbringing and education of their children in their early and formative years have a high place in our society." These can outweigh even strong state interest in universal education. See *Wisconsin v. Yoder,* U.S. 205, 213 (1972) discussed in Frederick LeClerq, "The Monkey Laws and the Public Schools: A Second Consumption?" *Vanderbilt Law Review* 27 (March 1974): 242.

43. Peter Dow, "MACOS: The Study of Human Behavior as One Road to Survival," *Phi Delta Kappan* 57 (October 1975): 81.

44. Letter from D. E. Martz to *Science,* 9 March 1973, p. 953. A series of similar letters were printed in *Science* with respect to the creationist conflict.

45. Susan Marshner, *Man: A Course of Study—Prototype for Federalized Textbooks?* (Washington, D.C.: The Heritage Foundation, July 1975).

46. James T. McKenna, *"Serrano v. Priest:* Where Have You Led Us?" *Imprimis* 3 (March 1975): 13.

47. T. M. Moudy, *Report to Committee on Science and Technology,* U.S. House of Representatives.

12

Science and Personal Beliefs

We resent the widespread philosophical prejudice that arises from the *a priori*, non-scientific assumption that there can be no divine intervention with the working of the universe and that the scientists' method is the only way to truth.[1]

Religious fundamentalists of the 1930s wanted to prevent the teaching of evolution theory because it threatened their theological views. They succeeded. Textbook publishers virtually ignored evolution theory for some thirty years. Today, fundamentalists, in the guise of "scientific creationists," are once again influencing the teaching of science. And evolution theory, the central organizing principle of modern biology, continues to be a vulnerable target, perceived as a direct and explicit threat to personal morality and religious belief.

Images of Science

The extension of personal beliefs and democratic principles to science suggests a public image of science at odds with the perceptions of scientists themselves. Scientists are amazed at the idea that questions of fairness in the representation of beliefs should determine the substance of scientific education: Can quacks be entitled to equal time? Should Christian Scientism appear in health books, the stork theory in books on reproduction, and astrological lore in expositions of astronomy?

To scientists, concepts of pluralism, of equity, of "fairness," of wide-open participatory democracy as practiced in a political context are irrelevant to the context of science. Science is based on the assumption that nature is comprehensible by objective observation. Decisions are based on the existence of an organized body of knowledge, and on an intricate network of procedures accepted by a community of scientists who share values concerning appropriate behavior and standards of acceptable truth. These values are founded on a view of science as an autonomous system distinct from political or personal beliefs. Robert Merton, whose work has laid the foundation of the sociology of science, described these values as universalism (claims of truth are subject to impersonal criteria); communism (the findings of science belong to the community of science); disinterestedness (claims are based on the testable character of science); and organized skepticism (methodological and institutional mandates require suspending temporary judgments until beliefs are tested in terms of empirical and logical criteria).[2]

Scientists accept theories and teach them, not because they represent "truth," but because they are accepted by the scientific community as useful explanations of reality. Theories can never be proven correct for all time, nor must they necessarily explain all evidence. While much of the evidence for evolution theory is circumstantial and incomplete, it is solidly supported by research in such diverse disciplines as genetics and biochemistry.[3] The important point for biologists is that research consistently confirms the evolutionary hypothesis and that it remains a powerful predictive instrument whether or not the evidence supporting it is complete.

In this context, only collegial acceptance can validate one theory and reject another; the views of those outside the community are irrelevant. Moreover, while science is an open system in terms of social criteria, scientific recognition depends on achievement and rigorous evaluation; indeed, the internal standards of performance in science may run counter to egalitarian notions.

The extent of creationist influence, the fact that many people are sympathetic toward the creationists' demands of "equal time," raises questions about the public understanding of science. What do people know about science, about its process and its methods? Is public support of research based on any rational understanding of the scientific endeavor? How is scientific knowledge received by the public that supports it?

Years ago, Oscar Handlin suggested that science was hardly assimilated even in the cultures of advanced industrial societies. Those who voted federal funds for its support had no understanding of its character, for science had advanced beyond common sense and empirical reality.

> Paradoxically the bubbling retort, the sparkling wire and the mysterious dials are often regarded as a source of a grave threat . . . the machine which was a product of science was also magic, understandable only in terms of what it did, not of how it worked. Hence the lack of comprehension or of control; hence also the mixture of dread and anticipation.[4]

Acceptance of the authority of scientific judgment continues to coexist with mistrust and fear. Roszak contrasts the romantic view of the scientist as "a modern magician, a miracle man who can do incredible things" with persistent negative images:

> Dr. Faustus, Dr. Frankenstein, Dr. Moreau, Dr. Jekyll, Dr. Cyclops, Dr. Caligari, Dr. Strangelove. . . . In these images of our popular culture resides a legitimate public fear of the scientist's stripped-down, depersonalized conception of knowledge—a fear that our scientists will go on being titans who create monsters.[5]

Ambivalence persists despite the post-Sputnik interest in science, and, in fact, public skepticism toward science has increased since 1957. The National Science Foundation has sponsored a public-opinion survey that differentiates between the "attentive public" (those identified as having interest in and knowledge about science—about one person in five) and the nonattentive public. Between 1957 and 1979, the percentage of the attentive public believing that "On balance the benefits of scientific research have outweighed the harmful results" declined from 96 percent to 90 percent. Among the nonattentive public, it declined from 87 percent to 66 percent, an erosion of 1 percent a year. More important for our purposes, the percentage of those believing that "scientific discoveries tend to break down people's ideas of right and wrong" increased: among the attentive group 11 percent agreed with this statement in 1957; 27 percent in 1979. Among the general public agreement with this statement increased dramatically from 24 percent to 42 percent in 1979.[6]

Daniel Yankelovich, an analyst of social trends and public attitudes, also finds a growing pattern of skepticism about science and technology, and a shift in cosmological outlook away from unqualified belief in science and technology as instruments of progress. He reports that in 1980, 27 percent of the public believed everything has a logical scientific explanation; 48 percent said they used to believe that all mysteries of life would eventually be explained by science, but now they believed that some things could be understood in a nonrational way. The rest believed that life is controlled by "strange and mysterious forces that decide our fate." Yankelovich finds that better-educated people—that is, those who are immersed in a technological outlook—are most likely to embrace nonrational explanations and to question the scientific world view.[7]

These attitudes are matched by confused comprehension. Surveys by the National Assessment of Educational Progress indicate that facts are far better assimilated and recalled than understanding of scientific process; few respondents show more than limited comprehension of the methods of scientific inquiry or the differences between facts, theories, and hypotheses. (See Appendix 2.) This is apparent among creationists who use the language of science but seem to understand little about its methods and underlying assumptions. Indeed, the creation controversy illustrates two common beliefs about science that bear on its acceptance: (1) that science can be defined as a collection of facts, and (2) that it can be evaluated in terms of its influence and implications.

The belief persists that "value-free" truths are derived from an accumulation of evidence. In this light, concepts in biology and the social sciences are especially prone to public criticism, for even theories that are well accepted within the scientific community may be based on untestable assumptions and indirect evidence. Like Darwin's contemporaries, modern creationists fail to understand that useful theories in science need not have definitive support if they have powerful predictive capacity, that indirect evidence may constitute support for certain theories that cannot be verified by direct observation. For those who miss the subtle relationships between fact and theory, acceptance of scientific theory remains a matter of faith. Thus creationists can argue with conviction that evolution is but a form of faith no more valid than their own religious beliefs.

While defining science as a collection of facts, creationists evaluate it in terms of its moral and political implications. People seek in their beliefs about nature the values that will guide their behavior.[8] Scientists themselves encourage this association between knowledge and values by claiming extensive territory for the concepts and tools of their disciplines—a tendency especially evident in efforts to extend tentative concepts in genetics to generalizations about man and society.[9] Such hubris is a source of success within science, but it also fosters public misconceptions and blurs the conventional distinction between science and its ideological and social content.[10] It further encourages the exploitation of science by creationists and other groups who believe that any systematic practice that is in some way conceived to "work," such as faithhealing, patent medicine, or transcendental meditation, can be justified on "scientific grounds."

Problems in the Communication of Science

The persistence of these images of science derives in part from problems in communication. Historically and methodologically, much of science developed in opposition to the dogmatism of religion, and most scientists understand their own work as approximate, conditional, and open to critical scrutiny. This is in striking contrast to the frequent public representation of science as authoritative, exact, and definitive. Science, in the original version of a

California textbook, "is the total knowledge of facts and principles that govern our lives." The organized skepticism toward scientific findings that is tacitly understood by those who practice science contrasts sharply with its public image.

Perhaps the most difficult concept to convey to those who are not scientists is the delicate balance between certainty and doubt that is so essential to the scientific spirit. Textbooks tend to convey a message of certainty, for in the process of simplification, findings may become explanations, explanations may become axioms, and tentative judgments may become definitive conclusions.[11] Preoccupied with communicating a scientific view of nature, textbooks often neglect the concepts of critical inquiry. The new science curricula tried to compensate for this tendency by emphasizing inquiry-oriented instruction and the concepts and methods that characterize "real" scientific research. But the image of science conveyed in textbooks seldom includes analyses of the organization of research, the personal motivations of scientists, or the relationship of science to cultural and social norms.

The recent explosion of popular science magazines and books hardly broadens the image. In the tradition of "news as entertainment," they portray science as a set of dramatic "results," as a source of hopeful promises, or as a cause of dire threat. The structure of science as a social process, less dramatic, is ignored. Indeed, the individualistic tradition in science leads its practitioners to minimize the importance of the social and cultural processes involved.[12] One historian of science has suggested, only partly tongue-in-cheek, that "the history of science be rated X," for a proper study of the historical development of scientific concepts and their underlying nonscientific values and assumptions would do violence to the professional ideals and public image of science.[13]

Scientists themselves seldom speculate about the assumptions that underlie their work, and would indeed be paralyzed if they constantly had to question hypotheses that lie deeply embedded in the structure of their disciplines. Convinced of the rationality and merit of their methods, they are constantly dismayed by the popularity of nonscientific approaches to nature. In 1975, for example, 186 scientists signed a statement criticizing astrologers. They were puzzled that "so many people are prone to swallow beliefs without sufficient evidence," and concerned that "generations of students are coming out without any idea that you have to have evidence for your beliefs."[14] The persistence of creationism reminds us that beliefs need no evidence; that, indeed, people are most reluctant to surrender their personal convictions to a scientific world view.

To those whose personal beliefs are challenged, the social and moral implications that can be drawn from a scientific theory assume far greater importance than any details of scientific verification. Indeed, increased technical information is unlikely to change well-rooted beliefs.[15] Creationists, as we have seen, avoid, debunk, or disregard information that would repudiate their preconceptions, preferring to deny evidence rather than to discard their beliefs. A great deal of social reinforcement helps them maintain their views in the face of repeated frustration, and opposition only strengthens their religious convictions.[16]

Confronted with conflict, scientists tend to forget the differences between the structures, meritocratic processes of science and the pluralistic processes of political disputes. They prefer to deny the perennial conflict between science and religious values (e.g., by bringing clergymen to public hearings to argue the compatibility of religion and science). They dismiss criticism of biology and social science as evidence of ignorance or educational failure; the arguments for design based on the intricacy and beauty of nature are "spurious and irrelevant," and belief in an intelligent designer is "as blasphemous as it is far fetched."[17] But then they respond to criticism with their own kind of fundamentalism, emphasizing the neutrality and apolitical character of science and the weight of evidence that supports scientific authority.

However, in the heat of public debate, this neutrality breaks down. The rhetoric of the creation-evolution controversy is far from neutral. Biologists and creationists alike claim the other bases its beliefs on faith; each group argues with passion for its own dispassionate objectivity; and each bemoans the moral, political, and legal implications of the alternative ideology. The influence of alternative assumptions on religious equality, as well as on educational practice, concerns both groups as they bring their social and political concerns to the conflict over teaching evolution. (See Table 12.1.)

TABLE 12.1.
Contrasting Arguments of Creationists and Evolutionists*

Creationist Argument	Evolutionist Argument
On Scientific Methodology	
Creation theory is as likely a scientific hypothesis as evolution. Neither theory can be supported by observable events, neither can be tested scientifically to predict the outcome of future phenomena, nor are they capable of falsification. Evolutionists, while claiming to be scientific, confuse theory and fact. And it is unscientific to present evolution as a self-evident truth when it is based on unproven *a priori* faith in a chain of natural causes. Based on circumstantial evidence, evolution theory is not useful as a basis for prediction. It is rather, "a hallowed religious dogma that must be defended by censorship of contrary arguments." The situation is a trial of Galileo in reverse.[1]	Creationism is a "gross perversion of scientific theory." Scientific theory is derived from a vast mass of data and hypotheses, consistently analyzed; creation theory is "Godgiven and unquestioned," based on an *a priori* commitment to a six-day creation. Creationists ignore the interplay between fact and theory, eagerly searching for facts to buttress their beliefs. Creationism cannot be submitted to independent testing and has no predictive value, for it is a belief system that must be accepted on faith.
On Moral Implications	
Man is a higher form of life made in the image of God. To emphasize the genetic similarity between animals and man is socially dangerous, encouraging animal-like behavior. As a "religion of relativism," evolution theory denies that there are absolute standards of justice and truth and this has disastrous moral implications.	"Tampering with science education by insisting on the priority of feeling over reason, of spontaneity over discipline, of irrationality over objectivity, the honorable man wrecks his own ideals. By attempting to redefine science for his own purposes, the honorable man finds himself in the company of a young hippie radical representing the counterculture, who indiscriminately is throwing out a life of reason based on objectivity and thus gives himself license to live carelessly and dogmatically."[2]
On Political Implications	
Evolution is a scientific justification for "harmful" political changes. The evo-	Creationism is a form of right-wing conservatism, as evident in the role of

lutionary philosophy, which substitutes concepts of progress for the "dignity of man" has been responsible for "some of the crudest class, race and nationalistic myths of all times: the Nazi notion of master race; the Marxist hatred for the bourgeoisie; and the tyrannical subordination of the worth of the individual to the state."[3]

Reagan appointees in the California Board of Education. "Attempts to legislate belief systems through controlling printed materials in the public schools have frequently been a part of fascism."[4]

On Legal Implications[5]

Public schools cannot legally deal with questions of origin that are the domain of religion. They infringe on constitutional rights as guaranteed under the "establishment of religion" and "free exercise" clauses of the First Amendment, the "equal protection" and due process clauses of the Fourteenth, and constitutional guarantees of freedom of speech. Teaching evolution amounts to the establishment of "secular religion," interfering with free exercise of fundamentalists' truths and violating parental rights. Moreover, restricting the teaching of alternate theories violates the free-speech right of teachers.

Exclusion of creation theory in science classes is justified by the First and Fourteenth Amendments. It is unconstitutional to teach children in a way that would blur the distinction between church and state. Creationism is non-scientific and religious, and therefore to include it would amount to "the establishment of religion." Imposing non-scientific demands would restrict the freedom of teachers to teach and students to learn. To require equal time for doctrines that have no relation to the discipline of biology would impose unconstitutional constraints on the teacher's freedom of speech.

On Religious Equality

To select one set of beliefs over another is to suggest that one group of people is superior to another. Creationists are a persecuted minority. In view of the wide range of beliefs among Americans, teaching evolution is divisive and inequitable and reflects the dogmatism of an established group. "Science has been oversold in Western culture as the sole repository of objective truth . . . the authoritarianism of the medieval

Creationist demands that their beliefs be taught in public schools represent the tyranny of a minority; a few people are using democratic protections to subvert majority interests. To teach creation theory would violate the beliefs of other religious groups. Justice, in this case, would also require teaching hundreds of other mythologies reflecting the belief of the American Indians, Hindus, Buddhists, Moslems, and so church has been replaced by the authoritarianism of rationalistic materialism."[6]

on. Religions can co-exist with science because they operate at a different level of reality.

On Sound Educational Practice

Education in biology is "indoctrination in a religion of secular humanism." It is a breach of academic freedom to prevent the teaching of arguments that have withstood challenges for 6,000 years. "Science demands that our children be taught an unproven, undocumentable theory. There is neither a scientific nor moral base upon which to refuse our school children access to another, much documented theory—the theory of *Genesis* creation." Sound educational practice requires teaching creation as an alternate theory so that students can decide what to believe for themselves.

To include creation theory in scientific classes would be poor pedagogy leading to ridicule and rejection of both science and religion. If creation were presented as an alternate hypothesis, even less would be taught about science than is taught today. Furthermore, it would be a breach of academic freedom to require to teach what is essentially a belief system. In-depth studies of the relationship between science and religion are too sophisticated for public schools. It is sound educational practice to focus on an accurate presentation of scientific fact and leave the teaching of religion to the home.

*SOURCE: From statements at the *Public Hearings on California Biology Textbooks,* Sacramento, 9 November 1972, and from the *BSCS Newsletter* (November 1972), unless otherwise indicated
[1]John N. Moore, "Evaluation, Creation and the Scientific Method," *American Biology Teacher* 35 (January 1973); and editorial, *Christianity Today* 17 (January 1973).
[2]David Ost, "Statement," *American Biology Teacher* 34 (October 1972): 414.
[3]Carl Henry, "Theology and Evolution," in *Evolution and Christian Thought Today,* ed. R. Mixter (Grand Rapids: Erdmans, 1959), p. 218.
[4]Ost, *op. cit.*
[5]Discussion of the legal issues appears in F. S. LeClercq, "The Monkey Laws and the Public Schools: A Second Consumption?" *Vanderbilt Law Review* 27 (March 1974): 209–242.
[6]Duane Gish, "Creation, Evolution and the Historical Evidence," *American Biology Teacher* 35 (March 1973): 140.

The battles between evolutionists and creationists continue—today's expression of the perennial warfare between science and religion. Their persistence suggests that the truce between science and religion, based on the assumption that they deal with separate domains, may be a convenient but unrealistic myth. Religion as well as science purports to be a picture of reality, a means through which people render their lives and the world around them intelligible. The heart of the religious perspective, argues anthropologist Clifford Geertz, is "not the theory that beyond the visible world there lies an invisible one; . . . not even the more diffident opinion that there are things in heaven and earth undreamt of in our philosophies. Rather it is the conviction that the values one holds are grounded in an inherent structure of reality."[18] It is clear that scientific explanations of reality, often unrelated to personal experience, leave many people on very shaky ground. Failing to find a sense of personal integration from scientific beliefs, they grope for more fulfilling constructs.

Faith in science persists when it satisfies a social need, but for many people science has lost its credibility, threatening the plausibility of nonrational beliefs, but hardly removing the uncertainties that seem to call for such beliefs. Thus the revival of fundamentalism fills a social void. The creationists are part of this revival, reflecting a quest for order and authority in a society increasingly influenced by the censors of the right. Using representations that are well adapted to the twentieth century and claiming scientific respectability, they offer intellectual plausibility as well as salvation and the authority of science as well as the certainty of Scripture. Fusing three venerated traditions of American culture—science, religion, and populist democracy—their influence is likely to persist.

Notes

1. Letter from E. G. Lucas to *Science,* 9 March 1973, p. 953.

2. Robert Merton, "Science and Technology in a Democratic Order," *Journal of Legal and Political Sociology* 1 (1942): 115–126. See also Norman Storer, *The Social System of Science* (New York: Holt, Rinehart & Winston, 1966).

3. For a discussion of the nature of proof and explanation in biology, see Michael Ruse, *The Philosophy of Biology* (London: Hutchinson, 1973); *BSCS Newsletter* 49 (November 1972): 3; and also the discussion of the relationship between evidence and theory in Harvey Brooks, "Scientific

Concepts and Cultural Change," *Daedalus* (1964); S. B. Barnes, "On the Reception of Scientific Beliefs," in *Sociology of Science,* ed. S. Barnes (Harmondsworth: Penguin Books, 1972), p. 287.

4. Oscar Handlin, "Ambivalence in a Popular Response to Science," in *Sociology of Science, op. cit.,* pp. 253, 267.

5. Theodore Roszak, "Science Knowledge and Gnosis," *Daedalus* (Summer 1974): 31.

6. Jon Miller, Kenneth Prewitt, and Robert Pearson, *The Attitudes of the US Public Towards Science and Technology* (Chicago: National Opinion Research Center, University of Chicago, 1980). The survey was based on a national sample of 1,635 people over age eighteen.

7. Daniel Yankelovich, "Changing Public Attitudes to Science and the Quality of Life" (edited excerpts from a seminar), *Science Technology and Human Values* 39 (Spring 1982). For a review of various surveys, see Amitai Etzioni and Clyde Nunn, "The Public Appreciation of Science in Contemporary America," *Daedalus* (Summer 1974): 191–205.

8. See discussion in Clifford Geertz, *Islam Observed* (New Haven: Yale University Press, 1968), and *Interpretation of Culture* (New York: Basic Books, 1973).

9. R. M. Young, "Evolutionary Biology and Ideology: Then and Now," *Science Studies* 1 (1971): 177–206, discusses these tendencies to extend biology and, in particular, the implications of the work of Ardrey and Lorenz.

10. The physicist Victor Weisskopf has discussed some of the implications of overextending the scientific approach to deal with human experience in an address to the American Academy of Arts and Sciences, *Bulletin* 27 (March 1975).

11. James Raths, "The Emperor's Clothes Phenomenon in Science Education," *Journal of Research in Science Teaching* 10 (1973): 211. For problems in the communication of science, see also Philippe Roqueplo, *Le Partage du Savior* (Paris: Editions du Seuil, 1974). For reviews of the effectiveness of the new science curriculum, see A. L. Balzer et al., "A Review of Research on Teacher Behavior Relating to Science Education (Columbus: ERIC Information Analysis Center, Ohio State University December 1973), 87–93; D. Novak, "A Summary of Research and Science Education" (Columbus: ERIC Information Analysis Center, Ohio State University, December 1973), pp. 32–51. These studies also note the continuing emphasis on skills of recall in the science classroom despite the "inquiry-oriented" approach in the new curriculum.

12. This point is well developed by a study examining the history of the study of genetics in relation to widely held beliefs during different periods.

See W. Provine, "Genetics and the Biology of Race Crossing," *Science,* 23 November 1973, pp. 790–798.

13. Stephen G. Brush, "Should the History of Science Be Rated X," *Science,* 22 March 1974, pp. 164 ff.

14. Statement by Paul Kurtz, editor of *The Humanist,* in justifying the statement by 186 scientists calling astrologers "charlatans who have no rational basis for their beliefs." See *The Humanist* (October/November 1975).

15. Leon Festinger, *A Theory of Cognitive Dissonance* (Evanston, Ill.: Row Peterson, 1957).

16. Peter Berger, *Sacred Canopy* (New York: Doubleday, 1967), argues that a prerequisite for belief is social support—that definitions of social reality are real insofar as they are confirmed by day-to-day interaction.

17. G. Ledyard Stebbins, "The Evolution of Design," *American Biology Teacher* 35 (February 1973): 58.

18. Geertz, *Islam Observed, op. cit.*

Appendix 1

REV. BILL McLEAN, ET AL.   PLAINTIFFS

VS.   NO. LR C 81 322

THE ARKANSAS BOARD OF EDUCATION, ET AL.   DEFENDANTS

INJUNCTION

Pursuant to the Court's Memorandum Opinion filed this date, the defendants and each of them and all their servants and employees are hereby permanently enjoined from implementing in any manner Act 590 of the Acts of Arkansas of 1981.

It is so ordered this January 5, 1982.

William R. Overton

UNITED STATES DISTRICT JUDGE

IN THE UNITED STATES DISTRICT COURT
EASTERN DISTRICT OF ARKANSAS
WESTERN DIVISION

REV. BILL McLEAN, ET AL.   PLAINTIFFS
VS.   NO. LR C 81 322
THE ARKANSAS BOARD OF EDUCATION, ET AL.   DEFENDANTS

MEMORANDUM OPINION

Introduction

On March 19, 1981, the Governor of Arkansas signed into law Act 590
of 1981, entitled the "Balanced Treatment for Creation-Science and Evolution-Science Act." The Act is codified as Ark. Stat. Ann. §80-1663, *et
seq.*, (1981 Supp.). Its essential mandate is stated in its first sentence:
"Public schools within this State shall give balanced treatment to creation-
science and to evolution-science." On May 27, 1981, this suit was filed[1]
challenging the constitutional validity of Act 590 on three distinct
grounds.

First, it is contended that Act 590 constitutes an establishment of religion prohibited by the First Amendment to the Constitution, which is
made applicable to the states by the Fourteenth Amendment. Second, the
plaintiffs argue the Act violates a right to academic freedom which they
say is guaranteed to students and teachers by the Free Speech Clause of
the First Amendment. Third, plaintiffs allege the Act is impermissibly
vague and thereby violates the Due Process Clause of the Fourteenth
Amendment.

The individual plaintiffs include the resident Arkansas Bishops of the
United Methodist, Episcopal, Roman Catholic and African Methodist
Episcopal Churches, the principal official of the Presbyterian Churches in
Arkansas, other United Methodist, Southern Baptist and Presbyterian
clergy, as well as several persons who sue as parents and next friends of
minor children attending Arkansas public schools. One plaintiff is a high
school biology teacher. All are also Arkansas taxpayers. Among the or-
ganizational plaintiffs are the American Jewish Congress, the Union of
American Hebrew Congregations, the American Jewish Committee, the
Arkansas Education Association, the National Association of Biology

---

[1]The complaint is based on 42 U.S.C. §1983, which provides a remedy against any
person who, acting under color of state law, deprives another of any right, privilege
or immunity guaranteed by the United States Constitution or federal law.

This Court's jurisdiction arises under 18 U.S.C. §§1331, 1343(3) and 1343(4).
The power to issue declaratory judgments is expressed in 28 U.S.C. §§2201 and
2202.

Teachers and the National Coalition for Public Education and Religious Liberty, all of which sue on behalf of members living in Arkansas.[2]

The defendants include the Arkansas Board of Education and its members, the Director of the Department of Education, and the State Textbooks and Instructional Materials Selecting Committee.[3] The Pulaski County Special School District and its Directors and Superintendent were voluntarily dismissed by the plaintiffs at the pre-trial conference held October 1, 1981.

The trial commenced December 7, 1981, and continued through December 17, 1981. This Memorandum Opinion constitutes the Court's findings of fact and conclusions of law. Further orders and judgment will be in conformity with this opinion.

There is no controversy over the legal standards under which the Establishment Clause portion of this case must be judged. The Supreme Court has on a number of occasions expounded on the meaning of the clause, and the pronouncements are clear. Often the issue has arisen in the context of public education, as it has here. In *Everson v. Board of Education,* 330 U.S. 1, 15–16 (1947), Justice Black stated:

> "The 'establishment of religion' clause of the First Amendment means at least this: Neither a state nor the Federal Government can set up a church. Neither can pass laws which aid one religion, aid all religions, or prefer one religion over another. Neither can force nor influence a person to go to or to remain away from church against his will or force him to profess a belief or disbelief in any religion. No person can be punished for entertaining or professing religious beliefs or disbeliefs, for church-attendance or non-attendance. No tax, large or small, can be levied to support any religious activities or institutions, whatever they may be called, or whatever form they may adopt to teach or practice religion. Neither a state nor the Federal Government can, openly or secretly, participate in the affairs of any religious organizations or groups and *vice versa.* In the words of Jefferson, the clause . . . was intended to erect 'a wall of separation between church and State.' "

---

[2]The facts necessary to establish the plaintiffs' standing to sue are contained in the joint stipulation of facts, which is hereby adopted and incorporated herein by reference.

There is no doubt that the case is ripe for adjudication.

[3]The State of Arkansas was dismissed as a defendant because of its immunity from suit under the Eleventh Amendment. *Hans v. Louisiana,* 134 U.S. 1 (1890).

The Establishment Clause thus enshrines two central values: voluntarism and pluralism. And it is in the area of the public schools that these values must be guarded most vigilantly.

"Designed to serve as perhaps the most powerful agency for promoting cohesion among a heterogeneous democratic people, the public school must keep scrupulously free from entanglement in the strife of sects. The preservation of the community from divisive conflicts, of Government from irreconcilable pressures by religious groups, of religion from censorship and coercion however subtly exercised, requires strict confinement of the State to instruction other than religious, leaving to the individual's church and home, indoctrination in the faith of his choice."

McCollum v. Board of Education, 333 U.S. 203, 216–217 (1948), (Opinion of Frankfurter, J., joined by Jackson, Burton and Rutledge, J.J.).

The specific formulation of the establishment prohibition has been refined over the years, but its meaning has not varied from the principles articulated by Justice Black in *Everson.* In *Abbington School District v. Schempp,* 374 U.S. 203, 222 (1963), Justice Clark stated that "to withstand the strictures of the Establishment Clause there must be a secular legislative purpose and a primary effect that neither advances nor inhibits religion." The Court found it quite clear that the First Amendment does not permit a state to require the daily reading of the Bible in public schools, for "[s]urely the place of the Bible as an instrument of religion cannot be gainsaid." *Id.* at 224. Similarly, in *Engel v. Vitale,* 370 U.S. 421 (1962), the Court held that the First Amendment prohibited the New York Board of Regents from requiring the daily recitation of a certain prayer in the schools. With characteristic succinctness, Justice Black wrote, "Under [the First] Amendment's prohibition against governmental establishment of religion, as reinforced by the provisions of the Fourteenth Amendment, government in this country, be it state or federal, is without power to prescribe by law any particular form of prayer which is to be used as an official prayer in carrying on any program of governmentally sponsored religious activity." *Id.* at 430. Black also identified the objective at which the Establishment Clause was aimed: "Its first and most immediate purpose rested on the belief that a union of government and religion tends to destroy government and to degrade religion." *Id.* at 431.

Most recently, the Supreme Court has held that the clause prohibits a state from requiring the posting of the Ten Commandments in public school classrooms for the same reasons that officially imposed daily Bible reading is prohibited. *Stone v. Graham,* 449 U.S. 39 (1980). The opinion in *Stone* relies on the most recent formulation of the Establishment Clause test, that of *Lemon v. Kurtzman,*

> "First, the statute must have a secular legislative purpose; second, its principal or primary effect must be one that neither advances nor inhibits religion . . .; finally, the statute must not foster 'an excessive government entanglement with religion.' "

Stone v. Graham, 449 U.S. at 40.

It is under this three part test that the evidence in this case must be judged. Failure on any of these grounds is fatal to the enactment.

II.

The religious movement known as Fundamentalism began in nineteenth century America as part of evangelical Protestantism's response to social changes, new religious thought and Darwinism. Fundamentalists viewed these developments as attacks on the Bible and as responsible for a decline in traditional values.

The various manifestations of Fundamentalism have had a number of common characteristics,[4] but a central premise has always been a literal interpretation of the Bible and a belief in the inerrancy of the Scriptures. Following World War I, there was again a perceived decline in traditional morality, and Fundamentalism focused on evolution as responsible for the decline. One aspect of their efforts, particularly in the South, was the promotion of statutes prohibiting the teaching of evolution in public schools. In Arkansas, this resulted in the adoption of Initiated Act 1 of 1929.[5]

Between the 1920's and early 1960's, anti-evolutionary sentiment had

[4]The authorities differ as to generalizations which may be made about Fundamentalism. For example, Dr. Geisler testified to the widely held view that there are five beliefs characteristic of all Fundamentalist movements, in addition, of course, to the inerrancy of Scripture: (1) belief in the virgin birth of Christ, (2) belief in the deity of Christ, (3) belief in the substitutional atonement of Christ, (4) belief in the second coming of Christ, and (5) belief in the physical resurrection of all departed souls. Dr. Marsden, however, testified that this generalization, which has been common in religious scholarship, is now thought to be historical error. There is no doubt, however, that all Fundamentalists take the Scriptures as inerrant and probably most take them as literally true.

[5]Initiated Act 1 of 1929, Ark. Stat. Ann. §80–1627 *et seq.,* which prohibited the teaching of evolution in Arkansas schools, is discussed *infra* at text accompanying note 26.

a subtle but pervasive influence on the teaching of biology in public schools. Generally, textbooks avoided the topic of evolution and did not mention the name of Darwin. Following the launch of the Sputnik satellite by the Soviet Union in 1957, the National Science Foundation funded several programs designed to modernize the teaching of science in the nation's schools. The Biological Sciences Curriculum Study (BSCS), a nonprofit organization, was among those receiving grants for curriculum study and revision. Working with scientists and teachers, BSCS developed a series of biology texts which, although emphasizing different aspects of biology, incorporated the theory of evolution as a major theme. The success of the BSCS effort is shown by the fact that fifty percent of American school children currently use BSCS books directly and the curriculum is incorporated indirectly in virtually all biology texts. (Testimony of Mayer; Nelkin, Px 1)[6]

In the early 1960's, there was again a resurgence of concern among Fundamentalists about the loss of traditional values and a fear of growing secularism in society. The Fundamentalist movement became more active and has steadily grown in numbers and political influence. There is an emphasis among current Fundamentalists on the literal interpretation of the Bible and the Book of Genesis as the sole source of knowledge about origins.

The term "scientific creationism" first gained currency around 1965 following publication of *The Genesis Flood* in 1961 by Whitcomb and Morris. There is undoubtedly some connection between the appearance of the BSCS texts emphasizing evolutionary thought and efforts by Fundamentalists to attack the theory. (Mayer)

In the 1960's and early 1970's, several Fundamentalist organizations were formed to promote the idea that the Book of Genesis was supported by scientific data. The terms "creation science" and "scientific creationism" have been adopted by these Fundamentalists as descriptive of their study of creation and the origins of man. Perhaps the leading creationist organization is the Institute for Creation Research (ICR), which is affiliated with the Christian Heritage College and supported by the Scott Memorial Baptist Church in San Diego, California. The ICR, through the Creation-Life Publishing Company, is the leading publisher of creation science material. Other creation science organizations include the Creation Science Research Center (CSRC) of San Diego and the Bible Science Association of Minneapolis, Minnesota. In 1963, the Creation Research

[6]Subsequent references to the testimony will be made by the last name of the witness only. References to documentary exhibits will be by the name of the author and the exhibit number.

Society (CRS) was formed from a schism in the American Scientific Affiliation (ASA). It is an organization of literal Fundamentalists[7] who have the equivalent of a master's degree in some recognized area of science. A purpose of the organization is "to reach all people with the vital message of the scientific and historic truth about creation." Nelkin, *The Science Textbook Controversies and the Politics of Equal Time*, 66. Similarly, the CSRC was formed in 1970 from a split in the CRS. Its aim has been "to reach the 63 million children of the United States with the scientific teaching of Biblical creationism." *Id.* at 69.

Among creationist writers who are recognized as authorities in the field by other creationists are Henry M. Morris, Duane Gish, G. E. Parker, Harold S. Slusher, Richard B. Bliss, John W. Moore, Martin E. Clark, W. L. Wysong, Robert E. Kofahl and Kelly L. Segraves. Morris is Director of ICR, Gish is Associate Director and Segraves is associated with CSRC.

Creationists view evolution as a source of society's ills, and the writings of Morris and Clark are typical expressions of that view.

"Evolution is thus not only anti-Biblical and anti-Christian, but it is utterly unscientific and impossible as well. But it has served effectively as the pseudo-scientific basis of atheism, agnosticism, socialism, fascism, and numerous other false and dangerous philosophies over the past century."

Morris and Clark, *The Bible Has The Answer*, (Px 31 and Pretrial Px 89).[8]

Creationists have adopted the view of Fundamentalists generally that

[7] Applicants for membership in the CRS must subscribe to the following statement of belief: "(1) The Bible is the written Word of God, and because we believe it to be inspired thruout (sic), all of its assertions are historically and scientifically true in all of the original autographs. To the student of nature, this means that the account of origins in Genesis is a factual presentation of simple historical truths. (2) All basic types of living things, including man, were made by direct creative acts of God during Creation Week as described in Genesis. Whatever biological changes have occurred since Creation have accomplished only changes within the original created kinds. (3) The great Flood described in Genesis, commonly referred to as the Noachian Deluge, was an historical event, worldwide in its extent and effect. (4) Finally, we are an organization of Christian men of science, who accept Jesus Christ as our Lord and Savior. The account of the special creation of Adam and Eve as one man and one woman, and their subsequent Fall into sin, is the basis for our belief in the necessity of a Savior for all mankind. Therefore, salvation can come only thru (sic) accepting Jesus Christ as our Savior." (Px 115)
[8] Because of the voluminous nature of the documentary exhibits, the parties were directed by pre-trial order to submit their proposed exhibits for the Court's convenience prior to trial. The numbers assigned to the pre-trial submissions do not correspond with those assigned to the same documents at trial and, in some instances, the pre-trial submissions are more complete.

there are only two positions with respect to the origins of the earth and life: belief in the inerrancy of the Genesis story of creation and of a worldwide flood as fact, or belief in what they call evolution.

Henry Morris has stated, "It is impossible to devise a legitimate means of harmonizing the Bible with evolution." Morris, "Evolution and the Bible," *ICR Impact Series* Number 5 (undated, unpaged), quoted in Mayer, Px 8, at 3. This dualistic approach to the subject of origins permeates the creationist literature.

The creationist organizations consider the introduction of creation science into the public schools part of their ministry. The ICR has published at least two pamphlets[9] containing suggested methods for convincing school boards, administrators and teachers that creationism should be taught in public schools. The ICR has urged its proponents to encourage school officials to voluntarily add creationism to the curriculum.[10]

Citizens For Fairness In Education is an organization based in Anderson, South Carolina, formed by Paul Ellwanger, a respiratory therapist who is trained in neither law nor science. Mr. Ellwanger is of the opinion that evolution is the forerunner of many social ills, including Nazism, racism and abortion. (Ellwanger Depo. at 32–34). About 1977, Ellwanger collected several proposed legislative acts with the idea of preparing a model state act requiring the teaching of creationism as science in opposition to evolution. One of the proposals he collected was prepared by Wendell Bird, who is now a staff attorney for ICR.[11] From these various proposals, Ellwanger prepared a "model act" which calls for "balanced treatment" of "scientific creationism" and "evolution" in public schools. He circulated the proposed act to various people and organizations around the country.

Mr. Ellwanger's views on the nature of creation science are entitled to

[9] Px 130, Morris, *Introducing Scientific Creationism Into the Public Schools* (1975), and Bird, "Resolution for Balanced Presentation of Evolution and Scientific Creationism," *ICR Impact Series* No. 71, App. 14 to Plaintiffs' Pretrial Brief.

[10] The creationists often show candor in their proselytization. Henry Morris has stated, "Even if a favorable statute or court decision is obtained, it will probably be declared unconstitutional, especially if the legislation or injunction refers to the Bible account of creation." In the same vein he notes, "The only effective way to get creationism taught properly is to have it taught by teachers who are both willing and able to do it. Since most teachers now are neither willing nor able, they must first be both persuaded and instructed themselves." Px 130, Morris, *Introducing Scientific Creationism Into the Public Schools* (1975) (unpaged).

[11] Mr. Bird sought to participate in this litigation by representing a number of individuals who wanted to intervene as defendants. The application for intervention was denied by this Court. *McLean v. Arkansas,* _____ F. Supp. _____, (E.D. Ark. 1981), aff'd. *per curiam,* Slip Op. No. 81-2023 (8th Cir. Oct. 16, 1981).

some weight since he personally drafted the model act which became Act 590. His evidentiary deposition with exhibits and unnumbered attachments (produced in response to a subpoena *duces tecum*) speaks to both the intent of the Act and the scientific merits of creation science. Mr. Ellwanger does not believe creation science is a science. In a letter to Pastor Robert E. Hays he states, "While neither evolution nor creation can qualify as a scientific theory, and since it is virtually impossible at this point to educate the whole world that evolution is not a true scientific theory, we have freely used these terms—the evolution theory and the theory of scientific creationism—in the bill's text." (Unnumbered attachment to Ellwanger Depo., at 2.) He further states in a letter to Mr. Tom Bethell, "As we examine evolution (remember, we're not making any scientific claims for creation, but we are challenging evolution's claim to be scientific) . . ." (Unnumbered attachment to Ellwanger Depo. at 1.)

Ellwanger's correspondence on the subject shows an awareness that Act 590 is a religious crusade, coupled with a desire to conceal this fact. In a letter to State Senator Bill Keith of Louisiana, he says, "I view this whole battle as one between God and anti-God forces, though I know there are a large number of evolutionists who believe in God." And further, ". . . it behooves Satan to do all he can to thwart our efforts and confuse the issue at every turn." Yet Ellwanger suggests to Senator Keith, "If you have a clear choice between having grassroots leaders of this statewide bill promotion effort to be ministerial or non-ministerial, be sure to opt for the non-ministerial. It does the bill effort no good to have ministers out there in the public forum and the adversary will surely pick at this point . . . Ministerial persons can accomplish a tremendous amount of work from behind the scenes, encouraging their congregations to take the organizational and P.R. initiatives. And they can lead their churches in storming Heaven with prayers for help against so tenacious an adversary." (Unnumbered attachment to Ellwanger Depo. at 1.)

Ellwanger shows a remarkable degree of political candor, if not finesse, in a letter to State Senator Joseph Carlucci of Florida:

"2. It would be very wise, if not actually essential, that all of us who are engaged in this legislative effort be careful not to present our position and our work in a religious framework. For example, in written communications that might somehow be shared with those other persons whom we may be trying to convince, it would be well to exclude our own personal testimony and/or witness for Christ, but rather, if we are so moved, to give that testimony on a separate attached note." (Unnumbered attachment to Ellwanger Depo. at 1.)

The same tenor is reflected in a letter by Ellwanger to Mary Ann Miller, a member of FLAG (Family, Life, America under God) who lobbied the Arkansas Legislature in favor of Act 590:

". . . we'd like to suggest that you and your co-workers be very cautious about mixing creation-science with creation-religion . . . Please urge your co-workers not to allow themselves to get sucked into the 'religion' trap of mixing the two together, for such mixing does incalculable harm to the legislative thrust. It could even bring public opinion to bear adversely upon the higher courts that will eventually have to pass judgment on the constitutionality of this new law." (Ex. 1 to Miller Depo.)

Perhaps most interesting, however, is Mr. Ellwanger's testimony in his deposition as to his strategy for having the model act implemented:

Q. You're trying to play on other people's religious motives.
A. I'm trying to play on their emotions, love, hate, their likes, dislikes, because I don't know any other way to involve, to get humans to become involved in human endeavors. I see emotions as being a healthy and legitimate means of getting people's feelings into action, and . . . I believe that the predominance of population in American that represents the greatest potential for taking some kind of action in this area is a Christian community. I see the Jewish community as far less potential in taking action . . . but I've seen a lot of interest among Christians and I feel, why not exploit that to get the bill going if that's what it takes. (Ellwanger Depo. at 146–147.)

Mr. Ellwanger's ultimate purpose is revealed in the closing of his letter to Mr. Tom Bethell: "Perhaps all this is old hat to you, Tom, and if so, I'd appreciate your telling me so and perhaps where you've heard it before —the idea of killing evolution instead of playing these debating games that we've been playing for nigh over a decade already." (Unnumbered attachment to Ellwanger Depo. at 3.)

It was out of this milieu that Act 590 emerged. The Reverend W. A. Blount, a Biblical literalist who is pastor of a church in the Little Rock area and was, in February, 1981, chairman of the Greater Little Rock Evangelical Fellowship, was among those who received a copy of the model act from Ellwanger.[12]

---

[12]The model act had been revised to insert "creation science" in lieu of creationism because Ellwanger had the impression people thought creationism was too religious

At Reverend Blount's request, the Evangelical Fellowship unanimously adopted a resolution to seek introduction of Ellwanger's act in the Arkansas Legislature. A committee composed of two ministers, Curtis Thomas and W. A. Young, was appointed to implement the resolution. Thomas obtained from Ellwanger a revised copy of the model act which he transmitted to Carl Hunt, a business associate of Senator James L. Holsted, with the request that Hunt prevail upon Holsted to introduce the act.

Holsted, a self-described "born again" Christian Fundamentalist, introduced the act in the Arkansas Senate. He did not consult the State Department of Education, scientists, science educators or the Arkansas Attorney General.[13] The Act was not referred to any Senate committee for hearing and was passed after only a few minutes' discussion on the Senate floor. In the House of Representatives, the bill was referred to the Education Committee which conducted a perfunctory fifteen minute hearing. No scientist testified at the hearing, nor was any representative from the State Department of Education called to testify.

Ellwanger's model act was enacted into law in Arkansas as Act 590 without amendment or modification other than minor typographical changes. The legislative "findings of fact" in Ellwanger's act and Act 590 are identical, although no meaningful fact-finding process was employed by the General Assembly.

Ellwanger's efforts in preparation of the model act and campaign for its adoption in the states were motivated by his opposition to the theory of evolution and his desire to see the Biblical version of creation taught in the public schools. There is no evidence that the pastors, Blount, Thomas, Young or The Greater Little Rock Evangelical Fellowship were motivated by anything other than their religious convictions when proposing its adoption or during their lobbying efforts in its behalf. Senator Holsted's sponsorship and lobbying efforts in behalf of the Act were motivated solely by his religious beliefs and desire to see the Biblical version of creation taught in the public schools.[14]

---

a term. (Ellwanger Depo. at 79.)

[13]The original model act had been introduced in the South Carolina Legislature, but had died without action after the South Carolina Attorney General had opined that the act was unconstitutional.

[14]Specifically, Senator Holsted testified that he holds to a literal interpretation of the Bible; that the bill was compatible with his religious beliefs; that the bill does favor the position of literalists; that his religious convictions were a factor in his sponsorship of the bill; and that he stated publicly to the *Arkansas Gazette* (although not on the floor of the Senate) contemporaneously with the legislative debate that the bill does presuppose the existence of a divine creator. There is no doubt that Senator Holsted knew he was sponsoring the teaching of a religious doctrine. His view was

The State of Arkansas, like a number of states whose citizens have relatively homogeneous religious beliefs, has a long history of official opposition to evolution which is motivated by adherence to Fundamentalist beliefs in the inerrancy of the Book of Genesis. This history is documented in Justice Fortas' opinion in *Epperson v. Arkansas*, 393 U.S. 97 (1968), which struck down Initiated Act 1 of 1929, Ark. Stat. Ann. §§80-1627-1628, prohibiting the teaching of the theory of evolution. To this same tradition may be attributed Initiated Act 1 of 1930, Ark. Stat. Ann. §80-1606 (Repl. 1980), requiring "the reverent daily reading of a portion of the English Bible" in every public school classroom in the State.[15]

It is true, as defendants argue, that courts should look to legislative statements of a statute's purpose in Establishment Clause cases and accord such pronouncements great deference. See, e.g., *Committee for Public Education & Religious Liberty v. Nyquist*, 413 U.S. 756, 773 (1973) and *McGowan v. Maryland*, 366 U.S. 420, 445 (1961). Defendants also correctly state the principle that remarks by the sponsor or author of a bill are not considered controlling in analyzing legislative intent. See, e.g., *United States v. Emmons*, 410 U.S. 396 (1973) and *Chrysler Corp. v. Brown*, 441 U.S. 281 (1979).

Courts are not bound, however, by legislative statements of purpose or legislative disclaimers. *Stone v. Graham*, 449 U.S. 39 (1980); *Abbington School Dist. v. Schempp*, 374 U.S. 203 (1963). In determining the legislative purpose of a statute, courts may consider evidence of the historical context of the Act, *Epperson v. Arkansas*, 393 U.S. 97 (1968), the specific sequence of events leading up to passage of the Act, departures from normal procedural sequences, substantive departures from the normal, *Village of Arlington Heights v. Metropolitan Housing Corp.*, 429 U.S. 252 (1977), and contemporaneous statements of the legislative sponsor, *Fed. Energy Admin. v. Algonquin SNG, Inc.*, 426 U.S. 548, 564 (1976).

The unusual circumstances surrounding the passage of Act 590, as well as the substantive law of the First Amendment, warrant an inquiry into the stated legislative purposes. The author of the Act had publicly proclaimed the sectarian purpose of the proposal. The Arkansas residents who sought legislative sponsorship of the bill did so for a purely sectarian purpose. These circumstances alone may not be particularly persuasive, but when considered with the publicly announced motives of the legisla-

---

that the bill did not violate the First Amendment because, as he saw it, it did not favor one denomination over another.

[15]This statute is, of course, clearly unconstitutional under the Supreme Court's decision in *Abbington School Dist. v. Schempp*, 374 U.S. 203 (1963).

tive sponsor made contemporaneously with the legislative process; the lack of any legislative investigation, debate or consultation with any educators or scientists; the unprecedented intrusion in school curriculum;[16] and official history of the State of Arkansas on the subject, it is obvious that the statement of purposes has little, if any, support in fact. The State failed to produce any evidence which would warrant an inference or conclusion that at any point in the process anyone considered the legitimate educational value of the Act. It was simply and purely an effort to introduce the Biblical version of creation into the public school curricula. The only inference which can be drawn from these circumstances is that the Act was passed with the specific purpose by the General Assembly of advancing religion. The Act therefore fails the first prong of the three-pronged test, that of secular legislative purpose, as articulated in *Lemon v. Kurtzman, supra,* and *Stone v. Graham, supra.*

III.

If the defendants are correct and the Court is limited to an examination of the language of the Act, the evidence is overwhelming that both the purpose and effect of Act 590 is the advancement of religion in the public schools.

Section 4 of the Act provides:
Definitions. As used in this Act:

(a) "Creation-science" means the scientific evidences for creation and inferences from those scientific evidences. Creation-science includes the scientific evidences and related inferences that indicate: (1) Sudden creation of the universe, energy, and life from nothing; (2) The insufficiency of mutation and natural selection in bringing about development of all living kinds from a single organism; (3) Changes only within fixed limits of originally created kinds of plants and animals; (4) Separate ancestry for man and apes; (5) Explanation of the earth's geology by catastrophism, including the occurrence of a worldwide flood; and (6) A relatively recent inception of the earth and living kinds. (b) "Evolution-science" means the scientific evidences for evo-

---

[16]The joint stipulation of facts establishes that the following areas are the only *information* specifically required by statute to be taught in all Arkansas schools: (1) the effects of alcohol and narcotics on the human body, (2) conservation of national resources, (3) Bird Week, (4) Fire Prevention, and (5) Flag etiquette. Additionally, certain specific courses, such as American history and Arkansas history, must be completed by each student before graduation from high school.

lution and inferences from those scientific evidences. Evolution-science includes the scientific evidences and related inferences that indicate: (1) Emergence by naturalistic processes of the universe from disordered matter and emergence of life from nonlife; (2) The sufficiency of mutation and natural selection in bringing about development of present living kinds from simple earlier kinds; (3) Emergence by mutation and natural selection of present living kinds from simple earlier kinds; (4) Emergence of man from a common ancestor with apes; (5) Explanation of the earth's geology and the evolutionary sequence by uniformitarianism; and (6) An inception several billion years ago of the earth and somewhat later of life.(c) "Public schools" mean public secondary and elementary schools.

The evidence establishes that the definition of "creation science" contained in 4(a) has as its unmentioned reference the first 11 chapters of the Book of Genesis. Among the many creation epics in human history, the account of sudden creation from nothing, or *creatio ex nihilo*, and subsequent destruction of the world by flood is unique to Genesis. The concepts of 4(a) are the literal Fundamentalists' view of Genesis. Section 4(a) is unquestionably a statement of religion, with the exception of 4(a)(2) which is a negative thrust aimed at what the creationists understand to be the theory of evolution.[17]

Both the concepts and wording of Section 4(a) convey an inescapable religiosity. Section 4(a)(1) describes "sudden creation of the universe, energy and life from nothing." Every theologian who testified, including defense witnesses, expressed the opinion that the statement referred to a supernatural creation which was performed by God.

Defendants argue that: (1) the fact that 4(a) conveys ideas similar to the literal interpretation of Genesis does not make it conclusively a statement of religion; (2) that reference to a creation from nothing is not necessarily a religious concept since the Act only suggests a creator who has power, intelligence and a sense of design and not necessarily the attributes of love, compassion and justice;[18] and (3) that simply teaching about the concept

---

[17]Paul Ellwanger stated in his deposition that he did not know why Section 4(a)(2) (insufficiency of mutation and natural selection) was included as an evidence supporting creation science. He indicated that he was not a scientist, "but these are the postulates that have been laid down by creation scientists." Ellwanger Depo. at 136.

[18]Although defendants must make some effort to cast the concept of creation in non-religious terms, this effort surely causes discomfort to some of the Act's more theologically sophisticated supporters. The concept of a creator God distinct from the God of love and mercy is closely similar to the Marcion and Gnostic heresies, among the deadliest to threaten the early Christian church. These heresies had

of a creator is not a religious exercise unless the student is required to make a commitment to the concept of a creator.

The evidence fully answers these arguments. The ideas of 4(a) (1) are not merely similar to the literal interpretation of Genesis; they are identical and parallel to no other story of creation.[19]

The argument that creation from nothing in 4(a)(1) does not involve a supernatural deity has no evidentiary or rational support. To the contrary, "creation out of nothing" is a concept unique to Western religions. In traditional Western religious thought, the conception of a creator of the world is a conception of God. Indeed, creation of the world "out of nothing" is the ultimate religious statement because God is the only actor. As Dr. Langdon Gilkey noted, the Act refers to one who has the power to bring all the universe into existence from nothing. The only "one" who has this power is God.[20]

The leading creationist writers, Morris and Gish, acknowledge that the idea of creation described in 4(a)(1) is the concept of creation by God and make no pretense to the contrary.[21] The idea of sudden creation from nothing, or *creatio ex nihilo,* is an inherently religious concept. (Vawter, Gilkey, Geisler, Ayala, Blount, Hicks.)

The argument advanced by defendants' witness, Dr. Norman Geisler, that teaching the existence of God is not religious unless the teaching seeks

---

much to do with development and adoption of the Apostle's Creed as the official credal statement of the Roman Catholic Church in the West. (Gilkey.)

[19]The parallels between Section 4(a) and Genesis are quite specific: (1) "sudden creation from nothing" is taken from Genesis, 1:1-10 (Vawter, Gilkey); (2) destruction of the world by a flood of divine origin is a notion peculiar to Judeo-Christian tradition and is based on Chapters 7 and 8 of Genesis (Vawter); (3) the term "kinds" has no fixed scientific meaning, but appears repeatedly in Genesis (all scientific witnesses); (4) "relatively recent inception" means an age of the earth from 6,000 to 10,000 years and is based on the genealogy of the Old Testament using the rather astronomical ages assigned to the patriarchs (Gilkey and several of defendants' scientific witnesses); (5) Separate ancestry of man and ape focuses on the portion of the theory of evolution which Fundamentalists find most offensive, *Epperson v. Arkansas,* 393 U.S. 97 (1968).

[20]"[C]oncepts concerning . . . a supreme being of some sort are manifestly religious . . . These concepts do not shed that religiosity merely because they are presented as philosophy or as a science . . ." *Malnak v. Yogi,* 440 F. Supp. 1284, 1322 (D.N.J. 1977); *aff'd per curiam,* 592 F.2d 197 (3d Cir. 1979).

[21]See, e.g., Px 76, Morris, *et al, Scientific Creationism,* 203 (1980) ("If creation really is a fact, this means there is a *Creator,* and the universe is His creation.") Numerous other examples of such admissions can be found in the many exhibits which represent creationist literature, but no useful purpose would be served here by a potentially endless listing.

a commitment, is contrary to common understanding and contradicts settled case law. *Stone v. Graham,* 449 U.S. 39 (1980); *Abbington School District v. Schempp,* 374 U.S. 203 (1963).

The facts that creation science is inspired by the Book of Genesis and that Section 4(a) is consistent with a literal interpretation of Genesis leave no doubt that a major effect of the Act is the advancement of particular religious beliefs. The legal impact of this conclusion will be discussed further at the conclusion of the Court's evaluation of the scientific merit of creation science.

IV. (A)

The approach to teaching "creation science" and "evolution science" found in Act 590 is identical to the two-model approach espoused by the Institute for Creation Research and is taken almost verbatim from ICR writings. It is an extension of Fundamentalists' view that one must either accept the literal interpretation of Genesis or else believe in the godless system of evolution.

The two model approach of the creationists is simply a contrived dualism[22] which has no scientific factual basis or legitimate educational purpose. It assumes only two explanations for the origins of life and existence of man, plants and animals: It was either the work of a creator or it was not. Application of these two models, according to creationists, and the defendants, dictates that all scientific evidence which fails to support the theory of evolution is necessarily scientific evidence in support of creationism and is, therefore, creation science "evidence" in support of Section 4(a).

[22]Morris, the Director of ICR and one who first advocated the two model approach, insists that a true Christian cannot compromise with the theory of evolution and that the Genesis version of creation and the theory of evolution are mutually exclusive. Px 31, Morris, *Studies in the Bible & Science,* 102–103. The two model approach was the subject of Dr. Richard Bliss's doctoral dissertation. (Dx 35). It is presented in Bliss, *Origins: Two Models-Evolution, Creation* (1978). Moreover, the two model approach merely casts in educationalist language the dualism which appears in all creationist literature—creation (i.e. God) and evolution are presented as two alternative and mutually exclusive theories. See, e.g., Px 75, Morris, *Scientific Creationism* (1974) (public school edition); Px 59, Fox, *Fossils: Hard Facts from the Earth.* Particularly illustrative is PX 61, Boardman, *et al, Worlds Without End* (1971), a CSRC publication: "One group of scientists, known as creationists, believe that God, in a miraculous manner, created all matter and energy . . .

"Scientists who insist that the universe just grew, by accident, from a mass of hot gases without the direction or help of a Creator are known as evolutionists."

IV. (B)

The emphasis on origins as an aspect of the theory of evolution is peculiar to creationist literature. Although the subject of origins of life is within the province of biology, the scientific community does not consider origins of life a part of evolutionary theory. The theory of evolution assumes the existence of life and is directed to an explanation of *how* life evolved. Evolution does not presuppose the absence of a creator or God and the plain inference conveyed by Section 4 is erroneous.[23]

As a statement of the theory of evolution, Section 4(b) is simply a hodgepodge of limited assertions, many of which are factually inaccurate.

For example, although 4(b)(2) asserts, as a tenet of evolutionary theory, "the sufficiency of mutation and natural selection in bringing about the existence of present living kinds from simple earlier kinds," Drs. Ayala and Gould both stated that biologists know that these two processes do not account for all significant evolutionary change. They testified to such phenomena as recombination, the founder effect, genetic drift and the theory of punctuated equilibrium, which are believed to play important evolutionary roles. Section 4(b) omits any reference to these. Moreover, 4(b) utilizes the term "kinds" which all scientists said is not a word of science and has no fixed meaning. Additionally, the Act presents both evolution and creation science as "package deals." Thus, evidence critical of some aspect of what the creationists define as evolution is taken as support for a theory which includes a worldwide flood and a relatively young earth.[24]

IV. (C)

In addition to the fallacious pedagogy of the two model approach, Section 4(a) lacks legitimate educational value because "creation science" as defined in that section is simply not science. Several witnesses suggested definitions of science. A descriptive definition was said to be that science

[23]The idea that belief in a creator and acceptance of the scientific theory of evolution are mutually exclusive is a false premise and offensive to the religious views of many. (Hicks) Dr. Francisco Ayala, a geneticist of considerable renown and a former Catholic priest who has the equivalent of a Ph.D. in theology, pointed out that many working scientists who subscribed to the theory of evolution are devoutly religious.
[24]This is so despite the fact that some of the defense witnesses do not subscribe to the young earth or flood hypotheses. Dr. Geisler stated his belief that the earth is several billion years old. Dr. Wickramasinghe stated that no rational scientist would believe the earth is less than one million years old or that all the world's geology could be explained by a worldwide flood.

is what is "accepted by the scientific community" and is "what scientists do." The obvious implication of this description is that, in a free society, knowledge does not require the imprimatur of legislation in order to become science.

More precisely, the essential characteristics of science are:

(1) It is guided by natural law;
(2) It has to be explanatory by reference to natural law;
(3) It is testable against the empirical world;
(4) Its conclusions are tentative, i.e., are not necessarily the final word; and
(5) It is falsifiable. (Ruse and other science witnesses).

Creation science as described in Section 4(a) fails to meet these essential characteristics. First, the section revolves around 4(a)(1) which asserts a sudden creation "from nothing." Such a concept is not science because it depends upon a supernatural intervention which is not guided by natural law. It is not explanatory by reference to natural law, is not testable and is not falsifiable.[25]

If the unifying idea of supernatural creation by God is removed from Section 4, the remaining parts of the section explain nothing and are meaningless assertions.

Section 4(a)(2), relating to the "insufficiency of mutation and natural selection in bringing about development of all living kinds from a single organism", is an incomplete negative generalization directed at the theory of evolution.

Section 4(a)(3) which describes "changes only within fixed limits of originally created kinds of plants and animals" fails to conform to the essential characteristics of science for several reasons. First, there is no scientific definition of "kinds" and none of the witnesses was able to point to any scientific authority which recognized the term or knew how many "kinds" existed. One defense witness suggested there may be 100 to 10,000 different "kinds". Another believes there were "about 10,000, give or take a few thousand." Second, the assertion appears to be an effort to establish outer limits of changes within species. There is no scientific explanation for these limits which is guided by natural law and the limitations, whatever they are, cannot be explained by natural law.

[25]"We do not know how God created, what processes He used, for *God used processes which are not now operating anywhere in the natural universe.* This is why we refer to divine creation as Special Creation. We cannot discover by scientific investigation anything about the creative processes used by God." Px 78, Gish, *Evolution? The Fossils Say No!,* 42 (3d ed. 1979) (emphasis in original).

The statement in 4(a)(4) of "separate ancestry of man and apes" is a bald assertion. It explains nothing and refers to no scientific fact or theory.[26] Section 4(a)(5) refers to "explanation of the earth's geology by catastrophism, including the occurrence of a worldwide flood." This assertion completely fails as science. The Act is referring to the Noachian flood described in the Book of Genesis.[27] The creationist writers concede that *any* kind of Genesis Flood depends upon supernatural intervention. A worldwide flood as an explanation of the world's geology is not the product of natural law, nor can its occurrence be explained by natural law.

Section 4(a)(6) equally fails to meet the standards of science. "Relatively recent inception" has no scientific meaning. It can only be given meaning by reference to creationist writings which place the age at between 6,000 and 20,000 years because of the genealogy of the Old Testament. See, e.g. Px 78, Gish (6,000 to 10,000); Px 87, Segraves (6,000 to 20,000). Such a reasoning process is not the product of natural law; not explanable by natural law; nor is it tentative.

Creation science, as defined in Section 4(a), not only fails to follow the canons defining scientific theory, it also fails to fit the more general descriptions of "what scientists think" and "what scientists do." The scientific community consists of individuals and groups, nationally and internationally, who work independently in such varied fields as biology, paleontology, geology and astronomy. Their work is published and subject to review and testing by their peers. The journals for publication are both numerous and varied. There is, however, not one recognized scientific journal which has published an article espousing the creation science theory described in Section 4(a). Some of the State's witnesses suggested that the scientific community was "close-minded" on the subject of creationism and that explained the lack of acceptance of the creation science arguments. Yet no witness produced a scientific article for which publication had been refused. Perhaps some members of the scientific community are resistant to new ideas. It is, however, inconceivable that such a loose knit group of independent thinkers in all the varied fields of science could, or would, so effectively censor new scientific thought.

[26]The evolutionary notion that man and some modern apes have a common ancestor somewhere in the distant past has consistently been distorted by anti-evolutionists to say that man descended from modern monkeys. As such, this idea has long been most offensive to Fundamentalists. See, *Epperson v. Arkansas,* 393 U.S. 97 (1968).
[27]Not only was this point acknowledged by virtually all the defense witnesses, it is patent in the creationist literature. See, e.g., Px 89, Kofahl & Segraves, *The Creation Explanation,* 40: "The Flood of Noah brought about vast changes in the earth's surface, including vulcanism, mountain building, and the deposition of the major part of sedimentary strata. This principle is called 'Biblical catastrophism.' "

The creationists have difficulty maintaining among their ranks consistency in the claim that creationism is science. The author of Act 590, Ellwanger, said that neither evolution nor creationism was science. He thinks both are religion. Duane Gish recently responded to an article in *Discover* critical of creationism by stating:

> "Stephen Jay Gould states that creationists claim creation is a scientific theory. This is a false accusation. Creationists have repeatedly stated that neither creation nor evolution is a scientific theory (and each is equally religious)." Gish, letter to editor of *Discover,* July, 1981, App. 30 to Plaintiffs' Pretrial Brief.

The methodology employed by creationists is another factor which is indicative that their work is not science. A scientific theory must be tentative and always subject to revision or abandonment in light of facts that are inconsistent with, or falsify, the theory. A theory that is by its own terms dogmatic, absolutist and never subject to revision is not a scientific theory.

The creationists' methods do not take data, weigh it against the opposing scientific data, and thereafter reach the conclusions stated in Section 4(a). Instead, they take the literal wording of the Book of Genesis and attempt to find scientific support for it. The method is best explained in the language of Morris in his book (Px 31) *Studies in The Bible and Science* at page 114:

> " . . . it is . . . quite impossible to determine anything about Creation through a study of present processes, because present processes are not creative in character. If man wishes to know anything about Creation (the time of Creation, the duration of Creation, the order of Creation, the methods of Creation, or anything else) his sole source of true information is that of divine revelation. God was there when it happened. We were not there . . . Therefore, we are completely limited to what God has seen fit to tell us, and this information is in His written Word. This is our textbook on the science of Creation!"

The Creation Research Society employs the same unscientific approach to the issue of creationism. Its applicants for membership must subscribe to the belief that the Book of Genesis is "historically and scientifically true in all of the original autographs."[28] The Court would never criticize or discredit any person's testimony based on his or her religious beliefs. While anybody is free to approach a scientific inquiry in any fashion they choose,

[28]See n. 7, *supra,* for the full text of the CRS creed.

they cannot properly describe the methodology used as scientific, if they start with a conclusion and refuse to change it regardless of the evidence developed during the course of the investigation.

IV. (D)

In efforts to establish "evidence" in support of creation science, the defendants relied upon the same false premise as the two model approach contained in Section 4, i.e., all evidence which criticized evolutionary theory was proof in support of creation science. For example, the defendants established that the mathematical probability of a chance chemical combination resulting in life from non-life is so remote that such an occurrence is almost beyond imagination. Those mathematical facts, the defendants argue, are scientific evidences that life was the product of a creator. While the statistical figures may be impressive evidence against the theory of chance chemical combinations as an explanation of origins, it requires a leap of faith to interpret those figures so as to support a complex doctrine which includes a sudden creation from nothing, a world-wide flood, separate ancestry of man and apes, and a young earth.

The defendants' argument would be more persuasive if, in fact, there were only two theories or ideas about the origins of life and the world. That there are a number of theories was acknowledged by the State's witnesses, Dr. Wickramasinghe and Dr. Geisler. Dr. Wickramasinghe testified at length in support of a theory that life on earth was "seeded" by comets which delivered genetic material and perhaps organisms to the earth's surface from interstellar dust far outside the solar system. The "seeding" theory further hypothesizes that the earth remains under the continuing influence of genetic material from space which continues to affect life. While Wickramasinghe's theory[29] about the origins of life on earth has not received general acceptance within the scientific community, he has, at least, used scientific methodology to produce a theory of origins which meets the essential characteristics of science.

The Court is at a loss to understand why Dr. Wickramasinghe was called in behalf of the defendants. Perhaps it was because he was generally critical of the theory of evolution and the scientific community, a tactic consistent with the strategy of the defense. Unfortunately for the defense, he demonstrated that the simplistic approach of the two model analysis of the origins of life is false. Furthermore, he corroborated the plaintiffs'

[29]The theory is detailed in Wickramasinghe's book with Sir Fred Hoyle, *Evolution From Space* (1981), which is Dx 79.

witnesses by concluding that "no rational scientist" would believe the earth's geology could be explained by reference to a worldwide flood or that the earth was less than one million years old.

The proof in support of creation science consisted almost entirely of efforts to discredit the theory of evolution through a rehash of data and theories which have been before the scientific community for decades. The arguments asserted by creationists are not based upon new scientific evidence or laboratory data which has been ignored by the scientific community.

Robert Gentry's discovery of radioactive polonium haloes in granite and coalified woods is, perhaps, the most recent scientific work which the creationists use as argument for a "relatively recent inception" of the earth and a "worldwide flood." The existence of polonium haloes in granite and coalified wood is thought to be inconsistent with radiometric dating methods based upon constant radioactive decay rates. Mr. Gentry's findings were published almost ten years ago and have been the subject of some discussion in the scientific community. The discoveries have not, however, led to the formulation of any scientific hypothesis or theory which would explain a relatively recent inception of the earth or a worldwide flood. Gentry's discovery has been treated as a minor mystery which will eventually be explained. It may deserve further investigation, but the National Science Foundation has not deemed it to be of sufficient import to support further funding.

The testimony of Marianne Wilson was persuasive evidence that creation science is not science. Ms. Wilson is in charge of the science curriculum for Pulaski County Special School District, the largest school district in the State of Arkansas. Prior to the passage of Act 590, Larry Fisher, a science teacher in the District, using materials from the ICR, convinced the School Board that it should voluntarily adopt creation science as part of its science curriculum. The District Superintendent assigned Ms. Wilson the job of producing a creation science curriculum guide. Ms. Wilson's testimony about the project was particularly convincing because she obviously approached the assignment with an open mind and no preconceived notions about the subject. She had not heard of creation science until about a year ago and did not know its meaning before she began her research.

Ms. Wilson worked with a committee of science teachers appointed from the District. They reviewed practically all of the creationist literature. Ms. Wilson and the committee members reached the unanimous conclusion that creationism is not science; it is religion. They so reported to the Board. The Board ignored the recommendation and insisted that a curriculum guide be prepared.

In researching the subject, Ms. Wilson sought the assistance of Mr. Fisher who initiated the Board action and asked professors in the science departments of the University of Arkansas at Little Rock and the University of Central Arkansas[30] for reference material and assistance, and attended a workshop conducted at Central Baptist College by Dr. Richard Bliss of the ICR staff. Act 590 became law during the course of her work so she used Section 4(a) as a format for her curriculum guide.

Ms. Wilson found all available creationists' materials unacceptable because they were permeated with religious references and reliance upon religious beliefs.

It is easy to understand why Ms. Wilson and other educators find the creationists' textbook material and teaching guides unacceptable. The materials misstate the theory of evolution in the same fashion as Section 4(b) of the Act, with emphasis on the alternative mutually exclusive nature of creationism and evolution. Students are constantly encouraged to compare and make a choice between the two models, and the material is not presented in an accurate manner.

A typical example is *Origins* (Px 76) by Richard B. Bliss, Director of Curriculum Development of the ICR. The presentation begins with a chart describing "preconceived ideas about origins" which suggests that some people believe that evolution is atheistic. Concepts of evolution, such as "adaptive radiation," are erroneously presented. At page 11, figure 1.6, of the text, a chart purports to illustrate this "very important" part of the evolution model. The chart conveys the idea that such diverse mammals as a whale, bear, bat and monkey all evolved from a shrew through the process of adaptive radiation. Such a suggestion is, of course, a totally erroneous and misleading application of the theory. Even more objectionable, especially when viewed in light of the emphasis on asking the student to elect one of the models, is the chart presentation at page 17, figure 1.6. That chart purports to illustrate the evolutionists' belief that man evolved from bacteria to fish to reptile to mammals and, thereafter, into man. The illustration indicates, however, that the mammal from which man evolved was *a rat.*

Biology, A Search For Order in Complexity[31] is a high school biology text typical of creationists' materials. The following quotations are illustrative:

---

[30]Ms. Wilson stated that some professors she spoke with sympathized with her plight and tried to help her find scientific materials to support Section 4(a). Others simply asked her to leave.

[31]Px 129, published by Zonderman Publishing House (1974), states that it was "prepared by the Textbook Committee of the Creation Research Society." It has a disclaimer pasted inside the front cover stating that it is not suitable for use in public schools.

"Flowers and roots do not have a mind to have purpose of their own; therefore, this planning must have been done for them by the Creator."—at page 12.

"The exquisite beauty of color and shape in flowers exceeds the skill of poet, artist, and king. Jesus said (from Matthew's gospel), 'Consider the lilies of the field, how they grow; they toil not, neither do they spin . . .' "
Px 129 at page 363.

The "public school edition" texts written by creationists simply omit Biblical references but the content and message remain the same. For example, *Evolution—The Fossils Say No!,*[32] contains the following:

Creation. By creation we mean the bringing into being by a supernatural Creator of the basic kinds of plants and animals by the process of sudden, or fiat, creation.

We do not know how the Creator created, what processes He used, *for He used processes which are not now operating anywhere in the natural universe.* This is why we refer to creation as Special Creation. We cannot discover by scientific investigation anything about the creative processes used by the Creator."—page 40

Gish's book also portrays the large majority of evolutionists as "materialistic atheists or agnostics."
Scientific Creationism (Public School Edition) by Morris, is another text reviewed by Ms. Wilson's committee and rejected as unacceptable. The following quotes illustrate the purpose and theme of the text:

Forward
————

"Parents and youth leaders today, and even many scientists and educators, have become concerned about the prevalence and influence of evolutionary philosophy in modern curriculum. Not only is this system inimical to orthodox Christianity and Judaism, but also, as many are convinced, to a healthy society and true science as well."

* * *

'The rationalist of course finds the concept of special creation insufferably naive, even 'incredible'. Such a judgment, however, is warranted

[32]Px 77, by Duane Gish.

only if one categorically dismisses the existence of an omnipotent God." at page 17.

Without using creationist literature, Ms. Wilson was unable to locate one genuinely scientific article or work which supported Section 4(a). In order to comply with the mandate of the Board she used such materials as an article from *Readers Digest* about "atomic clocks" which inferentially suggested that the earth was less than 4½ billion years old. She was unable to locate any substantive teaching material for some parts of Section 4 such as the worldwide flood. The curriculum guide which she prepared cannot be taught and has no educational value as science. The defendants did not produce any text or writing in response to this evidence which they claimed was usable in the public school classroom.[33]

The conclusion that creation science has no scientific merit or educational value as science has legal significance in light of the Court's previous conclusion that creation science has, as one major effect, the advancement of religion. The second part of the three-pronged test for establishment reaches only those statutes having as their *primary* effect the advancement of religion. Secondary effects which advance religion are not constitutionally fatal. Since creation science is not science, the conclusion is inescapable that the *only* real effect of Act 590 is the advancement of religion. The Act therefore fails both the first and second portions of the test in *Lemon v. Kurtzman,* 403 U.S. 602 (1971).

IV. (E)

Act 590 mandates "balanced treatment" for creation science and evolution science. The Act prohibits instruction in any religious doctrine or references to religious writings. The Act is self-contradictory and compliance is impossible unless the public schools elect to forego significant portions of subjects such as biology, world history, geology, zoology, botany, psychology, anthropology, sociology, philosophy, physics and chemistry. Presently, the concepts of evolutionary theory as described in

[33]The passage of Act 590 apparently caught a number of its supporters off guard as much as it did the school district. The Act's author, Paul Ellwanger, stated in a letter to "Dick," (apparently Dr. Richard Bliss at ICR): "And finally, if you know of any textbooks at any level and for any subjects that you think are acceptable to you and also constitutionally admissible, these are things that would be of *enormous* [use] to these bewildered folks who may be caught, as Arkansas now has been, by the sudden need to implement a whole new ball game with which they are quite unfamiliar." (sic) (Unnumbered attachment to Ellwanger depo.)

4(b) permeate the public school textbooks. There is no way teachers can teach the Genesis account of creation in a secular manner.

The State Department of Education, through its textbook selection committee, school boards and school administrators will be required to constantly monitor materials to avoid using religious references. The school boards, administrators and teachers face an impossible task. How is the teacher to respond to questions about a creation suddenly and out of nothing? How will a teacher explain the occurrence of a worldwide flood? How will a teacher explain the concept of a relatively recent age of the earth? The answer is obvious because the only source of this information is ultimately contained in the Book of Genesis.

References to the pervasive nature of religious concepts in creation science texts amply demonstrate why State entanglement with religion is inevitable under Act 590. Involvement of the State in screening texts for impermissible religious references will require State officials to make delicate religious judgments. The need to monitor classroom discussion in order to uphold the Act's prohibition against religious instruction will necessarily involve administrators in questions concerning religion. These continuing involvements of State officials in questions and issues of religion create an excessive and prohibited entanglement with religion. *Brandon v. Board of Education,* 487 F. Supp 1219, 1230 (N.D.N.Y.), *aff'd.,* 635 F.2d 971 (2nd Cir. 1980).

V.

These conclusions are dispositive of the case and there is no need to reach legal conclusions with respect to the remaining issues. The plaintiffs raised two other issues questioning the constitutionality of the Act and, insofar as the factual findings relevant to these issues are not covered in the preceding discussion, the Court will address these issues. Additionally, the defendants raised two other issues which warrant discussion.

V.(A)

First, plaintiff teachers argue the Act is unconstitutionally vague to the extent that they cannot comply with its mandate of "balanced" treatment without jeopardizing their employment. The argument centers around the lack of a precise definition in the Act for the word "balanced." Several witnesses expressed opinions that the word has such meanings as equal time, equal weight, or equal legitimacy. Although the Act could have been more explicit, "balanced" is a word subject to ordinary understanding. The proof is not convincing that a teacher using a reasonably acceptable understanding of the word and making a good faith effort to comply with the Act will be in jeopardy of termination. Other portions of the Act are arguably vague, such as the "relatively recent" inception of the earth and life. The evidence establishes, however, that relatively recent means from 6,000 to 20,000 years, as commonly understood in creation science literature. The meaning of this phrase, like Section 4(a) generally, is, for purposes of the Establishment Clause, all too clear.

V.(B)

The plaintiffs' other argument revolves around the alleged infringement by the defendants upon the academic freedom of teachers and students. It is contended this unprecedented intrusion in the curriculum by the State prohibits teachers from teaching what they believe should be taught or requires them to teach that which they do not believe is proper. The evidence reflects that traditionally the State Department of Education, local school boards and administration officials exercise little, if any, influence upon the subject matter taught by classroom teachers. Teachers have been given freedom to teach and emphasize those portions of subjects the individual teacher considered important. The limits to this discretion have generally been derived from the approval of textbooks by the State Department and preparation of curriculum guides by the school districts.

Several witnesses testified that academic freedom for the teacher means, in substance, that the individual teacher should be permitted unlimited discretion subject only to the bounds of professional ethics. The Court is not prepared to adopt such a broad view of academic freedom in the public schools.

In any event, if Act 590 is implemented, many teachers will be required to teach material in support of creation science which they do not consider academically sound. Many teachers will simply forego teaching subjects which might trigger the "balanced treatment" aspects of Act 590 even though they think the subjects are important to a proper presentation of a course.

Implementation of Act 590 will have serious and untoward consequences for students, particularly those planning to attend college. Evolution is the cornerstone of modern biology, and many courses in public schools contain subject matter relating to such varied topics as the age of the earth, geology and relationships among living things. Any student who is deprived of instruction as to the prevailing scientific thought on these topics will be denied a significant part of science education. Such a deprivation through the high school level would undoubtedly have an impact upon the quality of education in the State's colleges and universities, especially including the pre-professional and professional programs in the health sciences.

V.(C)

The defendants argue in their brief that evolution is, in effect, a religion, and that by teaching a religion which is contrary to some students' religious views, the State is infringing upon the student's free exercise rights under the First Amendment. Mr. Ellwanger's legislative findings, which were adopted as a finding of fact by the Arkansas Legislature in Act 590, provides:

"Evolution-science is contrary to the religious convictions or moral values or philosophical beliefs of many students and parents, including individuals of many different religious faiths and with diverse moral and philosophical beliefs." Act 590, §7(d).

The defendants argue that the teaching of evolution alone presents both a free exercise problem and an establishment problem which can only be redressed by giving balanced treatment to creation science, which is admittedly consistent with some religious beliefs. This argument appears to have its genesis in a student note written by Mr. Wendell Bird, "Freedom of Religion and Science Instruction in Public Schools," 87 Yale L.J. 515 (1978). The argument has no legal merit.

If creation science is, in fact, science and not religion, as the defendants claim, it is difficult to see how the teaching of such a science could "neutralize" the religious nature of evolution.

Assuming for the purposes of argument, however, that evolution is a religion or religious tenet, the remedy is to stop the teaching of evolution; not establish another religion in opposition to it. Yet it is clearly established in the case law, and perhaps also in common sense, that evolution is not a religion and that teaching evolution does not violate the Establishment Clause, *Epperson v. Arkansas, supra, Willoughby v. Stever,* No. 15574-75 (D.D.C. May 18, 1973); *aff'd.* 504 F.2d 271 (D.C. Cir. 1974); *cert. denied,* 420 U.S. 924 (1975); *Wright v. Houston Indep. School Dist.,* 366 F.Supp. 1208 (S.D. Tex. 1978), *aff'd.* 486 F.2d 137 (5th Cir. 1973), *cert. denied* 417 U.S. 969 (1974).

V.(D)

The defendants presented Dr. Larry Parker, a specialist in devising curricula for public schools. He testified that the public school's curriculum should reflect the subjects the public wants taught in schools. The witness said that polls indicated a significant majority of the American public thought creation science should be taught if evolution was taught. The point of this testimony was never placed in a legal context. No doubt a sizeable majority of Americans believe in the concept of a Creator or, at least, are not opposed to the concept and see nothing wrong with teaching school children about the idea.

The application and content of First Amendment principles are not determined by public opinion polls or by a majority vote. Whether the proponents of Act 590 constitute the majority or the minority is quite irrelevant under a constitutional system of government. No group, no matter how large or small, may use the organs of government, of which the public schools are the most conspicuous and influential, to foist its religious beliefs on others.

The Court closes this opinion with a thought expressed eloquently by the great Justice Frankfurter:

> "We renew our conviction that 'we have staked the very existence of our country on the faith that complete separation between the state and religion is best for the state and best for religion.'" *Everson v. Board of Education,* 330 U.S. at 59. If nowhere else, in the relation between Church and State, 'good fences make good neighbors.'" *McCollum v. Board of Education,* 333 U.S. 203, 232 (1948).

An injunction will be entered permanently prohibiting enforcement of Act 590.

It is so ordered this January 5, 1982.

William R. Overton

UNITED STATES DISTRICT JUDGE

Appendix 2

Public Knowledge of Science: Report of a Survey by the National Assessment of Educational Progress[1]

To what extent has the increased dissemination of sophisticated materials in science changed the level of knowledge about science and the understanding of its methods and concepts? The most thorough effort to assess public understanding of science in the United States was conducted by the National Assessment of Educational Progress (NAEP) in a sequence of surveys in 1969–1970 and 1972–1973. The surveys were administered to a national sample of students, ages nine, thirteen, and seventeen, and to a fourth group of young adults, aged twenty-four to thirty-five. They were intended to test the implementation of educational objectives, students' knowledge of fundamental facts and principles of science, their ability to engage in science, their understanding of its investigative nature, and their attitudes. The survey developers assumed that appropriately educated students would understand that science depends on observation and experiment directed intelligently within a logical theoretical framework. They would understand the role of theory in the process of analyzing observations and in making predictions.

The findings of the survey suggest that facts were far better assimilated and recalled than an understanding of the character of science, that students showed only limited understanding of scientific method and were confused about the function of scientific models, theories, hypotheses, and facts. For example, more than half of the respondents in each age group failed to answer correctly questions probing the differences among facts, theories, models, and empirical laws. Given a list of statements, fewer than half of the seventeen year olds could correctly differentiate a description of a model from a list of empirical observations. Only 58.7 percent of the seventeen year olds and 45.3 percent of the adults tested in 1973 appeared to understand the difference between facts and hypotheses with sufficient subtlety to select the correct answers among multiple-choice items. In one question, students were asked what a scientist might *not* do when beginning a scientific problem (the correct answer being that a scientist would not list the conclusions to be proved). In 1973, only 25 percent of the seventeen year olds responded correctly; this represented a 5.8 percent decline in the number of correct answers since the previous survey in 1969.

A number of questions dealt directly with the understanding of evolution theory. One classic question called for explaining the length of the giraffe's neck in terms of the theory of natural selection; 57.1 percent of seventeen year olds selected the correct answer, but a statistician, calculating the likelihood of guesses for this question, estimates that probably no more than 40 percent really understood the response. "Even the most optimistic interpretation . . . indicates that 40–50 percent of the nation's seventeen-year-olds did not give evidence of understanding this basic idea of western science . . . a concept [that] requires almost no technical knowledge to understand."[2] Answers to other questions pertaining to evolution also demonstrated considerable ignorance. For example, 68 percent of seventeen year olds and 63 percent of adults associated the idea of natural selection with Darwin; but in a more sophisticated question ("How could a fossil of an ocean fish be found on a mountain?"), only 39 percent of the adults chose the correct answer that the mountain was raised after the fish was dead. Most respondents believed that the fossil was carried by a flood to the mountain. And in a question about how long man has lived on the earth, 24.6 percent of adults estimated less than 100,000 years and 21.3 percent claimed not to know.[3]

Regional differences in the responses to questions on evolution suggest the possible influence of religious values as well as overall differences in educational quality. Students from the southeastern United States scored about 5 percent lower in the entire survey than respondents from the country as a whole, but they were especially weak in biology. In one exercise concerning what scientists learn from studying fossils, there was a striking 23 percent difference between the southeast and the rest of the nation in the number of correct responses.

In the four years between the two surveys (1968–1969 to 1972–1973), performance in the science survey declined by about 2 percent, interpreted by the NAEP as "significant" and well outside the margin of error, corresponding to a loss of six months "learning experience." Scores declined most systematically in questions relating to the nature of the scientific process. Averaging all the questions in this area, we find that the number of correct answers decreased by about 6 percent among both seventeen year olds and young adults.

Notes

1. The NAEP is part of the Education Commission of the States, a consortium of state education officials. Funded by the Office of Education, its offices are in Denver, Colorado. The survey covered 90,000 students and is described in NAEP reports.

2. NAEP, "Gilberts Discusses Meaning of Science Results," *Newsletter* (March–April 1974): 6–7.

3. BBC held a similar survey in 1958. Two thirds of their sample had some knowledge of the concept of evolution and defined it in terms of change; one third could volunteer no information at all. Only one in three could associate the theory with Darwin. And in a question about why giraffes have long necks, 50 percent of the response indicated belief in special creation theory, 16 percent in Lamarckian theory, and 33 percent in Darwinian evolution theory. The study concluded that the average viewer 'believes in evolution which for him means not much more than that man has descended from monkeys." Described in Stuart Blume, *Toward a Political Sociology of Science* (New York: The Free Press, 1974), pp. 255–256.

Appendix 3

Proposed Creationist Revisions of the California *Science Framework* for 1976

The following document is from a position paper submitted by the Creation Science Research Center to the California Curriculum Development and Supplemental Materials Commission in October 1975. Proposals for changes in the 1976 guidelines were made by crossing out statements in the original *Science Framework* and by underlining statements creationists wished to add. The few statements neither crossed out nor underlined were regarded as acceptable.

Science Framework *Changes*

~~Another example of the interdependence of the structure and function is found in evolution. Cause and effect evolutionary theories were at first misinterpreted by Lamarck when he predicted that function gave rise to~~

~~structural adaptations. Experimental research indicates that structures evolved that made some organisms more adaptable to their environment than others. Organisms that evolved parts that did not successfully function within their environment did not survive.~~ The interdependence of structure and function is also believed to be demonstrated in evolution. Lamarck proposed a cause-and-effect relationship between the function of the bodily parts of living organisms and the appearance of structural adaptations in their offspring. Ecological studies suggest that some organisms tend to adapt to changes in their environment better than do other organisms. Those that are less successful in adapting do not survive. In Lamarck's theory the need, use, or disuse of a given capacity or organ caused not merely adaptation but the evolution of new organs and structures in succeeding generations. This theory is yet to be supported by experimental evidence.

Another order of interactions is that of supposed evolutionary events, which are believed to have produced ~~produce~~ predictable changes in certain kinds of objects over long periods of time. One theory claims that atoms, interacting with one another and evolving over eons of time, gave rise to the present assemblage of various kinds of elements. Another evolutionary thesis describes the progress of stars all the way from young gaseous nebulae to pulsating dying stars. ~~There is much continuing debate among scientists concerning evolutionary theories of cosmogenesis because of the numerous theoretical problems which remain unsolved and because the postulated developmental process cannot be reproduced experimentally.~~ Still another interacting series of events has produced the ~~evolution~~ transformation of rocks from igneous to sedimentary and metamorphic.

~~Interactions between organisms and their environments produce changes in both.~~ Changes in ~~the~~ earth environment are readily demonstrable on a short-term basis; i.e., over the period of recorded history (circa 5,000 years). ~~These~~ Such changes also have been inferred from geologic evidence over a greatly extended period of time (billions of years). ~~although the further back we go, the less certain we can be. Prehistoric processes were not observed, and replication is difficult.~~ Interaction between populations of organisms and their environments produced changes in both. During the past century and a half, the earth's crust and the fossils preserved in it have been studied intensively by scientists. Fossil evidence shows that many organisms populating the earth have not always been structurally the same. The differences are ~~consistent with~~ interpreted in terms of the theory that anatomical changes have taken place through time. The Darwinian theory of organic evolution postulates a genetic basis for the biological development of complex forms of life in the past and present and the changes ~~noted~~ inferred through time. This theory, since it deals with postulated prehistoric events and processes which neither were observed by man nor can be repeated and controlled by man, is not subject to possible falsification by experimental test, a normal requirement for scientific theories.

The concepts that are the basic foundation for this theory are (1) that inheritable variations exist among members of a population of like organisms; and (2) that differential successful reproduction (i.e., survival) is occasioned by the composite of environmental factors impinging generation after generation upon the population. The theory is used to explain the many similarities and differences that exist between diverse kinds of organisms, living and extinct. The actual variations in living populations observed experimentally and in the field during the decades of modern biological research appear to be limited by rigid genetic boundaries. The theory, therefore, involves the idea of large-scale evolution by the extrapolated accumulation over vast periods of geologic time of limited variations of the type which have actually been observed.

~~The theory of organic evolution, its limitations not withstanding, provides a structural framework upon which many seemingly unrelated observations can be brought into more meaningful relationships.~~ Biologists also have developed, from experiments and observations, hypotheses concerning the origination of life from nonliving matter (e.g., the heterotroph hypothesis). These ideas together with the Darwinian theory in its modern form constitute the explanation for the origin and development of life based upon a materialistic interpretation of the data from pertinent sciences. The theory of organic evolution, its limitations notwithstanding, provides a structural framework within which many seemingly unrelated observations can be brought into more meaningful relationships. There are, nevertheless, data from the biological and physical sciences which are difficult to fit into the materialistic and evolutionary framework of interpretation which has been adopted by a majority of scientists over the past century since Darwin's time.

Another interpretative framework has been adopted by that minority of scientists who hold a theistic and creationist rather than a materialistic and evolutionary philosophy. They believe that the data of the sciences can better be understood and the origin of life better explained in terms of a theory of divine creation in accord with an intelligent, purposeful plan. This theory, in common with the evolutionary theory, is not subject to experimental falsification because it contains postulated events and processes which neither were observed by nor can be repeated by man. Also,

there are data from the sciences which are difficult for the creationist to
fit into his framework.

Philosophic and religious considerations pertaining to the origin, meaning, and values of life are not within the realm of science, because they
cannot be analyzed or measured by the present methods of science.

In view of the fact that the theistic and materialistic philosophies are
equally religious and/or anti-religious and because both the evolutionary
and creationist theories of the origin and development of life are equally
inaccessible to falsification by experimental test, both should be studied in
the light of the scientific data. The essential philosophy underlying each
interpretive system should be clearly identified, but these should not be the
subject of study in the science classroom.

Index

Abington School District v. *Schempp*, 107

Ackworth, Captain, 84

Act 590, *see* Balanced Treatment for Creation-Science and Evolution-Science Act (1981)

Acts and Facts, 82

Agassiz, Louis, 27

Alaska, 124

Ambassador College, 61, 62

American Anthropological Association, 160

American Association for the Advancement of Science (AAAS), 72, 160, 161

American Biology Teacher, 157–58

American Civil Liberties Union (ACLU), 31, 100

Balanced Treatment Act and, 137, 140–45

American Council of Learned Societies, 48

American Institute of Biological Sciences (AIBS), 44–47

American Library Association, Office for Intellectual Freedom of, 68

American Nuclear Society, 170

American Scientific Affiliation (ASA), 77–78

America's Future, 58

America United for the Separation of Church and State, Inc., 98

Apter, David, 149

Archibald, George, 127, 134–35

Arizona, 124

Arkansas, 155–56

creationist legislation in, 17, 18, 31, 34, 100, 102

Armstrong, Herbert W., 61, 62

Ashford, John, 127

astrologers, scientists' view of, 190–91

astronauts, as creationists, 61, 86

Awake, 62

Balanced Treatment for Creation-Science and Evolution-Science Act (1981), 17, 18, 100

Arkansas trial for, 137–46

Memorandum Opinion on, 201–28

Barnes, T. G., 65

Bauman amendment, 131

Bestor, Arthur, 58

Bible, literal interpretation of, 30, 31, 71, 77, 79, 156, 166

Bible Science Association, 80, 83–84

Bible Science Newsletter, 83

Big Daddy, 62–63

Biological Sciences Curriculum Study (BSCS), 42, 86, 175

creationism considered in, 159

Curriculum Study (BSCS) development of, 44–47

as target of textbook watchers, 64, 126, 153

Willoughby suit and, 101, 171

biology textbooks, changes recommended in, 114–16

Bird, Wendell, 99–100, 139, 143, 144
Black, Hugo, 143
Blount, W. A., 139, 144
Bob Jones University, 83
Boosters of True Education, 94
Borman, Frank, 86
Braun, Wernher von, 86
Bruner, Jerome, 48–51, 125
Bryan, William Jennings, 31–32
Bube, Richard, 113
businesses, natural selection in, 29

California, 21
  board of education of, 17, 79,
    101–2, 107–19, 152, 158, 171
  Curriculum Development and
    Supplemental Materials
    Commission of, 108–13
  Guidelines for Moral Instruction in,
    108
  Science Framework for schools in,
    102, 108–12, 116, 118, 158, 160,
    167, 171, 233–36
  textbook selection in, 72, 93–94,
    124, 167, 171
California, University of, Academic
    Senate of, 160
Cape Canaveral, Fla., 61
Carnegie, Andrew, 29
catastrophism, 26, 27
Catholicism, science vs. religion in,
    28–29
CBE Bulletin, 66
Chance and Necessity (Monod), 23
Christian Broadcasting Network, 66–67
Christian Heritage College, 80–81
Citizens for Scientific Creation, 117
Civil Rights Act (1964), 108
Clark, Steve, 141, 144
Clark, Thomas C., 107
Colorado, University of, 45, 100–101
Columbus (Ohio) School Board, 94
comic books, antievolution, 62
Committees of Correspondence, 162
communist scare, evolution theory
    and, 32, 34, 123

Congress, U.S., 17–18, 43, 99
  MACOS and, 127–35
Conlan, John, 127–35, 168
  amendment proposed by, 129–30
Connally, John, 46–47
conservative religions, growth of,
    59–63
Constitution, U.S.:
  First Amendment to, 31, 47, 98,
    99–100, 101, 102, 137, 139–46,
    193
  Fourteenth Amendment to, 98, 193
Coors, Joseph, 65–66
Corinth, N.Y., MACOS conflict in
    schools of, 121–124, 126
Council for Basic Education (CBE),
    58, 66, 128
Creation-Life Publishers, 82
Creation Research Science Education
    Foundation, Inc., 84, 94
Creation Research Society (CRS),
    78–79, 143
Creation Science Legal Defense Fund,
    141, 144
Creation Science Research Center
    (CSRC), 79–80, 82
creation theory, 71–73
  activists for, 84–90
  "equal time" for, 17, 18, 100,
    137–46, 173–79, 187, 201–28
  organizations for, 77–84; see also
    specific organizations
  as science vs. religion, 73–77, 100,
    110, 140–46, 156–57
  in textbooks, 114–16, 153–54
cults, scientific validation in, 166
curriculum reform:
  in biological sciences, 42, 44–47
  of CSRC, 79–80
  in physical sciences, 40–41
  in social sciences, 43, 47–51, 118
Cuvier, Georges, 26

Dade County, Fla., 46
Dallas Times Herald, 151–52
Däniken, E., Von, 59

Darrow, Clarence, 31–32
Darwin, Charles, 25, 29–30, 111,
    153–54, 161
  evolution theory of, 26–28
Darwin, George, 111
Day, Howard, 109
Dayton, Tenn., 32, 97
Deen, Braswell, 168
Depression, Great, 32
Deward, Douglas, 84
direct-mail campaigns, conservatives'
    use of, 66–67, 80
Doolittle, Russell, 152
Dyson, Freeman, 76

Eagle Forum, 66–67
education, as ideological instrument,
    20, 39, 58, 67
Educational Development Center
    (EDC), 48–51
Educational Research Analysts,
    64–65, 84
Ellwanger, Paul, 99–100, 138–39
"Emergence of Man" exhibit, 101
Epperson, Susanne, 34, 138
Epperson v. *Arkansas,* 138
"equal time," public-opinion polls on,
    116–17
Evolution Protest Movement (EPM),
    83
evolution theory:
  of Darwin, 26–28
  early history of, 25–30
  modern resistance to, 19–22
  in textbooks, 114–16, 153–54; *see
    also* Biological Sciences
    Curriculum Study; Man: A
    Course of Study
Exorcist, The, 166

Falwell, Jerry, 144
Faubus, Orval E., 34
Federal Communications Commission
    (FCC), Fairness Doctrine of,
    174–75
Fischer, Robert, 113

FitzGerald, Frances, 66
Fleming, Sir J. Ambrose, 84
Florida, 124
Follett Publishers, 130
Ford, John, 109, 111, 113, 117
Fosdick, Harry Emerson, 31–32
Four Dialogues (Lippman), 105
fundamentalism:
  evolution viewed in, 30–31, 61–63
  growth of, 20–21, 30–33
  literal interpretation of Bible in, 30,
    31, 71, 77, 79, 156, 166
  renewal of, 63, 195
Fundamentals, 30

Gabler, Mr. and Mrs. Mel, 63–65,
    126, 171
Gateway to the Stars, 61
Geertz, Clifford, 195
Geisler, Norman, 142
General Accounting Office (GAO), 133
Genesis School of Graduate Studies, 83
genetics:
  creationist view of, 75
  evolution theory and, 26
geology, early theories of, 26
Georgia, 144
  "equal-time" legislation in, 99
  textbook selection in, 94
Georgia Ontological Association for
    the Protection of Evolution (GO
    APE), 156
Gillispie, Charles, 27
Gish, Duane, 81, 85, 86, 140, 144,
    152
Gosse, P. H., 28
Gould, Stephen Jay, 76
Gray, Asa, 27
Great Society, 48
Grebe, John J., 65
Grose, Vernon, 86, 109–11, 167–68
*Guidelines for Moral Instruction in
    California Schools,* 108

Handlin, Oscar, 187
Hardin, Garrett, 76, 116

Hargis, Billy James, 62
Harward, Thomas, 109
Hays, Arthur Garfield, 31
Helms, Jesse, 133–34
Heritage Foundation, 65–66, 96, 128, 134, 176
High Flight, 61, 84
Holsted, James L., 139, 144
Holt, Marjorie, 127
Hopper, Barbara, 116
Hubbard, David, 109, 113
Huntsville, Ala., 99
Hutton, James, 26
Huxley, Julian, 29

Idaho, 124
Ideology and Discontent (Apter), 149
Indiana, textbook selection in, 94
In Search of Noah's Flood (TV film), 152
Institute for Creation Research (ICR), 80–83, 99–100
Internal Revenue Service (IRS), 162–63
Iowa Academy of Sciences, 162
Irwin, James, 86

Jehovah's Witnesses, 32, 59, 170
Watch Tower Society of, 62
John Birch Society, 123

Kanawha County, W.Va., textbook conflict in, 95–97, 130, 172
Kilpatrick, James, 126, 130
Kumamoto, Junji, 111

LaHaye, Tim, 81
Lamarck, Jean Baptiste de, 26
Lammerts, Walter, 107
Lang, Walter, 83
Leadership Action, Inc., 66, 128
LeClercq, Frederic, 98
Lemmons, Reuel, 46–47
Lester, Lane, 85–86
LeTourneau, Richard, 65
libraries, censorship and, 68

Link Lizard Defeats Evolution, 62
Lippincott Publishers, 130
Lippman, Walter, 105
Little Rock Ministerial Association, 138
Longview, Texas, 63–64
Los Angeles Times, 109, 113
Louisiana, creationist legislation in, 17, 18, 100
Lyell, Charles, 26, 73

McCarthy, Joseph, 155
McGraw, Ona Lee, 126
McIntire, Carl, 61
McKenna, James, 176
McLaughlin, Roy, 140, 144
McLean, Rev. Bill, v. Arkansas Board of Education, 199
Major Barbara (Shaw), 55
Man: A Course of Study (MACOS):
congressional action on, 127–35
development of, 47–51
evolutionary approach in, 168–69, 175–77
local protests against, 121–27
as target of textbook watchers, 65, 171
Maryland, 124
Mayer, William, 159
mechanics, laws of, creationist views on, 75–76
Merton, Robert, 186
Methodists, 30
Michigan State University, 83
Minnesota Association for Improvement of Science Education, 162–63
Mississippi:
creationist legislation in, 31, 34, 144
textbook selection in, 94
Missouri Association for Creation, 84
Mitchell, Edgar, 86–87
Monod, Jacques, 23
Moore, John A., 156
Moore, John N., 83
Moral Majority, 66–67

Morris, Henry, 81, 84–85, 174
Morris, John, 82–83
Mosher, Charles A., 129
Moudy, T. M., 132
Moudy Committee, 171–72, 176
Mount Ararat, creationist tours to, 80, 82–83
Muller, Herman J., 33
mysticism, 20, 59, 166

Nägeli, Karl, 26
National Academy of Sciences (NAS), 159–60, 161–62
National Assessment of Educational Progress, 188
  public knowledge of science report of, 229–31
National Association of Biology Teachers (NABT), 72, 98, 101
  creationism and, 157–63
National Bible Knowledge Association, 144–45
National Education Association (NEA), 29–30, 172
National Foundation of Fairness in Education, 144–45
National Opinion Research Center, 166
National Science Board, 133, 134
National Science Foundation (NSF), 19, 66, 171
  appropriations to, 128–35
  lawsuit against, 100–101, 176
  public knowledge of science survey of, 187–88
  science curriculum reform of, 19, 40–47, 59, 66, 118, 154
National Science Teachers Association, 34, 154–55
natural selection:
  in business, 29
  see also evolution theory
Nature, 156
Nature Study Movement, 39
Netsilik Eskimos, 48, 50, 127, 169
New Mexico, board of education of, 46
New Right, 66–68, 154, 155, 161

news media, creationism covered in, 18, 83, 102, 128, 139, 145–46, 151–52, 174
Newton Scientific Organization, 84
New York, 124
  Board of Regents exam of, 94
Nixon, Richard M., 134
Noachian Deluge, as historical event, 79, 82–83, 156
Noah's Ark, ICR and, 82–83

Oregon, 124
  School Board of, 94
Origin of Species (Darwin), 25, 27
Overton, William R., 143–44
Owen, Sir Richard, 28

"Paluxy Man," 76
Parker, Gary, 86
Pennsylvania, 124
Perluss, Irving, 102
Physical Science Study Committee (PSSC), 40–41
pi, value of, 31
Piel, Gerard, 132
Plain Truth, 62
progressive education movement, 39, 58
Proxmire, William, 129–30

radioisotope dating, 75, 76
Rafferty, Max, 108
Ragle, Eugene, 109
Reagan, Ronald, 18
Reagan administration, 134–35, 173
  Heritage Foundation and, 66
Revolution, American, 162
Rickover, Hyman, 39
Riecken, Henry W., 43
Roberts, Oral, 59
Robertson, Pat, 144
Rockefeller, John D., 29
Roszak, Theodore, 187

Save Our Schools, 123
Schlafly, Phyllis, 66–67
Schlei, Norbert A., 108

Science, 152
science:
  ambivalent views of, 18–22, 87,
    166–70, 187–89
  hostility to authority of, 31, 61,
    170–73, 189–91
  methodological conflicts in, 140–41,
    192
  public knowledge of, 188, 229–31
  values influenced by, 124–25, 168,
    176, 188–89, 192
Science and Scripture, 80
Science Framework, 102
  proposed creationist revisions of,
    233–36
Scientific American, 152
Scientific Creationism Association of
  Southern New Jersey, 84
scientific creationists, identified, 88–90
Scientific Integrity, 162
scientists, creationism rejected by,
  156–63, 186–87
Scopes trial, 20, 31–34, 154
Scott, Gary, 34
secular humanism, 59, 64, 67, 87,
  101, 135, 169
Sedgwick, Adam, 27–28
Segraves, Kelly, 118, 152
Segraves, Nell, 107, 152
Seventh-Day Adventists, 32, 116–17
Shaw, George Bernard, 55
Smith, D. O., 34
Smithsonian Institution, 101, 144–45
Southern Illinois University, 83
Spencer, Herbert, 29
Sputnik, 39, 58
Steinbacher, John, 126
Stever, H. Guyford, 100–101, 129
Sumrall, Jean, 107
Supreme Court, U.S., 34, 58, 98, 101
  pornography decision of, 67, 172
  school prayers decision of, 107
Symington, James W., 129

Talks to Teachers, 50
Teague, Olin, 129, 132, 171

Tennessee, 32, 124
  creationist legislation in, 31, 34,
    97–98, 101
Texas, 21, 31
  textbook selection in, 46–47, 93–94,
    124, 126, 153, 167
Texas Education Policy Act, 1974
  amendment to, 65
textbook publishers, 65, 151
  economics of, 153–54
  evolution theory and, 18, 40
  MACOS and, 51, 130
textbook reform, changes for, 114–16
theistic evolution, 85
Triangle Association for Scientific
  Creationism, 84
Turkey, creationist tours to, 82–83
Twentieth Century Reform
  Movement, 61

Unbiased Presentation of
  Creation-Science and
  Evolution-Science Bill, 18
uniformitarianism, 26, 27, 75
Ussher, James, 26

Velikovsky, I., 59
Vermont, 124
Viguerie, Richard, 67

Waddington, C. H., 29
Wakely, Sir Cecil, 84
Wall Street Journal, 145, 152
Washington Post, 128
Watergate affair, 128, 130, 134, 173
Weber, George, 66
Welch, Claude, 158–59
West Virginia, textbook conflict in,
  95–97, 130, 172
White, Frank, 137, 139
Wickramasinghe, Chandra W., 142–43
Willoughby, William, 100–101, 176

Yankelovich, Daniel, 188

Zacharias, Jerrold, 40